The 21st Century

ENTREPRENEUR

HOW TO OPEN YOUR OWN STORE

MICHAEL ANTONIAK

A Third Millennium Press Book

AVON BOOKS NEW YORK

THE 21ST CENTURY ENTREPRENEUR: HOW TO OPEN YOUR OWN STORE is an original publication of Avon Books. This work has never before appeared in book form.

AVON BOOKS, INC.
1350 Avenue of the Americas
New York, New York 10019

Copyright © 1994 by Third Millennium Press, Inc.; Stephen Pollan and Michael Antoniak
Published by arrangement with Third Millennium Press, Inc.
Cover art by Nick Gaetano
ISBN: 0-380-77076-8
www.avonbooks.com

Library of Congress Cataloging in Publication Data:
Antoniak, Michael.
  The 21st century entrepreneur: how to open your own store / by Michael Antoniak.
    p.—cm.
1. Retail trade—United States—Management. 2. Stores, Retail—United States. I. Title.
II. Title: Twenty-first century entrepreneur.
HF5429.3.A58   1994   94-4078
658.87—dc20   CIP

First Avon Books Trade Paperback Printing: August 1994

AVON TRADEMARK REG. U S. PAT. OFF. AND IN OTHER COUNTRIES, MARCA REGISTRADA, HECHO EN U S A.

Printed in the U.S.A.

OPM 10 9 8 7 6 5

I'd like to thank the hundreds of retailers who so generously shared their insights, experiences, and frustrations with me over the years. Also, thanks to Stuart Krichevsky and Saverio Perri for their consultation and support, Jim Leonard for the detailed budget analysis in Chapter 6, Stephen Pollan for his expertise and encouragement, and especially Mark Levine for his personal and professional friendship. Finally, heartfelt appreciation to my parents for getting me started, and Liz and our children for keeping me going.

Michael Antoniak

❧ CONTENTS ❧

RETAILING IN THE 21ST CENTURY

Owning and operating a store remains one of the best opportunities if you're intent on going into business for yourself—just as it has been throughout our nation's history.

Long before they were called entrepreneurs, independently minded men and women found careers and financial freedom by running retail businesses. They were merchants who plied the trade routes, bearing exotic goods from distant lands. They were blacksmiths shoeing the horse and selling the hinge. And they were weavers making and marketing cloth for citizens of town and country.

In our American history, now forgotten retailers, the proprietors of general stores and peddlers roaming the countryside in wagons, helped tame the land. They provided the pioneers access to the tools and goods that couldn't be carried along on the western advance. And when the wilderness was conquered, there could be no surer sign of the victory than a street lined with shops addressing the needs and indulging the wants of a civil society. Success as a retailer then required a special combination of confidence, marketing and management skills, and gut instinct about what customers would buy. And that's still what's required.

Today, the products available through retailers large and small help define our time and aspirations. At the heart of any city are the shops and stores that mirror its diversity and culture. The border between city and suburb is often lined with expansive malls and shopping centers—their stores serving as places to be as much as places to buy. In the country, any trip into town invariably becomes a trip to shop some local store. And where you find a

faded downtown, it's a sign the community's vital retail establish-
ments opted for another location, taking the crowds with them.

AN ESSENTIAL SERVICE

Whatever the era, wherever situated, independent retailers provide an essential service to the community and its citizens. Your
mission as a retailer, whether you're selling from a flea market
booth, a strip shopping center, or a dazzling storefront, is to provide the buying public access to goods and services. People will
pay handsomely for that access. That's fortunate since, as a retailer, you'll make your living, and hopefully your fortune, off
the difference between what you pay for goods and what you can
sell them for.

If you're the type of person who can sense what that public
wants, and you're willing to assume the responsibility to find and
deliver it, owning and operating a retail store will prove a rewarding and challenging profession. As the owner of a small store,
you'll be in charge of your career and your life. You'll only answer
to the man or woman in the mirror. If you long for that kind of
self-determination, your own retail store offers a promising path
to independence.

In the consumer marketplace, there's always room for the store
owner who can keep the customer satisfied. You may not think
that's true when you first glance at today's retail landscape, where,
if there's a predominant trend, it's toward "super" stores and
warehouse clubs. But those giants' "everything under one roof"
approach to selling goods is at once their greatest strength and
potential weakness. People shop those stores for bargains. But in
exchange for that good price, they must also be willing to accept
the selection on hand. These retail generalists stock a little of
everything but not much of anything.

SMALL STORES, BIG OPPORTUNITY

What about the shopper who doesn't really know what she
wants? The shopper who wants more selection than can be found

in stores that strive to be all things to all people? She needs the help of the sales clerk who can suggest the best software to enhance her child's education. He likes the idea that the guy who sells the family bicycles will also be there when repairs are needed. She'll buy from the local merchant she knows on a first-name basis, and will take advantage of the free door-to-door delivery service.

In other words, for the very reasons that today's retail giants prosper, consumers need independently owned specialty stores. Many observers feel retailing is at a crossroad, heading in two different directions as we enter the new millennium. Down one road are the giant stores pushing price without service. Down the other are smaller, highly specialized shops requiring the dedication, skills, and vision of the entrepreneur.

Specialty stores thrive by offering consumers unrivaled selection in a distinct category of merchandise, and all related goods and services. It's a business that demands the attention of a hands-on operator, the entrepreneur who will devote him or herself to becoming the expert on what consumers need in that category, and answering those demands. This book is about opening one of those specialty stores, the best retail opportunity for the 21st Century entrepreneur.

Before you get lost in dreams of that wonderful opportunity, remember life's rewards are earned, not granted. Running your own store asks nothing short of hard work, long hours, and occasional spates of high anxiety. But if you cherish challenge, and enjoy the process of building a business as much as the fruits of success, you can make it in retailing today.

Still, if you're going to succeed, you need to realize that when it comes to specializing, it's no longer enough to simply open a clothing store, an electronics store, or a bookstore. Those concepts may still work in the few underserved population centers that remain, but they're guaranteed tickets to failure in areas where competition already reigns. To survive and thrive, you must focus on the narrow markets within markets; and then become the unquestionable expert within that narrow internal market.

While your city probably doesn't need another women's apparel store, it might need a specialist in clothing for big women. It might not need another electronics store, but how about a home office center? And while there might not be room for another bookstore, what about the best-stocked music book and score store in the land?

Whatever subcategory you choose, service will prove as critical to survival as the products you sell.

THE SERVICE ADVANTAGE

Personal service, be it advice on the right color or prompt in-home delivery, is one advantage you, as an independent retailer, will always enjoy over a larger store. Today's social and demographic trends dictate the need for the services only the specialty store can provide. And demand will only grow in the years ahead.

Everyone seems caught up in a rush to juggle schedules and accomplish more than the day allows. What a welcome respite it can be for a customer to step into a store and be greeted by name. To have the clerk show her a new color in that style she liked so much last month. To be asked how his grandchildren are doing, or if he enjoyed that vacation trip. And then he finds exactly what he needed. Why would he shop anywhere else? The specialty store is built on such relationships.

Experience teaches consumers there's no substitute for quality. Shoppers want the best, but don't always enjoy the luxury of time to find out what that is. They'll give their business to an expert who earns their trust.

Your success as an independent retailer in the 21st Century depends on your ability to provide that expertise, and to use it to benefit your customers. In retailing you may be boss, but you work for everyone who walks into your store. While you don't need to worry about getting fired if you don't do your job for them, you do need to fear being ignored. If that happens, it's only a matter of time before you'll be investigating other lines of work.

On the other hand, if you follow the fundamentals of smart retailing and develop and implement a business plan that's right for your store, you'll share in the success that makes retailing one of the best opportunities any self-assured man or woman can enjoy.

FAVORABLE WINDS

Before you begin planning, take a moment to consider some of the outside forces—social and economic trends—at work in today's consumer marketplace. Awareness of these will help you determine what type of retailer you should become, and how you should reach and serve your customers.

THE BABY BOOM GENERATION IS GETTING OLDER

If you're one of the multitude tagged "baby boomers," a quick glance in the mirror should be enough to convince you society is aging. The baby boom generation is so large, it continually dominates and redefines the consumer marketplace. As boomers look to their middle years and beyond, they'll again have their say on how stores should serve them.

An aging population is more settled, home-oriented, and concerned with convenience. Baby boomers have been consumers long enough to realize the only guarantee worth having is a quality product. They'll accept nothing but the best in goods and services, and on that, they'll give you no room to err. Each of their visits to your store should be regarded as your only chance to please them. It will take a lot more than a smile at the cash register to keep them coming back to your store.

PEOPLE ARE LOOKING FOR SIMPLICITY COMBINED WITH LUXURY

Eventually some in this age group may opt for simpler lives, perhaps in more pastoral settings. But they won't want to surrender the little luxuries and conveniences they've become accustomed to. That fact, combined with today's faster and more efficient delivery services, dictates that you must think of your audience in a very broad sense.

Most of your customers will come from the area surrounding your shop. But if you successfully address a special product niche, you will sell to people living in a much wider area, as well. The owner of the specialty store in the 21st Century should offer such a comprehensive combination of product selection and service that people will seek out that store from near and far. Some will shop in the store, others may trade with you by phone, fax, or mail; all should recognize the store as their best source for whatever it is you sell.

People no longer must live where they work; they can now work where they live. Tomorrow's successful specialty store may need to enter mail order to exploit the potential of its market niche. All your customers, regardless of where they live or work, will expect prompt delivery of whatever they buy. And whether they live across town or across country, they'll demand that if your store sells a product, you'll also service or repair it, at their convenience.

AMERICA IS BECOMING A MORE DIVERSE SOCIETY

The dawn of the 21st Century will also present you with a more diverse society. Immigrants from around the world will continue to have their impact on American society and culture. But unlike past waves, which assimilated into America's melting pot, many of today's immigrants aspire to American citizenship without surrendering their cultures. The pot itself may be melting as we evolve into a society of societies retaining their individual ethnic identities.

If you're expecting to trade with these groups, you must be prepared to deal with them on their own terms. That means in their language, and being sensitive to their manners and customs. Of course, this should also be taken into consideration when hiring staff.

BUILDING THE RIGHT TEAM AND REPUTATION

Staffing itself poses both challenge and opportunity for you. Traditionally, small stores are staffed by family members or from the pool of unskilled or semiskilled labor: a transient labor market of mostly young people more interested in short-term employment than a career in retail. That pool of young prospective employees will soon shrink while the number of available mature workers will increase.

Whoever is hired, you'll need to offer employees more than an hourly wage. A specialty store depends on forging personal relationships with its clients. For those to endure, shoppers expect to see familiar faces. To establish and retain those relationships, you must do whatever you can, within reason, to retain staff. That could include offering a benefit package attractive enough to make the job in the store a career, or offering star employees a profit-sharing plan or limited interest in the store's long-term performance.

You'll also be expected to be a good neighbor to your community and customers. That means much more than sponsoring a Little League team. Environmental awareness and concern for the underprivileged, once regarded as political activities, today speak of your commitment to your community. Today's consumer expects involvement. They'll prefer to spend their money with firms that share their sense of social responsibility.

And when such joint purpose is evident, consumers will voice their approval with their dollars. Tomorrow's shoppers will spend to make a statement about their concerns and themselves. They'll spend for products that add comfort to their homes, and insulate them from a harsh world. And they'll spend on hobbies and pursuits that reaffirm their individuality.

Every consumer believes he's special and expects the appropriate special handling from the specialty retailers he supports. Think of customers as subscribers to the philosophy behind your store. Just as a magazine's fate ultimately rests with its readers, yours rests with your customers. You need to do everything to attract their business and to keep them coming back. Every time they exit your store they must leave with cause to renew their patronage, to come back again.

To serve them to that level, you'll need to know your customers intimately. You'll need to recognize how your customers and their tastes are changing and how to position your store to anticipate rather than react to market trends.

THE UP SIDE OF A DOWN ECONOMY

You don't need a degree in finance to know the economy hit some rough patches in recent years. Regardless of how fast we emerge from these doldrums, the recession will have a lingering impact on business and attitudes for years to come. Gone forever are the days of reckless spending with no sense of accountability. The only guarantee about the future is that it'll bring more change.

When faced with uncertainty about their finances, consumers tend to watch how and what they spend. They demand quality and real value for their dollar. Some thoroughly investigate their options before any major purchase decision. All want an expert's advice.

Knowledge about what you sell, and everything related to it, is the most important service you must offer customers. They recognize the importance that knowledge should play in their decision to buy. Savvy shoppers have been bombarded with so many advertising claims that they doubt them all. Honestly sharing what you know about the products you sell will be regarded as service that sets your store apart.

Convenience is another consideration that will influence the shopper's decision on where to shop. You must do everything possible to make the shopping experience enjoyable and painless for the customer. That means you may need to offer delivery service, accept phone orders, or sponsor seminars to familiarize customers with new products or services. You must work with as well as for customers, perhaps opening at odd hours or by appointment to accommodate pressing schedules.

Today's business environment can help you become a 21st Century retailer in ways you may not yet recognize. One of the results of the economic transitions of recent years is that many qualified people are out of work, eager for employment. The store owner who seeks mature, experienced help should find it easy to attract a competent staff, as long as you offer the right incentives. (We'll thoroughly discuss staffing strategies in Chapter 9.) For some, retirement is not the eagerly awaited milestone it once seemed. Others, who lost their jobs, are embarking on second or third careers, whether by necessity or choice. Search among the ranks of these mature professionals and you may find someone who spent years developing the very skills you need to make your business a success.

Such individuals could prove willing mentors and concerned employees. Some entrepreneurs should consider entering business with an older, experienced person as a partner. Such a joint venture may provide just the seasoning you need to give your store a solid start. The insight experience brings will certainly prove an asset if you must seek outside financing for your venture into retail.

When selecting a location for your store, expect to meet developers and landlords eager to please. The unbridled confidence of the 1980s did not include plans for the recession and slow growth that greeted the 1990s. Right now, retail and office spaces are overbuilt in many areas. Expect to be dealing with a landlord who'll eagerly negotiate rather than dictate terms. In commercial real estate, it's a buyer's or renter's market for the foreseeable future.

In fact, thanks to the recession, the playing field is now more level than ever for anyone who wants a chance to play the retail game. From your potential suppliers to the contractor who can renovate your space, anyone with goods or services to sell needs your business. The economic climate says you should be able to negotiate a fair price and command quality work and service from everyone you deal with. If someone refuses to accommodate you, rest assured there's someone else waiting in line behind him who will.

INFORMATION AND ACCESS RATHER THAN LOCATION

With a good computer system and the right software, you'll be able to know which customers are buying what and why, right up to that very minute. That knowledge is power for you; power that provides leverage when dealing with suppliers.

This information age will also knock down the notion of the critical importance of location to a specialty store. If you choose, and your category of preference warrants it, you can operate tomorrow's store in two neighborhoods. First, there's the physical neighborhood where the store is situated. And second, there's the electronic neighborhood of instant access by phone, fax, or modem. Today's overnight courier services make it as easy to ship products across borders as across town. Since your store's success will depend on your ability to identify and relentlessly pursue a distinct niche of the consumer market, you must do everything within your means to exploit that commitment. If shoppers in your town or city will turn to you because you're the best source in your category, why wouldn't "teleshoppers" enjoy the same options? That means success with a retail store in the 21st Century will owe as much to access as location.

MINIMIZE YOUR RISKS, MAXIMIZE YOUR OPPORTUNITIES

Despite the new watchwords of information and access, and the old stress on location, the fundamental core of any retail business is, was, and remains providing a selection of products a sufficient number of consumers want, backed by personal service. Selling those goods represents both risk and opportunity. Retailing by its nature is a risky business. Think back twenty years. How many of the stores you remember shopping are still in business? Did the owners cash in and move on to something bigger and better? Or did they fall victim to the risks inherent in running a retail store?

This book is about minimizing those risks. Owning and operating a retail business can carry entrepreneurs to independence. But it's also one of the riskiest ventures anyone can make without proper planning. Master the fundamentals outlined in the pages that follow. Recognize your opportunities and seize them. Do that and you'll increase your odds of long-term success. And success as a retailer can be incredibly rewarding.

You'll be in control of your own income and your own destiny. You'll no longer be eager to leave work at the end of the day, no longer constantly be looking for ways to escape from your occupation. Rather than avoiding tasks, you'll seek them out. You'll find yourself working, or at least thinking about working, continuously. From the moment you rise to the moment you go to bed, you'll be wrapped up in your retail venture. And when you go to sleep, you'll dream about it. You'll be working harder than ever before—and loving every minute of it.

❧ 2 ❧
RETAILING 101

To be a citizen is to be a shopper. That truth could lead you to believe you already know enough about retailing to get your store up and running.

Maybe so. But whether you've dreamed of owning your own store all your life, hail from a long line of merchants, or have arrived at this juncture as a last resort in your quest for self-employment, it's important to take a few minutes and read this quick review of some basic concepts behind retailing. At the very least, refreshing your memory about the processes you're about to become a part of will help you fine-tune the plans for your store and put that plan into action.

Let's start at the beginning. Anyone who sells products to an end user is a retailer. That user, known as the customer, can be an individual, a group, or a business. What the retailer does is actually put the product in a customer's hands. The transaction revolves around an exchange of money, or its paper or plastic equivalent, for goods. That's a sale.

(Please note: This chapter is intended as a brief overview of the varied aspects of retailing discussed in subsequent chapters of this book. Throughout the chapter you'll see references to subsequent chapters of the book in which the topic is covered in greater detail.)

THE MANY FACES OF RETAILING

While you may think first of a retailer as a store owner, many other types of entrepreneurs can claim the label: the couple who spend their weekends at arts and crafts shows selling their home-made pottery; the consultant who visits your office, determines the company's computer needs, then puts together and sells a turnkey system; the street vendor hawking costume jewelry on the corner; and the owner of the downtown department store brimming with the latest goods.

Each of these individuals, and everyone else who sells products at retail, provides much-needed services. For consumers, retailers are the source of almost every product in the market. For suppliers—manufacturers and importers—retailers serve as the critical final link in the product distribution pipeline. The store is where the product meets the public.

As a retailer, you'll be a vital cog in the economic wheels of the nation. It's consumer purchases that help drive those wheels. A good year for retailers means a good year for the economy; the two are forever entwined.

WATCHING THE MONEY FLOW

The retail marketplace is one of the main channels allowing the flow of cash through our economy. For example, suppose a woman visits a local store and buys a new coat for one hundred dollars. A portion of that sale covers the store's overhead and operating expenses, and contributes to the store owner's income.

Most of the $100 goes to the distributor, the retailer's immediate supplier, to cover the retailer's cost of the coat. The distributor takes his cut for handling the merchandise, then pays the manufacturer. The distributor's profit from the sale helps meet expenses, including the salaries of his staff, and contributes to the distributor's income.

When the supplier—a manufacturer or importer—finally receives her payment for the coat, it pays for everything related to manufacturing it: raw materials, factory equipment, shipping, employee salaries and benefits, advertising, transportation, etc. As it was for the dealer and distributor, anything left after expenses is profit.

The actual retail cycle is obviously a bit more complicated, but that's basically how it works.

What happens at your store affects people around the country and world. When lots of women buy lots of coats, there's lots of money moving around. The retailer can give his clerks a raise and start thinking about a redesign of the store to attract more shoppers. The distributor sees enough business to invest in computerizing operations to handle the volume. The supplier adds a second shift at her factories to keep up with soaring demand for coats. She also designs a couple of new styles to give the shoppers more selection, hoping an additional increase in sales will follow.

While retail helps drive the national financial trends, your store can have an even more telling and immediate impact on your local economy. Any successful store owner lives off the profits from his business. He purchases all his goods and services, pays taxes, and makes donations to charity with money generated by store sales. When his store concept succeeds, he also creates jobs in the community, giving other people a livelihood. All this because the retailer can supply consumers with goods they want, but can't obtain directly from the supplier.

FRONTLINE OBSERVERS

As a retailer, your primary value to your suppliers is in creating a marketplace for their products. (Relationships with suppliers are covered in Chapter 11.) Without stores stocking and selling its products, a supplier would be forced to develop some alternative system to reach the consumer. The expense involved would drain her resources, demanding more in staff and expenditures than she could afford. Even then, she couldn't hope to place her products before as many consumers as she could with a national network of independent retailers carrying her products in every town and city.

One problem with the supplier's use of distributors and dealers is that she has little direct contact with the end users of her products. Some suppliers strive to offset that knowledge gap through extensive market research and consumer focus groups.

Nevertheless, it's you, the retailer, who mans the front line in the consumer market. Day in, day out, you'll observe firsthand what shoppers are buying, and why. Long before the marketing departments at corporate headquarters sense a new market trend, you'll know consumer attitudes have changed. Your insight can be of immeasurable use to suppliers, enabling them to fine-tune their products to the changing consumer tastes. Its value will become even more important as new computer technology allows you and other retailers to track developing trends with the cold precision of science.

THE QUID PRO QUO

You won't be serving your suppliers in these ways simply out of gratitude for products to sell. You'll be demanding product and marketing support in return for carrying the supplier's goods. The minimum: a quality product backed by a reasonable warranty or guarantee.

Since inventory will tie up your money, you'll look to your suppliers to share some of the financial burden. (Inventory selection is addressed in Chapter 8.) Some will, serving as both the source and financier of purchases. Suppliers may be a little wary of extending credit to the new shop in town, but once you demonstrate staying power, more favorable terms for payment can be negotiated.

In fiercely competitive markets of high-priced goods, smaller retailers, like you, try to shift as much of the financial burden to suppliers as possible. The recession's toll on retail forced many specialty store owners to adopt a "just-in-time" approach to inventory. Instead of committing to one large order for a selling season, these retailers placed smaller orders more frequently. When something moved off the shelf, they ordered another. And they expected delivery within days. You'll be adopting this just-in-time approach from day one.

All retailers look to their larger suppliers to "presell" recognized brand-name products through a combination of advertising and promotions. When the programs work, the store traffic that results helps all aspects of the retailer's business. For local advertising, many manufacturers offer "co-op" finds to offset the retailer's costs of advertising the manufacturer's products in local media. (Chapter 13 focuses on all your marketing tools: advertising promotions and public relations.)

Some also supply product literature imprinted with the store's name and location. As enticement to get store personnel behind their products, manufacturers run incentive programs: Sell so many Brand X televisions and you "win" a trip to Hawaii for two.

All these promotions and advertising are designed to help move products off your store's shelves. Consumers shop stores as sources of those goods. But despite all the ambitious planning that guides a marketing program, you'll serve as the shopper's main source for product information. Most people don't decide what to buy until they're standing in the aisle. (Customer service and customer relations are topics covered in Chapter 12.)

Successful specialty store owners, servicing a narrow market niche, know everything about their category of choice and anything related to it. (You'll find information on selecting your market niche in Chapter 4.) Shoppers will turn to you and your sales staff for help in selecting the product right for them. For the specialty store, this service before the sale is critical to survival. Once customers trust your store's advice, they develop a sense of loyalty that keeps them coming back.

By default, your store is the consumer's sounding board when she has complaints or praise for a product. To the shopper, you're accountable for any purchase made in the store. A poor-quality product may be the manufacturer's fault, but it's your problem until that customer is satisfied.

A STORE FOR EVERY SHOPPER

What does it take to ensure customer satisfaction? There are as many answers as there are shoppers. That's why our marketplace supports such a wide variety of stores. Each is developed around a distinct retail concept that caters to a particular group of shoppers.

Discount stores emphasize price over customer service. "Hypermarkets" and warehouse clubs take this approach to the extreme. Pallets filled with products is about as far as these stores go in the service category.

In department stores, there's more attention paid to the needs of the individual shopper. They market goods by category in departments staffed by employees well versed in the products.

Take the department out of the department store, add breadth to its selection and service, give it a catchy name, and you've got a specialty store. Specialty stores concentrate on a niche of the market, a select class of products thoroughly understood by the staff. For you, the trick is to take this concept as far as possible. Opening a store for fly-fishing gear, rather than sporting goods, immediately tells shoppers: "We are the experts."

RETAIL SUPPLY AND DEMAND: IN THEORY AND PRACTICE

Ideally, retail follows the theory of supply and demand. Say the summer's hot movie features an endearing black ferret. Suddenly every kid who sees the movie wants a black ferret. Some parents indulge their offspring's wants. Pet stores experience an unexpected run on ferrets. There are only so many ferrets to go around, though. Demand outpaces the supply, so the prices on all ferrets climb. Black ferrets sell for more than they ever have, or ever will again. It's a banner year for pet shop owners.

The theory holds with respect to products that aren't widely distributed. When you get into mass-market products, there's "intercompetition" among all classes of retailers for the same business. Eventually that situation forces someone to cut prices to boost sales. Better to sell at a lower price than not sell at all, is how the reasoning goes. It's a game only the largest retailers can hope to win.

As a retailer, you'll make your money from the difference between what you pay for a product and what you sell it for. This is called the profit margin, and is measured in points. Points are actually the percentage above what an item costs you that you're able to sell it for.

For instance, if you're a specialty dealer and you buy a hat for five dollars and sell it for ten dollars, your margin is one hundred points. That translates into a 100 percent markup. If a discount store pays the same for a comparable hat and sells it for six dollars, the margin is twenty points. The volume-oriented discounter must now sell five hats to realize the same profit you saw from one.

The immediate advantage is actually with the discounter. Most people shop price first. For them to spend more, you'll need to offer the consumer some compelling reason to buy your hat. Maybe you're the only one in town with a particular brand or style hat, or maybe you stock a broader selection of colors. Perhaps your hats are custom-fitted for customers.

Before you can begin adding up your profits, you must settle accounts with everyone else your business depends on. (Expenses and overhead are among the topics covered more thoroughly in Chapters 6 and 7.) The landlord, utilities, employees, advertising, etc. Then, what's left is your profit. That's not all going to pay for a family weekend in the Florida Keys, however. When you decide you want to expand the store, or add another location, you'll need to pay for that out of profits. Where else, short of a bank loan, can you get the money? Certainly not from suppliers. Their main concern is selling you products so consumers will have a place to buy them. As long as they're assured of sell-through at retail, they can keep their factories running.

THE MEN AND WOMEN IN THE MIDDLE

Suppliers use a variety of strategies to sell to and service their retail network. The type of individual you deal with depends on the distribution system endorsed by that company. Some small companies sell direct to dealers from the factory, without any middle man.

Most suppliers employ some form of sales staff for handling retail accounts. Anyone representing a supplier can be considered as a potentially valuable source of information about that company, its products, and trends in their industry. All salespeople get around. They have regular contact with a variety of retailers, and develop a good sense of what's happening in the marketplace.

Milk them for information, but closely scrutinize what salespeople tell you. Remember, their income depends on convincing you to stock what they sell.

Some suppliers employ their own field sales forces, staffed by regional sales managers and traveling salesmen and saleswomen. They visit stores on a regular basis, updating retailers on the company's products and promotions, and offering free advice on how to sell even more of their products.

Other companies rely on independent sales representatives—commonly called reps—to develop, service, and sell to their retail network. Reps function much like a company's own sales force. Usually they represent the product lines of companies too small for a dedicated sales staff, or for suppliers without sales staff in a particular region of the country. Reps usually handle only one brand in a product category. They may represent several suppliers in an industry as long as those products are not in direct competition. This can give them a much broader sense of trends; reps are especially well attuned to what's happening at retail.

Most salespeople don't actually deliver the goods they sell. Your order will get passed on to the supplier's own warehouse, or to a distributor who fills the order. Some distributors function as shipping warehouses for the manufacturer. Others operate as product wholesalers, a retailer to the retailer. Some distributors publish a catalog detailing the variety of products available for order and delivery.

Since they're more often specialists in a category rather than a particular manufacturer's line of product, distributors often have the best insight into market trends. Other salespeople work in the field and spend a lot of time traveling. Distributors take orders by phone, fax, or modem. They may hear from more retailers in a day than the field sales staff can visit in a week.

While their primary function is to sell, anyone serving as the supplier's middle man should be regarded as an ally in developing your store's marketing program. They're a good source for information on what products will be promoted, when, and how. They can help you acquire everything related to product support, from literature and ad slicks to co-op dollars for local advertising.

Occasionally you may deal with an individual who actually

makes the products he wants your store to sell. This is especially true for stores marketing arts and crafts or other one-of-a-kind products. The often self-employed producers of these goods usually lack the resources to extend the payment terms available from distributors and manufacturers. The best they can do is agree to supply you with goods on consignment. The maker of the craft sets her price, and you're free to add whatever margin seems reasonable. When the product sells, the artist gets paid. This strategy benefits both parties, especially when either is building a business. Selling on consignment gives the supplier a market to prove the worth of the product. For you, it's a risk-free opportunity to experiment with new inventory.

DEFINED BY PRICE

Regardless of how your store acquires its stock, one of the toughest challenges facing you is establishing a pricing strategy. Price sends consumers a loud message about who you want to be. People shop specialty stores for the combination of selection and service not found elsewhere. They expect to pay a little more for that privilege. Pricing should be a reasonable response to the trends in the market and an acknowledgment that your store offers something more. The specialty store owner who cuts margins close in a pitch for sales undercuts the reasons the store exists.

Price must allow room to cover expenses and provide a living wage. If the store concept cannot deliver that much return, you chose the wrong niche. Consider the expenses to be covered by the difference between what you pay and sell goods for: rent or mortgage, insurance, utilities, computers, advertising, upkeep and improvements on the store. Add to that your responsibilities as an employer. (These are covered in Chapter 11. For advice on hiring staff, see Chapter 9.) Staff deserves a decent wage. A benefits package is smart, too; it's cheaper to hold on to your old employees than find, hire, and train new ones. Only after you've met all those obligations can you start thinking about your own salary. So if your pricing doesn't allow room to cover all the basics, there won't be much of anything in the till by the time you dip into it for your compensation.

THE MASTER OF ALL TRADES

Getting paid is but one among your many concerns. Large retailers have people to worry about every aspect of the business. You must be a master of all trades: management and marketing; advertising and promotion; purchasing and collections; display and delivery; selection and service; personnel and customer relations.

Who said self-employment had anything to do with freedom from work? All those little responsibilities others leave at the office belong to the small business owner to take with him wherever he goes. Success as an independent retailer requires a clairvoyant's eye and a fisherman's patience. Not only must you sense what the customers want, but when and how much.

Every retail operation, every type of store, is a seasonal business. For most the holiday rush is the make-or-break period. Others depend on summer vacations or the whims of fashion with the changing seasons. Knowing what to stock, when, and how to promote it for maximum sales is a survival skill you'll need to refine, over time, into an art.

The dynamics of retailing offer opportunities to those rare individuals with a mind for business and a personality for people. Supreme confidence and optimism are requisites for anyone willing to surrender the security of employment to make their own careers.

Still interested? Then it's time to assess your skills and begin building the foundation for your retail empire.

❦ 3 ❦

HAVE YOU GOT WHAT IT TAKES?

Eager to work seven days a week, at least fifteen hours a day? Looking for the chance to spend even less time with family members and loved ones than you already do? Ready to give up vacations or holidays for the next year . . . or two . . . maybe five? Can you muster enthusiasm about surrendering the security of employment for the personal and financial risks of self-employment? Do you cherish an opportunity to toil harder, longer, and possibly for less money, so you can be your own boss?

If you can answer yes to these questions—and that doesn't scare you—you've got the attitude to make it as a retail entrepreneur. For if there's one trait shared by every entrepreneur, evident in every success story you've ever read, it's a singular determination to pursue one's dream, one's goal, whatever the odds. In layman's terms: You must be willing to do a lot of hard work.

Hard work isn't enough to secure your store's future, though. There are other business skills and personality traits that will help you bring your dream to life. What skills you lack, you can develop. But without an entrepreneur's unshakable drive, the challenges that go into opening your store will overwhelm you.

THE ENTREPRENEURIAL SPIRIT

The entrepreneur doesn't get discouraged. You can be stubborn to a fault, but you must be honest enough to admit when you're wrong. You must be goal-oriented, and willing to do whatever is required to nurture your dream to life. You'll need to stick with

22

a strategy as long as you're convinced it best serves your goal. But if you're shown a better way, you'll need to eagerly surrender yesterday's plan for today's solution.

If you're an entrepreneur, what will matter is success, on your terms. You'll need to believe in yourself and your business dreams, absolutely. Your motivation must be the opportunity to realize a personal vision, not convincing the rest of the world of your vision's merits. What the world thinks now shouldn't matter to you; the world will catch up, eventually. You're preoccupied with achieving personal goals that will bring you a more reward-ing career. Your commitment is complete; and you'll throw your-self into achieving that goal, entirely.

Your enthusiasm should be contagious, because you love what you're doing. It also springs from your drive to provide meaning-ful service to the community through retailing. The entrepreneur finds the better way of doing things, and draws rewards and fulfill-ment when the public recognizes his contribution. These are spirit-ual rewards, the emotional satisfaction a business brings that you can't define in dollars and cents.

You're in it for the money, surely. But that should be more the symbol than substance of your success. Your drive demon-strates your dissatisfaction with the status quo. The security of a nine-to-five job, a measured climb up the career ladder—that's right for somebody else, not you. You'll work longer hours, and perhaps make less money, for the independence that comes only with controlling your own career.

Psychologists, psychiatrists, and academics have long tried to identify the personal traits that separate the entrepreneur from the crowd. More than anything else, their studies suggest the entrepre-neur is an individual driven by challenge. The entrepreneur is self-made, not born. If there's a trait common to all, it's singular dedication to the hard work that will realize their particular dream. Entrepreneurs come in all shapes, colors, and sizes; some young and some old; men and women; and at every skill level. What all entrepreneurs share is a strong sense of faith in themselves, their abilities, and their vision.

The entrepreneur is the athlete of the business world. The indi-vidual who summons every resource, every skill and experience, and patiently applies all of this to reaching his goal. He cherishes the challenge as much as the progress in making his way. The entrepreneur is at once the contestant and opponent, runner and referee. It's her race and prize. Tempered by disappointment, the entrepreneur never loses sight of the goal, no matter what the odds.

Everyone loves a success; no one cares about a success in the making. Until you arrive, you'll face a long and lonely road. The climb to the top, to the realization of your dream, is one demanding self-reliance. You should know, or you'll learn, to trust none but yourself. Entrepreneurial experience teaches the essential truth of the proverb ''If you want something done, do it yourself.'' The reach for independence and self-determination is the entrepreneur's response to the world. If you're truly an entrepreneur, you want more for yourself than anyone else can deliver. In the early stages of building the business, you alone are the keeper of the dream.

You'll make demands of everyone, but no more than of yourself. The challenges you'll face are greatest at the outset, but they never abate. Certain characteristics, innate traits, tilt the scales in favor of success for the individual who possesses them. You need a positive attitude, a certain cockiness built of confidence, unshakable determination and enthusiasm. Beyond that, the skills required for success can be developed or hired.

What separates the achievers from the aspirants is awareness of their own limitations. Stubborn to a fault, single-minded, immune to criticism, you must also possess the instinctive sense to recognize when to turn to outside help. That's a point of strength, not an admission of defeat. Nature endows but few of us with everything required to make a success of our dreams. The entrepreneur is the one who can build on strengths by compensating for weaknesses.

Recognizing which skills you have, and which you lack, is a necessary first step in that process. The retail entrepreneur must be both an effective business manager and a skilled marketer. Your management and marketing skills will either support the vision through to success, or crumble from the stress that results when one takes on more than one should, or strives to do more than one could.

THE RETAIL MANAGER

Every business depends on an effective manager, the decision maker who directs the operation, supervises the staff, plans for the future, and ensures the entire operation runs smoothly. The retail manager must effectively manage store operations and manage people. Each requires certain skills and attitude. Review the following sections before filling out the skills assessment at the end of the chapter. It will help you identify the skills you need to improve or develop if you are to give your store a fair chance of success.

BEING THE BOSS MEANS YOU HAVE TOTAL RESPONSIBILITY

As the owner/operator, you're heir to every responsibility related to managing your store. You have all the responsibility, all the authority for building success. You own whatever headaches and triumphs the business brings.

As your business grows, or if business start-up resources allow it, you may decide to hire staff to handle some of the key areas of responsibility like running your business office, supervising the sales floor, or buying inventory. But if you're like most start-up retailers, you can expect to wear all hats and catch all the grief and what little praise falls your way. As the manager, you'll handle all the decision making related to running the business: everything from buying light bulbs to balancing the books and seeing Uncle Sam gets his due. Each area of management responsibility demands a certain level of awareness and skills, if not absolute expertise.

YOU'LL NEED TO MANAGE THE MONEY

Where's the money coming from? Where's it going? What's left? From long before the store formally opens its doors to closing day, finances should top your concerns. Just as money drives the national economy, cash flow keeps your store on the road to success.

You don't need to be a certified public accountant, but familiarity with basic principles of bookkeeping is strongly advisable. You should know how to project costs, read and keep a balance sheet, and analyze financial records for insight into the business. Your financial responsibilities will also entail controlling spending activities, budgeting expenses, and reconciling records and accounts. Managing finances means accurately projecting how much funding the store will need, and when. (We'll be covering all this in Chapter 7.)

These skills can be self-taught from books like this one, learned in night courses, and mastered through experience. You can also make it a computer-learning process, developing your skills as you learn how to run your business with a computer system. Computer hardware and software should be considered the basic tools of business management in the 21st Century. (We'll discuss your computer needs in Chapter 8.) For now, it's enough to say few retailers will be able to conduct business without them, and remain competitive. Computers are work savers. The right program, or application, will help organize all management responsibilities, do the books, reconcile accounts, and provide you with up-to-the-minute insight into any aspect of the business.

YOU'LL NEED TO MANAGE THE INVENTORY

All stores sell something. Products are your business, so everything related to what you sell and why is your decision. Managing inventory begins with selecting the right product mix. You'll need to respond to trends, seasonal and otherwise. What everyone wants this month, you won't be able to give away next month. You must know how much to order, when, and then when to reorder. When something starts to languish on the shelves, you must sense when it's time to drop prices and cut losses.

To a certain degree, experience will endow such instincts. From the beginning, though, you should develop a practice of maintaining accurate inventory records. Any retailer who enters business today thinking he can keep the stock records in his head is inviting in thieves or misfortune. In either event, you won't really know how much you lost. Again, a computer system, as an organizational tool and time saver, is recommended. (We'll be examining inventory management in Chapters 8 and 9.)

Success as a retailer in the 21st Century will owe much to the science of specialization. One of your ongoing challenges will be to keep pace with the latest developments in your category. It won't be enough for you to visit trade shows for an annual update on your industry. Your viability as the expert demands you constantly sift through manufacturer announcements, distributor catalogs, trade journals, and the business section of the local paper in pursuit of the next competitive advantage. With that, you'll continually monitor the competition, both through their advertising and inside their stores.

As inventory manager, you'll pull together the product mix that differentiates your store from every other store handling the same products. Once that mix is determined, and the products are in stock, you'll also need to set up displays that draw shoppers to the products. You'll decide what receives prominent play on the sales floor, and when it's appropriate to rotate the merchandise.

If the sales strategy includes telemarketing sales or mail order, inventory management also entails delivery service: packing and shipping products by the cheapest carrier and making sure they reach their destination. As if you didn't have enough to contend with.

YOU'LL NEED TO MANAGE PEOPLE

Since retailing is a people business, you'll need to be a "people person": an effective communicator, ever the charmer, yet able to draw the line and stand your ground when the situation demands it.

Managing relations with people will put you in contact with three groups: staff, suppliers' representatives, and customers. When dealing with anyone, the ability to communicate directly and effectively, in writing, person to person, or over the phone, is the basis of rewarding relationships. When you need to convey a point—whether placing an order or setting employee policy—the message should be above debate.

Managing staff requires responsiveness to their needs. Effective managers inspire rather than direct others. They let others know exactly what is expected of them. They promote spirit and team so people want to contribute to the common good. A team is composed of individuals; the smart manager recognizes the potential and limits of each player. He asks without demanding, and helps people test their skills and develop their potential. Still, the effective manager establishes definable benchmarks of what's expected and what will be accepted from others. The manager remains gracious to a point, but firm beyond that.

In dealings with suppliers, you'll have certain expectations, yet you'll need to recognize your own obligations. You must remain a loyal customer as long as that loyalty is rewarded. You must be open to suggestions on how to help your business. You'll need to be honest and open with suppliers in all dealings, and demand the same respect from those you trade with.

These same attitudes will guide your relations with customers. In the early history of most retail operations, the store owner is the store to shoppers. She's the salesperson, the stock clerk, and cashier all rolled into one smiling individual. Enthusiasm always wins customers over. In all dealings with customers, store personnel should follow the owner's lead and maintain a degree of professionalism and warmth. No one enjoys dealing with a retail salesperson who comes across as slick and primed for any sale.

Managing people requires combining the psychological and intuitive skills mentioned earlier with an ability to communicate directly and effectively. You'll need to be a skilled observer, able to read faces and interpret body language, cognizant of how the pause in the conversation defines intent. You need the innate ability to hear what shoppers say, and understand what they aren't saying.

Such skills must be cultivated. Your classroom could be any public place where people interact. But since stores are your future, that's where you should begin your education. Even before you know what type of store you want to run, visit all stores as an observer of the people who work and shop them. Solicit the help of salespeople. Test their knowledge and skills, and learn from their responses. Your experiences should give you direction and insight on how to treat your customers, and how they expect to be treated.

Stop by the customer service desk. Listen to shoppers and their frustrations. Watch their behavior. How do the clerks handle them? What works, and what doesn't? Is there anything you would do to improve relations?

The store owner who understands people, what they want and how to please them, is one whose business enjoys a head start. The skills required for business management and marketing can be acquired through training or experience. Anyone who emphasizes those over "people" skills is denying the reason all stores exist and prosper: to serve the shopper.

The retail manager demonstrates a certain respect for others and an interest in them. To sell to people, you must like them, generally and individually. After all, that's what retailing is all about: serving people. (We'll cover dealing with people in greater depth in Chapter 10.)

THE RETAIL MARKETER

Put a good selection of products in a well-designed store and you'll soon starve . . . if that's all you do. Why? Because before shoppers buy from your store, they must know it's there. Telling them about the store, what it offers and why they should shop there, is a make-or-break challenge for you. As the store owner and its business manager, your marketing responsibilities are as critical to the fate of the business as your management skills.

It's not enough to develop, nurture, and manage your vision of the perfect store, you must also sell others on the concept, continually. Whenever you seek financial backing for your store—be it from banks to finance your dream or the customers you hope will flock to your latest sale—you're involved in marketing.

Marketing is as much about public relations as promotions. It shapes the best face you put before your customers, the store image that invites them in or keeps them away. The store name, logo, design, and displays, special promotions and sales, community involvement, and advertising all fall within your realm as retail marketer. (And all will be covered thoroughly in Chapter 13.)

If you're serious about going into business for yourself, you already possess the basic skill of marketing: confidence in your abilities and vision. If you don't believe in your store concept, and question your ability, read no further. This book is written for people who know they can make it on their own. How can you hope to convince others of your store if you don't completely believe in it yourself?

If you have that confidence, you shouldn't have trouble summoning the enthusiasm to promote the concept. Effective marketing requires your confidence and enthusiasm. These are qualities you won't find in any book, and you can't get them from night school. They must be part of your psyche from the outset. The successful retail marketer has such a great store, with such a great selection, that she's bursting to let the world know where it is.

In getting that word out, you'll be challenged to use public relations, promotions, and advertising to create the positive perceptions that will win loyal customers for your store.

THE MYTH OF FREEDOM

Now that you're familiar with the breadth of responsibility that goes with running a store, perhaps it's worth pausing a moment to reflect on your dream of freedom through retailing.

As demonstrated in the previous pages, running your own retail store is all about hard work, dedication to long days, and uncertain gains. If your definition of freedom holds no place for these, then you should not assume the risks of starting your own retail business. The freedom the store promises is the sense of liberation that comes with controlling your destiny. Certainly hard work is required, but you're the sole beneficiary of that dedication, not some guy in the big office at the end of the hall on the fifth floor.

When you wake up in the morning, when you go to bed at

night, as the store owner, you're in charge. You may work long hours, you may lose a few hairs, but your success, or failure, is entirely your own. And when there's another generation hungry to climb up the career ladder, there won't be anyone who can push you out of the business you nurtured and brought to success yourself.

If that sounds like freedom to you, running your own store definitely promises a better future than the alternative.

HONING YOUR SKILLS

That said, the faster you develop your skills, the faster you'll be able to set that dream in motion. One of the most valuable attributes you can possess is an ability and willingness to recognize personal limitations. When there's something you can't do, better to hire the person who can than stumble deeper into a maze of your making.

Most of these skills required of you can be developed on your own, either through self-education or by attending evening courses or professional development seminars. You must be realistic in terms of personal expectations and obligations, though. You can study store design at night school for a semester, or hire a consultant who can do the job in two weeks. Your time is your most important asset. If you're smart, you'll manage time as a limited resource.

Take a few moments to fill out the skills evaluation chart at the end of the chapter. Be honest and thorough with your answers; you want to identify your weaknesses so you can improve your skills. Use your time now, as you begin investigating your options and planning your store, to improve your skills. Observe and learn from the success of other retailers. Talk to store owners about the business of retailing. Fill out the skills assessment chart and use it as a guide, then begin working to improve your skills in the management areas where you recognize your own weaknesses. Enroll in business classes if your time allows, or become a regular customer at the self-help section of the local bookstore. If you already own and use a computer, investigate accounting and business management software. As you'll see in Chapter 10, the computer will prove an invaluable tool in every phase of planning and managing your store, and save you time in the process.

And time is the one commodity you'll always need more of. The varied responsibilities that go with being the store owner/operator will soon make ample demands on yours.

SKILLS ASSESSMENT Chart

Use the following chart as a guide in honestly evaluating your skills as a retail manager and marketer. Simply check off the categories in which you have sufficient experience to fulfill the responsibilities as store owner.

BUSINESS/OFFICE MANAGEMENT

Accounting/Payroll _____
Purchasing _____
Billing _____
Collecting _____
Taxes _____
Record Keeping _____
Computers/Business Software _____

PERSONNEL

Hiring _____
Firing _____
Motivating/Scheduling _____

RETAILING

Sales _____
Customer Service _____
Buying _____
Pricing _____
Sales Planning _____
Dealing with Salespeople _____
Negotiating/Tracking Sales _____
Tracking Competitors _____
Display _____

MARKETING

Advertising/Public Relations _____
Promotion _____
Writing/Composing Ads/Media Contact _____
Media Buying _____
Tracking Responses _____

☙ 4 ❧

CHOOSING YOUR MARKET

If you've pushed this far into the book, you're obviously serious about opening your own store. The workload described in the last chapter wasn't enough to scare you off, and you realize opening your own store carries both risks and opportunity. From here you'll start putting theory into practice, and you'll plan your store.

The process begins with choosing your market. Your store's identity, and your future as the retail entrepreneur, depends on the mix of products you sell, the services you provide, and the customers you serve. In this chapter we'll focus on the initial research you should do as you investigate your best retail opportunity. Ideally the store you open builds on your present skills and interests, the local and national trends in the product market that interests you, and the competition that exists on the local level for sales in that market.

Your first step is to begin keeping a notebook or set up a computer file devoted to your retail store. When you put your thoughts and plans on paper, and can return to them, they assume a greater sense of urgency. Written plans and established goals provide a yardstick with which to measure your progress, or lack of it. For some of us, writing things down helps organize our thoughts and plans. Once recorded for posterity, they're there as a reference, either to jog your memory or refamiliarize you with something once learned but forgotten.

You can increase your chances for success if you enter a product market already familiar to you. So the investigation begins with an assessment of what you bring to the venture in background, skills, and interest. This information should provide insight on the products or product categories you are best suited to sell.

In your first entry, describe yourself: age, income, family, interests, things you enjoy doing, things you hate doing, and anything else you would use to describe you. Include your major accomplishments or disappointments, as well as your personal and financial goals.

Next, compose a few lines summarizing why you want to go into business for yourself. What's so bad about your present job? How will owning your business improve that? What do you want from your store? What will it take to make you happy? What strengths do your bring to business? What skills do you need to improve? What kind of income are you looking for? What excites you most about being in business for yourself? Least? What do you expect to gain, professionally and personally, from opening your own store?

Finally, focus on your present thoughts about your store. Do you have any particular store or store type in mind, or do you just want to open "a store?" What will you sell? Where will it be? Who are your customers?

SELL WHAT YOU KNOW

Unless your plans for a career in retailing are built around buying an established store, your responses to the last set of questions demand a great deal of time and thought and will evolve in the process. Deciding what type of store you'll open, selecting your merchandise, and identifying your market niche, when taken together, amount to defining your business.

As mentioned earlier, today's retail marketplace offers distinct opportunities for the specialty store concept. There are certain store types that, given the right location, will usually succeed: the combination convenience store/gas station sitting at the exit ramp of a busy interstate; the pharmacy/health and beauty aid store across the street from the major medical center; and the newsstand/candy shop at the entrance of the commuter railway station. Unfortunately, the prime real estate that all but guarantees prosperity for certain retail ventures has by now all been claimed. Sure, the occasional new interstate or major shopping mall will still be built. But today the typical independent retailer has to rely on more than location to deliver customers. The store itself must possess some compelling feature that makes people want to shop there.

Today's trend of huge, generalist discount stores and price clubs creates a real need for the smaller specialty store. You can, and must, focus your business on a narrow segment of the market, defined either by interest, age group, or demographic profile. That's the market upon which you can build a business. It's not enough to put together a selective assortment of merchandise and wait to tally sales. To be successful you must present shoppers with solutions to their purchase needs. That may be as frivolous as a new doodad to display on their mantel, or as necessary as a new liner for the chimney. The successful specialty store gains a reputation as the unrivaled source for selection and related services in a select category of merchandise.

Whatever the category, you'll need to be fully familiar with the products you sell, and their applications. It's not enough to know what is available in your selected market niche, however. The specialty retailer must know all there is about the products the store sells, their use, and how to help consumers get the most benefit from these purchases. Remember, the specialty store exists to provide solutions for a distinct group of customers. Your knowledge and enthusiasm are an important aspect of what the store offers.

For that reason, if you want to open a store, but aren't yet sure what type it should be, you should begin the planning process with a thorough evaluation of your interests and experience. Look within, first, for anything in your background, experience, or hobbies that might lend itself to a retail store. The gourmet knows food and how to prepare it. The outdoorsman, camping equipment. The working woman respects the challenge of balancing career and family.

In each case above, the individual could develop a store concept around the interest, immediately identifiable by shoppers: The Gourmet Pantry of special kitchen tools and condiments; Trips and Trails, the backpacker's warehouse; Mother's Helper, where women find everything from quick meals to games for quality family time. Whenever an entrepreneur develops a store concept around a personal interest or concern, the store gains a mission. The owner brings genuine passion to the endeavor, and that can prove contagious to shoppers. And in pursuing your own interests and helping others in that pursuit, running the store is not a job, but a pleasure. Such fortunate retailers can't wait to get to work, and they have trouble leaving at the end of the day.

Creating your store around something you already know and enjoy strengthens the business. It's easier to get enthusiastic about something fondly familiar than something entirely new. By selling what you know, you give yourself a head start and cut down on the time required to learn an entirely new category of goods. To succeed as a 21st Century retail entrepreneur, you must be the recognized expert on what you sell. That expertise should be rooted in your own experience and interests.

The specialty store draws its appeal from the combination of product selection and related services available only there. Camera stores stock cameras, accessories, and frames, and offer camera repair and film processing. Computer stores sell hardware and software along with such services as repair, installation, and training. Use your own shopping experience as an aid in identifying potential market opportunities. Compare your needs for selection and service with what you've found in the marketplace.

So if you want to open a store, but aren't yet certain what kind, get out your notebook and start jotting down notes. Where are your real interests and experience? Is there anything there that lends itself to a specialty store? Have you ever experienced trouble locating what you need for a hobby? Was it a major hassle the last time you set out to purchase a particular type of equipment? If there's already a store that addresses your interests locally, is there something it does that leaves customers like you unhappy with the shopping experience? If you come up with yes answers to the last few questions, other people probably share that experience. Like you, they would support a retailer who does a better job catering to their particular interest and need. Take the success of telephone specialty stores as an example. Telephones and related products—answering machines, fax machines, cables and other accessories—can be found in every type of retail outlet today. But no other single source offers the breadth of selection and related services as the telephone specialty shop. Whatever the consumer wants in a telephone product can be found there. These retailers provide either installation service or ''how to'' advice for the consumer. For those shopping for a telephone, the shop offers one-stop convenience with enough of a selection to please every shopper and the service support they require to enjoy the full benefits of their purchases.

Now identify all local sources for products required for your interests or work background. Are there any local gaps in availability? Review the list and your response to the preceding questions, matching the products and services that could be brought under one roof. Based on your notes, suggest some store types you feel a need for, or think others might want to shop. Consider these entries as you identify the best fit for your interests, skills, and experience. Compile a prioritized list of the type of store you would like to open. Use it as a guide for investigating your options. Are there stores that match your suggestions in the area? If so, visit them. Later, write down your impressions, as a shopper, of their strengths and weaknesses. If no such store exists locally, ask why. You may be on to something, or it may be that the area's economy can't support such a venture.

CHOOSING YOUR MARKET Work Sheet

This form can help you identify market opportunities in your area. Start by listing the product or product category that interests you, followed by a list of related products and services, and a description of whom you envision as the typical customer. Then conduct an informal survey of stores in your area stocking this product, noting the selection, prices of goods, and service support available at each. The information you compile should help you determine if a gap in availability exists that could be addressed by a specialty store. If it does, you should pursue the additional research (see Chapter 5) that will help you select the right location.

Product(s): _____

_____

Related products: _____

_____

Related services: _____

_____

Suppliers or manufacturers (for each category of product, accessory, or service): _____

_____

Typical customer(s):
   Sex _____ Age _____ **Household situation** _____

   Income level _____

   _____

These products are currently available at the following store(s): _____

_____

(complete this section for each potential competitor)

Store name and location:_____

_____

Selection by manufacturer model and price: _____

_____

Service support: _____

_____

Was salesperson knowledgeable about product?: _____

_____

Products and services not available at this location: _____

_____

_____

KNOW WHAT YOU SELL

Once you identify the type of specialty store that seems to represent your best retail opportunity, you need to thoroughly investigate the types of products the store would handle. This involves a look at what's being sold by potential competitors as well as what is available from suppliers.

As you investigate products and suppliers, you're gathering information that will be of vital use when you actually begin planning the store you'll open.

Before you proceed with planning, you need a real sense of the forces at play in the product market you're considering.

Go back to your notebook and start writing again. Is there enough selection in that specialty to warrant a store devoted to it? Are there related products, or services, that could be handled in the same store? Who are the major and minor suppliers to the category? How widely distributed are their products? Are there more choices available than consumers need? What do you intend to offer that other retailers who stock those products don't? What type of advertising is being done?

Again, consider the telephone specialty store as a model. The selection there includes everything to do with telephones. The store's strength is its comprehensive selection, and the services that allow consumers to enjoy the full benefit of their purchases. Shoppers can buy phones anywhere today, but many prefer the specialty store because it has the combination of selection and service that makes it the most convenient place for them to shop.

As part of your research, visit every type of store that handles the products you're considering. If none exist locally, head out of town for a weekend. If you still can't find any, you may really be on to something.

WHO ARE YOUR CUSTOMERS?

Describe the people who'll buy from your store. Visualize the shopper who'll bring you success. When you know who you need to reach, you can begin thinking about how to present and market products, and where to situate the store.

You may be able to acquire a detailed profile of your typical customer by contacting the industry or retail trade group representing your selected product category. (For information on how to locate these groups, see Appendix B). Many trade groups conduct market research that enables them to develop a profile of the typical buyer of a product or group of products. You may also develop your own profile by describing the person you believe your store will serve.

Is your core customer male or female? Young? Old? What's his income? Where does he live? What are his interests? How and where does he shop? Why would he shop in your store? Can't he already get that somewhere else? What can your store give him, or do for him, that he can't get now? How far would he travel for such a store? Is there any way you can make the process more convenient for distant shoppers?

Consider where your customers presently shop. How easy is it now to find the products and services your store will sell? The specialty store draws on a much wider population base than the local supermarket. Everyone needs food, every week; people might patronize The Umbrella Stand once in a lifetime. If you're smart, you'll know who your customers are, where they live, and how to reach them before you hang your signs.

Opening any store asks serious financial investment with no absolute guarantee of return. Better to hold your store idea to the fire now, and test it for success or failure on paper, than spend the next year and your life savings on a great idea the numbers can't support. Conversely, if your evaluation of consumers, products, and the market indicates retail opportunity, you can proceed with a certain degree of optimism.

INVESTIGATING THE MARKETPLACE

You know what you want to sell, and who you want to sell it to. Now for the really tough question: Does the market need your store? Before you can answer that, find out some information on the individuals you've established will be your customers.

WHERE ARE YOUR TARGETED CUSTOMERS?

One of your best sources for demographic information is the census tract data published by the U.S. Census Bureau. This information provides a detailed analysis of a geographic area based on the census survey. In heavily populated areas, that area can be as concentrated as a single zip code. Another good resource for general insight on the consumer market is the publication *American Demographics*. This monthly magazine regularly publishes articles on population trends and their effect on consumer needs and attitudes. Such articles provide insight into consumer market trends, which people are buying what products, and what they'll be buying in the future. When you have an idea of who your potential customers are, you can find out where they live by researching the demographic data available from census records.

As long as we're discussing research, this seems as good a place as any to urge you to take advantage of all the resources available to you at your local public or college library's business resource center. Their shelves overflow with data valuable for the cautious business planner. Reference librarians enjoy nothing more than helping someone like you track down some useful information. In minutes they'll direct you to information it might take hours for you to locate unassisted.

If you've got computer proficiency, sign on with one of the on-line business database services. These put the world of business information, market research, and detailed data analysis within instant reach by modem. Contact your local computer user's group for information on what services are available in your area. When using an on-line service, remember the meter is running as long as you're connected. Research sessions can get surprisingly expensive. It's best to know what information you want, and where you're going to go for it, before you dial the connection.

Once you gather the demographic statistics, look for information that matches the profile you've created of your perfect customer. Start with census figures for the immediate area, and search until you identify an area or region where the people you need to reach live. Suppose the concept behind a store called Just the Fax is to put fax machines in the homes of married professionals.

The entrepreneur looks for areas with a heavy concentration of affluent, middle-aged working couples. When they're identified, she can start investigating suitable locations. (We'll cover the details of that search in Chapter 5.)

On the other hand, suppose the entrepreneur planning The Parachute Shoppe, which caters to young, thrill-seeking adventurers, learns there aren't enough potential customers residing in any combination of census tracts within a ten-mile radius. However, in his own experience as a jumper, he's met people from more than fifty miles away, who regularly travel to the local airport to pursue the sport. That indicates he should situate his dream store somewhere along the road leading to the airport where these thrill seekers gather for jumps.

Demographic information provides insight on where the people who match your envisioned customer profile live. It can help direct you to an appropriate location, and indicate how large an area you must reach with your advertising. (The prospective store owner would be wrong to assume everyone who lives in an area, and matches the profile, will actually shop at the store, however. Be conservative in your expectations. Better to be pleasantly surprised than bitterly disappointed later.)

Here again, the information gathered through your own research or available from trade groups can be of help. Of course, the number of customers your store needs, and the area in which they live, depends on what you sell. The retailer of antique Oriental rugs serves a much smaller audience, drawn from a much wider area, than the proprietor of the carpet store. Your research should help you determine how much surrounding population is required to give the store a reasonable chance of success. Remember, if your research reveals there's not enough concentration of customers in any area to support the store, but everything else convinces you the idea is viable, approach the development and store location issues differently. Stores can be so specialized that potential customers are scattered across the state or nation. Such retailers combine a physical store—showroom and warehouse—with retailing alternatives like catalog or telephone sales. You may still find success by being willing to adapt your idea to accommodate clients who may never actually step into your store. Before you begin fine-tuning your store concept to the needs of your customers, you need to understand who they are and where they live. That insight can only be gained through demographic research.

WHAT ARE THE RETAILING TRENDS?

Market demographics reveal only one part of the story. Other sets of numbers you should consider as you finalize your product selection are profiles of national retailing trends, and the failure and success rates for specific store types. The Department of Commerce produces detailed statistical analysis on just about every aspect of American business, including retailing. Dun & Bradstreet maintains and markets reports on small business, such as success and failure rates by retail store type. (For information, contact the Department of Commerce at (202) 377-2000, or Dun & Bradstreet at (201) 605-6000.) Remember, while the numbers contained in these reports are only as good as the information reported to the researchers, they're still strong indicators of the trends at play in the marketplace. An overabundance of stores similar to yours, or an unusually high failure rate for similar start-ups, should be regarded as red flags. These are all indicators that you may need to rethink your store concept, or field-test it before investing in opening a store. (Test options are suggested in Chapter 5.)

Whatever statistics you use when exploring the market, don't let the numbers alone shape your plans. An entrepreneur draws power from instinct as well as information. Numbers measure facts and report what's already happened. Statistics indicate trends in process or after the fact. They say nothing about changing attitudes or the whims of fashion. For those you'll need to rely on your instincts.

Once you're considering a particular retail specialty, start reading the trade magazines written for that industry. Some of these publications track the business from the retailer's perspective. Written for store owners and operators, retail trade publications cover the issues affecting retail, including business trends and marketing strategies. Manufacturers use trade books to announce products and programs through advertising. Their executives discuss trends shaping their business plans through the articles.

No single resource seems to list every magazine written for every industry. Ask your librarian for help compiling a list of publications for your field from several reference books. Also check the *Reader's Guide to Periodical Literature* and the business index listing for recent articles about the retail market you plan to enter. Read at least a year's worth of these articles to gain a sense of what's happening in the field.

Other information resources for the aspiring retailer include the varied trade organizations representing that industry. Gale Research publishes *The Encyclopedia of Associations,* which is available at most business reference centers. A *Directory of Business, Trade, and Public Policy Organizations* is available from the Small Business Administration. Trade groups vary greatly in intent and action. Some function as affiliations of people working within an industry. Others exist solely as lobbying arms for special interest groups. Most serve in some capacity as an information clearinghouse for that industry. They produce market trend reports and annual analysis of the health of their industry. A few publish their own monthly magazines. Get in touch with the right organizations, and request whatever information they can supply about the industry.

Industry trend reports contain an abundance of information, not all of it useful to the retailer. It's up to you to pick through the numbers. Some reports provide a detailed breakdown of the store types handling the industry's products and market share. Some reports produced by trade groups are quite expensive for nonmembers. Know what the report covers before you place an order. Ask for a previous year's report at no charge so you can study it before ordering this year's.

When reading trade reports and business journals, look for insight into how the industry operates. What are the issues or opportunities that could shape the outlook for your store? Closely read the magazine's letters from readers, and look for profiles and articles about retailers. That's where you'll learn about the real challenges of running a store in that industry, and how retailers deal with these problems. You may discover unexpected issues that should temper your plans.

SPEAK WITH YOUR POTENTIAL PEERS

People who enjoy what they do like to talk about their work. Retailers are no different. Consider speaking to those already in the retail category you want to enter. They're among your best sources for information and insight. The man or woman already operating a store like the one you want to open is the person with the most to teach you. Unfortunately for you, no intelligent businessperson will coach an upstart into becoming direct competition. That's why you should contact stores in the same business, but not in the same general area as where you want to locate. Visiting these stores, and talking to their owners, can prove a crash course in everything you need to know to realize your dream. In a larger city, you may only need travel across town for this learning experience. In less populated areas, the journey may take you a few hours away.

Contact the store owner before you visit. Briefly explain your store plans. If he sounds receptive, ask to arrange, at his convenience, a visit to the store and a short meeting. Offer to buy him a cup of coffee—successful retailers don't have time to go out for long lunches. Be honest and open about what you want to do, and what you hope he might share with you. When you get the chance to talk in detail, ask about business in general. How long has he been at it? What's the key to his success? If he could, would he open the same type of store again? Can he recommend this concept to you? Why?

Then move to some specifics about "the industry." How is the retailer treated by suppliers? Are there any problems with products, in terms of supply or quality? Do the suppliers support small retailers? Is there any trouble remaining competitive and profitable? What was the biggest headache in establishing the store? What are the retail trends for business, in the store owner's view?

Establish good rapport with other dealers and it'll benefit you throughout your retail career. As long as stores are not directly competing for the same consumer's dollar, a certain camaraderie exists among retail specialists serving the same category. They confide about business with one another, bounce ideas back and forth, and share suggestions on improving sales. The fact that you're interested in the same career is flattering. Some dealers will be glad to help a novice learn from, and avoid, their mistakes.

SPEAK WITH YOUR POTENTIAL SUPPLIERS

After speaking with retailers, contact suppliers whose products you may handle. Call corporate headquarters and ask for the person responsible for sales in your state or region. He may be on staff, working as an independent rep, or working out of a distributor's office. In any event, once that person picks up the phone, introduce yourself, mention your store plans, and request product information. Ask for a couple of minutes of the salesperson's time to discuss his company's product and sales policy. Find out what kind of year the company, and its dealers, are having. Is the market for its products growing, declining, or flat? What does the company do to support its dealer base? Does it control distribution? Do larger accounts get preferential treatment? Are there any special programs to support specialty dealers? Is there enough demand for its products to support another dealer in your area?

Remember, in this conversation you're dealing with a salesperson ever intent on gaining another account. Nevertheless, he or she has an implied obligation to be honest about business and the retail trends at work. Just to make sure, compare what you hear from him with what you've heard from retail contacts. If the answers agree, you're getting good information. If not, press the salesperson about discrepancies that concern you.

SPEAK TO POTENTIAL CUSTOMERS AND SEASONED OBSERVERS

Finally, talk to consumers about your store concept. That includes everyone you know: friends, family, acquaintances, and strangers. How do they see chances for a store like yours? Would they shop there? Forget the praise for your idea, it won't teach you anything. Carefully measure the criticism, though. It reveals perceptions and attitudes you'll continually confront as you build the business.

If you want to bounce your store idea off an independent observer, contact the local office of the Small Business Administration. SBA sponsors a mentor's program called SCORE (Senior Corps of Retired Executives). It brings together retired executives and people trying to launch a business within their realm of expertise. Their advice is free, impartial, and rooted in experience.

SIZING UP THE COMPETITION

By now your notebook will be swollen with opinions, observations, and cold hard facts about the business you want to be in. You still need to investigate yet another of the determining factors in the ultimate success or failure of your store: the competition. If your research to this point convinces you your store concept is so unique, you face no competition, move on to the next chapter and start thinking about where to set up shop. Most aspiring retailers, though, must take competition into account when deciding what type of store they want to open. Unless your store is so specialized it will be the *only* source for products (quite unlikely), you'll face some competition. And as we approach the turn of the millennium, you can expect much of this to be intercompetition in which all types of retailers compete for sales in some product categories.

Take the VCR as an example. It's available across the spectrum of retail outlets. The discount variety store stocks one or two models, inexpensively priced to appeal to the broadest group of buyers. Department stores sell VCRs as well, but the selection concentrates on mid-priced and high-end models that reflect their customers' tastes and budgets. The electronic superstore stocks a representative sampling of all models currently available, heavily promoting price on low-end models in an effort to attract shoppers and step them up to higher-priced, more profitable models. Finally, the audio/video specialist focuses on the absolute best in today's VCR technology, and packages it into an integrated home entertainment center. Although their customer bases differ, all these retailers are competing for the sale to the person simply shopping for a VCR. A similar situation will present itself in any product category that's widely distributed.

As a 21st Century retail entrepreneur, you must either offer consumers the selection and service no one else in your area is offering, or do what everyone else is doing, but better. Before you can develop the appropriate response strategy, you must first know how your potential competition approaches business. This education process begins with a visit to every store in the area handling the products you intend to sell. Record your impressions after each visit. How broad a selection does each offer? How are the products displayed, advertised, and promoted? What brands are carried where? What related products or services do these stores carry in support of that product? What about price and guarantees? How do they handle customers on the sales floor and at the return desk?

Track your competitors' advertising. How do they present themselves to consumers? What image do the ads convey? Who do the ads speak to? How do they hope to motivate people into the store? What kind of expectations do the ads create for shoppers?

The retail entrepreneur will design her store as a response to the competition's strengths and weaknesses. Her store will be strong in all the areas they're strong, and also strong where they're weak. Survival as a specialty retailer demands your store be all things to anyone interested in the products it sells.

SELECTING YOUR NICHE

Specialty store retailing, which is the real business opportunity for you, requires that you identify and pursue a distinct niche of the consumer marketplace. It may be a specialized line of products, or a combination of products and services that cater to a core group of consumers. Fish with a net, and you'll come up with something. Fish with a lure and you get the fish you're after. Specialty retailing is all about coming up with the right hooks, the right lures, for the prize catch.

In selecting a market niche, take everything you've learned into consideration: products, suppliers, competition, customers, demographics, and consumer attitudes. Focus your efforts where your interests, experience, and research indicate opportunity. Use your intellect, insight, and instinct as tools for adapting your store concept to consumer needs.

A market niche requires special handling, and appeals to a select group of people. The best specialty store concepts focus on a narrow segment of the market, but appeal to a broad segment of the population. A greeting card shop or child's shoe store are two good examples. Other good concepts focus on a narrow product base that appeals to only one portion of the population: Consider the success of eyeglass centers and craft supply stores. All children wear shoes; only a share of the population requires glasses; fewer still are interested in visiting a crafts store. Yet each of these represents a valid specialty store because they cater to only a small segment of the total consumer marketplace.

We'll talk about some of the ways to test your idea in the next chapter.

Regardless of the type of niche, the pricing strategy you choose will go a long way toward defining your market. Price plays a critical role in determining how the store is perceived in the minds of shoppers. Its importance cannot be overlooked, from the moment you begin to develop your business plan (Chapter 6) to the ongoing efforts of your marketing strategy (Chapter 13). The price structure you adopt defines who you want to be for your customers. Emphasis on low prices means no-frills shopping to many shoppers, while higher prices imply the consumer will find more for his money, in terms of selection and service, at the store.

Specialty stores often charge a premium because of the unique assortment of products found there. If you choose to price your products on the high end, you send a message that must be reinforced by the look of your store. A specialty store may stock top-quality merchandise, but if the store itself looks cheap, the goods will seem overpriced to most shoppers. By the same token, a share of bargain-hunting shoppers will never enter a store with expensive fixtures, even if it stocks an assortment of low-priced goods. The look of the store must announce the type of store it is. The store's viability hinges on product selection and service, and consumer perceptions created by pricing and the look of the store. If the retailer identifies and addresses a distinct market niche, these factors will all work together to guarantee success.

When choosing your niche for the 21st Century, you should also consider whether the store should be entirely dependent on in-store sales, or if other selling techniques can be utilized to your advantage. Services like mail and fax orders, telemarketing, even on-line sales, are now feasible endeavors for small retailers. As the specialist, the retail entrepreneur needs to sell to as broad a customer base as possible. That could force many who select a tightly focused niche to reach beyond the immediate geographic area for sales. They'll need to develop alternative means of sales and distribution.

Regardless of whether you're going to rely on in-store sales alone, or you'll use every possible means to pull in customers, you can't afford to lose sight of the three factors that always motivate shoppers: selection, service, and convenience. Always keep them in mind as you develop the strategy for serving your market niche. The way you apply them as you develop your store will give it an identity, and how consumers respond will determine how successfully you've addressed the market you choose.

SELECTION IS WHY CUSTOMERS COME

Shoppers support a store because that's where they find an assortment of goods. You'll need to offer shoppers all that's available within a well-defined category. That means more breadth and greater depth; every product in the category, and everything else related to it. The best source quickly becomes the only source, in the mind of the shopper.

SERVICE IS WHAT KEEPS CUSTOMERS COMING BACK

If selection is what draws people to the store, service is what keeps them coming back. That won't change in the 21st Century. What will change are the lengths to which you'll need to go to fulfill your service obligations to customers. From now on, retailers will need to do anything and everything that supports the customer's purchase, including delivery, repair, updates, and exchanges. Service is where shoppers most need the independent retailer, and where you must shine.

CONVENIENCE IS THE RESULT OF SELECTION AND SERVICE

Give people the best selection, back it up with every conceivable service, and you're running a pretty convenient place to shop. Convenience is all about making the shopping experience as enjoyable as possible.

To some people, shopping is a destination. They regard the store as a place to go for socializing and modest entertainment. For others, shopping is a process, an endured activity that gives them access to something they want. If your store will be a destination, its ambience will be one of the determining factors in your success. Your shoppers will expect more from the store than a place to buy things. They'll want an experience to go with it, experience found only there. Conversely, if the store exists primarily as the source, it is the delivery and access to goods you provide customers that must separate it from the retail pack.

Whatever market niche you choose, only continued success will demonstrate how well your concept matches consumers' changing needs and expectations of what a store should be. Before you can begin to test the concept, though, you must find the location that will serve your retail ambitions.

⤞ 5 ⤝

SELECTING YOUR SITE

Now that you've an idea of where to find your customers, turn your attention to where they'll find you. Nothing serves your store as well, during its first year, as the right location. And nothing can do as much to unravel your retail dreams as the wrong location. Selecting your site, then, may contribute as much to your immediate success as deciding what to market in your store.

Such an important decision warrants special attention. Begin by determining what you need in terms of space, and then you can concentrate on finding the location that promises to give your store the start it deserves.

LOCATION OR ACCESS?

An old saying holds "location, location, and location" as the three most important ingredients in a store's success. While that's still true for many retail businesses, it's no longer the universal rule. In fact, with today's electronic communications technology and mobile distribution network, "access" might have replaced location. Which is the most important—location or access—depends on what type of retailer you want to be. If your plans center around a retail store, then certainly the right location will make your dreams come quicker. On the other hand, if what you really want to run is a retail business, location may not be as important. You might be just as, if not more, concerned with developing a system that gives shoppers access to place orders by mail, phone, or fax.

The owner of a retail store requires an attractive store setting, easily accessible to shoppers, a place to showcase what the store sells. For the retail business, location is a secondary consideration. Its customers have no need to visit a store. Either the salesperson carries merchandise directly to them, or they order from catalogs by phone, fax, or mail.

Consider the situations of two people intent on opening bookstores, as examples. One enjoys reading, and lives in a rapidly developing suburb outside a major city. Over the past few years she has tired of heading into downtown every time she wants the latest book or magazine; there are no local sources. She has heard that complaint from others in the area. With a new mini-mall going up at the crossroads of the area's two main avenues, she has signed on as one of the first tenants for her store, Book Ends, a combination book, magazine, and stationery store.

He has mulled a career change for years, and has concluded there's a bookstore in his future, but of a much different sort. All his life he has been an avid reader of personal diaries and narratives of historical interest. It has always been trouble tracking them down, a frustration he has heard from other amateur historians who share his special interest. He plans The Diary Pages as the top source for published diaries in the country. His customers will be people like himself who have an abiding interest in history, as well as professional historians and book collectors eager to acquire rare or out-of-print first-person accounts. That audience, his core customers, is scattered all over the country.

Both retailers need a physical location for their businesses. Her business is totally dependent on in-store traffic. Sure, she can take orders by phone and ship them out, but her livelihood depends most on sales transactions in the store, at the cash register. For him, the situation is almost reversed. He'll need a storeroom with a limited sales floor. More important to him than the location is a system for interacting with customers all over the country. The money others spend on store design, fixtures, and display, he'll invest in a mailing list and publishing and distributing a catalog of available titles. Most sales will go to people living outside his immediate area. When these core customers want to visit the store, they'll seek it out, wherever it sits.

YOU NEED TO OPERATE IN BOTH A REAL AND AN ELECTRONIC NEIGHBORHOOD

Each of these scenarios demonstrates extremes of specialty retailing. Many retail entrepreneurs will draw a little from both concepts to survive and thrive in the 21st Century. To take full advantage of the store's sales potential, you'll want to serve two groups of customers. One will physically visit the store to view and sample products before making a purchase. The other group may regard the store more as a retail business, a source for products and services. Remember how important convenience will be to tomorrow's shopper. That means making the shopping experience as easy and enjoyable for your customers as possible.

Every "neighborhood" retailer will need to employ a modern equivalent to the delivery boy of another generation as basic service. Customers who regard the store as a retail business will expect the same level of service. They'll demand overnight delivery on orders by courier service and the same service support after the sale. Anything less in service will cost the retailer, dearly, in sales and reputation.

In the electronic neighborhood, the business will depend on efficient distribution and delivery of product to remote locations. You'll benefit by exploiting the potential of your expertise in the local marketplace, and a broader electronic marketplace as well. We'll talk more about how to cultivate those opportunities in Chapter 8. For now, suffice to say that for some retailer specialists, location is no longer the absolute determining factor it once was.

Before you set out in search of your store location, review your notes on your market and customers. Are you sure enough people live in your market area to support the store you want to open? Unless you're certain, and confident enough to risk your personal wealth, it may be wise to test consumer response to your concept before you make the full-scale investment a store requires. You may discover your market niche offers more sales potential when served by a retail business than by a specialty store.

TESTING YOUR CONCEPT

There are viable alternatives for a retail experiment that minimize your risks. So do you really need a storefront now? Isn't there another way you could market products to your customers without physically setting up shop? In the initial stages of developing your retail business, it may be in your best interest to start off smaller, "field-test" your concept, and cultivate a consumer market in the process. Several sales avenues warrant investigation.

OPEN A BOOTH AT A FLEA MARKET

One of the easiest ways to test your concept is to open a booth at an area flea market. Once the last stop for grandma's junk no one had the heart to throw out, flea markets are now the modern equivalent of the sales bazaars of the Old World. People of every description, and every income level, visit them for entertainment as much as for an opportunity to buy.

In the flea market you'll have a chance to gauge consumers' response for pennies on the dollar of the cost of a month's rent for store space. If you find an eager reception from shoppers, the booth will also serve as a forum for promoting your forthcoming store. On the other hand, if you set up several weekends and don't even recover your booth expenses, you may want to retool your concept. Before you do, try a couple of different flea markets. It may be that the first flea market failed to draw the people who'll support your business. If you still experience problems after trying two or three different flea markets, then rethink your business.

SET UP A KIOSK IN A MALL, OR RENT A MINISTORE

Many shopping malls in the country now open up their corridors to booth and kiosk sales, as well. Talk about a perfect place to test your concept! Floor space in the mall is by no means cheap, but requires much less investment than a store in the same mall. Some larger individual retailers also sublease minidepartments on their sales floor. For the mall or store, this is an easy way to offer a broader selection of merchandise in the hope of attracting more shoppers. Either of these options can be used to test both the location and your idea for a store. If the ministore fails in the aisles, where traffic is greatest, it certainly won't prosper as a full-size store set back into one of the available storefronts.

Another nice thing about this way of testing your idea is that it allows you to set up and take down your "store" with ease. You can move it around if need be, and experiment with different locations at one site or several sites. You can also try various display techniques and product mixes with a minimum of investment.

SELL FROM A PEDDLER'S WAGON

On the street, a peddler's wagon, loaded with a sampling of the goods you want to sell, is another way to sample the public response. If you take this route, you'll probably need a license to sell on the streets. Thoroughly investigate your obligations. Contact city hall and the local chamber of commerce as well as your state's small business assistance agency, and ask each what licenses or permits are required.

START OFF WITH MAIL ORDER

Another way to test your idea with minimal investment is to start as a mail-order business. Once again, you'll need to check into local regulations, licenses, and tax obligations. Mail order can provide you with an effective tool for testing your concept and in the process let you collect the names of potential customers for future sales. The toughest challenge in mail order is figuring out how to reach your audience. That can take time. You'll know you're getting your message to your audience when your mailbox is brimming with orders.

For more information on mail order, take a look at the following books:

- *Fifty-Nine Response-Profit Tips, Tricks & Techniques to Help You Achieve Mail Order Success,* by Galen Stilson (Premier, 1984)
- *Getting into the Mail-Order Business,* by Julian L. Simon (McGraw, 1984)
- *How I Grossed More Than One Million Dollars in Direct Mail & Mail Order Starting with Little Cash & Less Knowhow,* by Tyler G. Hicks (International Wealth, 1993)
- *How to Start & Run a Successful Mail Order Business,* by Sean Martyn (McKay, 1980)
- *Mail Order Legal Guide,* by Edwin J. Keup (Oasis, 1993)
- *Mail Order Moonlighting,* by Cecil C. Hoge, Sr. (Ten Speed, 1978)
- *Mail Order Riches Success Kit,* by Tyler G. Hicks (International Wealth, 1993)
- *Mail Order Selling: How to Market Almost Anything by Mail,* by Irving Burstiner (Prentice-Hall, 1989)
- *Money in Your Mailbox: How to Start & Operate a Successful Mail-Order Business,* by Perry L. Wilbur (Wiley, 1992)

ASSESSING YOUR NEEDS

Now let's proceed beyond the experimental mode. Assume your experience with one of these convinces you your retail concept is a real winner, or you've got so much unshakable confidence in your store, you know your store will make it. How do you go about finding the right location? Well, before you can begin answering that, you must know what you need in a storefront. You probably won't find any single location that meets all your needs—you'll need to settle for whatever location offers the closest match.

SHOULD YOU BUY OR RENT?

Before you begin your search, you must decide whether you want to buy or rent the space. That should be an easy decision, since you're just starting your business and you probably don't have extra barrels full of money. Rent. It's considerably less of a strain on your limited start-up budget, and until your business is up and running, you really don't know what to expect. Sure, your business could soar from day one, but then again, even after all your research, you may end up with the right store in the wrong place. Better to leave yourself the option to ease your way out of the situation.

Leasing also protects you against the unforeseen. Suppose the neighborhood undergoes an unexpected change. What if the city decides to embark on a one-year project widening the road that winds past your site? You could starve because of the inconvenience it causes shoppers. Leasing allows you the luxury of relocating your business should something about the location you select not live up to your expectations.

That said, recognize that your lease, or mortgage if you choose to purchase your site, will likely represent the single greatest fixed cost in running your business. For many retailers, location is the make-or-break factor in their business. You want the best possible location, and you need a landlord or seller who will work with you and share some of the financial burden and risk, with the promise of being paid back during the first year while you grow your business. In the process you also want to make sure your interests are fully protected, should you ever need to sell or close the store. (We'll thoroughly discuss the considerations you should make when negotiating a lease later in this chapter.)

DETERMINING WHAT YOU NEED IN A STORE LOCATION

Your responses to the following questions will help you narrow your search for a location to places that best match your needs.

Store name or type: _____

_____

Products sold: _____

_____

Planned days and hours of operation: _____

_____

Required utility connections: _____

_____

Store departments: _____

_____

Types of displays you will use on the sales floor: _____

_____

Estimated total space needs, in square footage: _____

_____

Amount used for:

   Sales floor _____

   Warehouse _____

   Office _____

   Employee area _____

Deliveries to store will be made:

 By truck _____

 By courier _____

For shipping and receiving I need a:

 Loading dock _____

 Back entrance _____

 Doesn't matter _____

Your ideal location is:

 In a mall _____

 Along a busy street_____

 In a shopping center or plaza _____

 A stand-alone site _____

 Doesn't matter _____

For display and promotion you need:

 A large sign out front _____

 Large display windows _____

Customers will arrive:

 By public transit _____

 By car _____

 Stroll in off street _____

I therefore need:

A wide sidewalk out front _____

Customer parking _____

Lighting at night _____

Other special considerations: _____

_____

DESCRIBE YOUR IDEAL STORE

Get out your notebook and describe your ideal store. Item by item, list the features you want and need. At minimum, how much space for the showroom? For the office? For the warehouse? What kind of display area will make the best presentation of your merchandise? Is it important you have large windows, or will a simple sign tell passersby all they need to know? Does your store need to be on the first floor, or could you rely on customers walking up or down a set of steps? Is your store a stand-alone destination, to which people will drive? Then they'll need places to park. Will it be helped greatly by the presence of other stores, some selling similar merchandise? Review these answers, along with your notes on the customers you need to reach, and where they live.

HIT THE STREETS

Then set out for your field investigations of your area. This is work you must do yourself. It's your observations that will enable you to make an informed decision when selecting a site. If your earlier research indicates certain areas are convenient to the types of consumers who'll support your store concept, visit them, notebook in hand. Stop by promising malls and shopping centers at different hours of the day throughout the week. Are there a lot of people? More important, are they buying things? What kind of cars do they drive? What are they wearing? What you see should support the demographic profile you've drawn of the area.

NARROW YOUR SEARCH TO AN INDIVIDUAL SHOPPING AREA

Compare the features of individual malls, blocks, or shopping centers within the general area. Here are some questions to ponder. Is the setting attractive? Does the look of the buildings work with your store concept? A look of glass and chrome lends itself to a trendy fashion boutique better than to an antiques store. Browse through the existing stores in buildings, malls, or shopping centers with vacancies. What's your first impression walking through the doors? Any foul or sharp odors? Do the spaces feel open or confined? Do you have trouble adjusting to the light?

If there are no apparent vacancies in an area you like, ask store owners if any store space will be available for rent soon. They may be aware of a renter's plans to move out long before the owner is. Contact local landlords as well. Express your interest, should any space in their building, mall, or shopping center become available. Once you determine an area suits your interests, track the commercial listings in the local paper. Visit every site that sounds like what you need.

Conversely, if you experience trouble finding suitable locations in your area of choice, contact a real estate broker specializing in commercial property. In doing so, accept that you may end up paying some form of finder's fee for the assistance. If you must resort to a broker's aid, contact several. Let each know you're in contact with competitors. Some will work harder if it's a race for your dollar. Be specific about your plans and space needs, as you

---

WARNING: At this point you'll probably have a fairly good idea of what rent will cost you for the kind of location you need for the business you've planned. Before you move forward and select a specific site, sign a lease, and implement all the subsequent advice in this chapter, you'll need to do some in-depth financial analysis and develop a business plan for your business. That's the subject of the next chapter, but for now, suffice it to say it should set out the broad goals for your business, and provide a financial time line by which you can measure your success. Since you won't be able to do that, however, until you've an idea of what your rent will cost, we've addressed the location issue first. When it comes to implementing the advice in this book, use the time between determining what your approximate rent will be and actually signing the lease to draft your business plan and arrange financing.

see them. Ask for suggestions, and listen to what you hear. A good commercial real estate broker understands the needs of people like you. She should be able to offer practical insight on the potential advantages and disadvantages of several locations. After you've visited a couple of suggested sites, you'll have a good idea if she can really be of any help.

EXPLORING SPECIFIC SITES

Whenever you visit a specific potential location, whether you found it on your own or with the help of a broker, think of it in terms of your business needs.

IS THE EXTERIOR WELCOMING TO CUSTOMERS?

Record your impressions of the exterior. In a mall or shopping strip, a location with good visibility could be one of your best marketing tools. How does the place look to passersby? Are the windows large enough to let people know what type of business it is? Do they leave ample room for display of merchandise? Is there a visible place for your sign? If it's a street location, how far is it from parking? Are the sidewalks wide enough to encourage people to walk along the street? Does the location carry any potential liabilities? What's the condition of the sidewalk and the exterior of the building? Must shoppers climb stairs to enter the building? Is it accessible to the handicapped? Are the storefront and parking lot well lit? Is there a place in the back where you can accept deliveries? How secure is that?

DOES THE INTERIOR HAVE EVERYTHING YOU NEED?

Proceed with an inspection of the interior. First consider the floor layout. An open, unencumbered space easily adapts to any store concept. If there are permanent fixtures, shelving, or angles, you may need to adapt your store to them. Look closely at the ceiling and floors for signs of water damage or leaks. Do the same with any plumbing connections that enter or leave the building. Ask a lot of questions. What kind of wiring does the building have? Will it handle your needs? Think ahead. If your business grows, will you be able to expand your space as needed?

LOOK AT THE SITE'S RELATIONSHIP TO THE LOCAL AREA

When you're relatively satisfied a site offers what you're looking for, step back and reconsider the site in relation to its surroundings. Are there stores nearby that will add to or detract from your store? Some specialty stores can effectively piggyback on a major retailer of related products in the area. The larger store is the main draw, but it stocks only a sampling of what the specialty dealer carries in depth. This can help sales. Does such a store exist? If so, is there easy access between the two? Can you place signs where they will draw attention to your store?

On the street, the direction a store faces can affect store traffic and the retailer's utility bills. A store facing north is easier to cool in summer, but needs more heat in the winter for lack of the sun's warming rays. Summer shade attracts sidewalk shoppers; winter shade can disperse them. Conversely, a store facing south is always well lit with natural light. The owner may need an awning in summer, but sunshine on a winter's day will add warmth and appeal.

OBSERVE PEDESTRIAN AND AUTO TRAFFIC PATTERNS

The next facet of your site investigation puts you in the observation post. Stop by the site a few times during the week and monitor the traffic patterns, during both day and night. Note the types of crowds, looking for the people you've already identified as your ideal customer. Do they appear, and if so, when? If the only time your ideal shopper strolls through is early Saturday morning, you may not be able to attract enough shoppers to support your business. Many purchases are made on impulse, but your customer must be in the area before that sudden urge to buy strikes. Note the type of crowds that gather in the area toward the evening hours. A group of boisterous teenagers may make you suddenly nostalgic for your own reckless youth, but they will also keep certain shoppers away.

If the storefront sits on the street, monitor the auto traffic. A busy road can prove too busy if the pace of traffic discourages drivers to slow down and turn in to your parking lot. Is there a turning lane, and a progression of traffic lights to regulate the flow? These can actually encourage people to pull off the road for a shopping diversion. How visible is the store and storefront from the road? With outdoor and stand-alone locations, be sure to check the night lighting. A dimly lit, inaccessible parking lot will discourage some night shoppers and invite after-hour thieves.

GETTING DOWN TO THE DETAILS

You've done all your homework, and you're still encouraged? Relay your interest to the landlord or his authorized representative and inquire about the property. Once you know the space is available, your first and foremost question will be "How much?"

THERE'S MORE TO COSTS THAN JUST RENT

Be aware, though, what initially appears to be a big bargain can cost money and business in the long run. With a conventional store, location serves as a main marketing tool. The wrong location will put you out of business. Visibility, accessibility, traffic patterns, and the condition of an area all help determine rent. Corner properties always command top dollar. Stores along the main drag rent for much more than those straddling a back alley.

Finding out what it will cost you to rent some space entails much more than establishing the monthly rent. It's your responsibility to determine what the rental agreement includes, and how far the landlord will go to accommodate you. For starters, what will you be getting for your money? Commercial leases are usually based on square footage. You should be paying only for usable floor space that can be carpeted. Get out your tape measure and make sure you can use every foot you'll be paying for. Then find out what the landlord will be willing to do for you. Will he take care of or contribute toward renovating the space for your needs, or will he simply supply you with an empty shell? What will that include, in terms of utility connections and other services? Will you be obligated to return the building to the condition you find it in if you ever decide to vacate? Is the store paneled or carpeted? Who pays to upgrade the utility service so it meets your needs? How are utilities billed? Are they included in the rental fee or billed separately? What about security patrol, alarm systems, and trash hauling? Will these carry additional, separate charges? What type of insurance does the landlord provide? What will you, as store owner, be required to carry? The answers can all provide you with points for negotiation when you sit down with the landlord to work out an agreement.

INVESTIGATE THE SITE'S COMMERCIAL HISTORY AND ZONING

Before you enter into final negotiations of a lease or sales contract, investigate the commercial history and zoning status of the property. How many stores occupied the site in the last five years? A progression of tenants says, proceed with caution. You may want to contact the owners of some of those businesses, particularly if one tried a store like yours at that location. Be sure to check the certificate of occupancy for the space that interests you and make sure you can use the site as you intend.

Stop by city hall to find out the zoning status of the property. Explain what type of business you plan to locate there and ask if there are any restrictions that should concern you. Also inquire about any restrictions on the size or placement of signs or billboard advertising at the location. A store that can't place signs is anonymous; in retailing, anonymity invites failure.

While at city hall, remember to ask if there are plans for immediate construction in the area, or any long-term improvement projects that will block or detour traffic in the area. Any of these could disrupt normal business long enough to put the start-up business at risk.

IF YOU'RE A BUYER, YOU'LL NEED TO DIG EVEN DEEPER

If, despite the earlier warnings, you're intent on purchasing a location for your store, you'll need to undertake an even more thorough investigation. Unless you find an outstanding bargain, buying your store site adds to the financial burden that goes with starting a store. Ideally you want to do whatever you can to minimize the risks during your first year of operation. So if you must buy the site, scrutinize everything about the site and your sales agreement closely to ensure you get exactly what you expect, with no hidden liabilities.

In addition to the history of the site, zoning, and possible future development, you'll need to investigate the structure itself. Ask that the seller produce an engineer's report on the condition of the building. Make sure the sale includes rights to adjacent parking. Examine the building with an eye to one day expanding your business. Will the usable space grow with your success, or could you one day face costly reconstruction or relocation? Any immediate renovation required will greatly add to your set-up costs. Things you must do to upgrade or improve the facility should be considered points of negotiation when setting the sale price.

For more information on buying a business, take a look at the following books:

- *Buying & Selling a Small Business,* by Michael M. Coltman (International Self Counsel Press, 1989)
- *Buying & Selling a Small Business,* by Verne A. Bunn (Ayer, 1979)
- *Buying or Selling a Business,* by Dana Herbison (Success, 1990)
- *Buying Your Own Small Business,* by Brian R. Smith and Thomas L. West (Viking Penguin, 1985)

NEGOTIATING THE LEASE
OR SALES CONTRACT

Understand that before you sign any contract, there are several things that it's in your best interest to negotiate. The standard commercial lease is entirely prolandlord. You want a contract that's fair, one that will help you give your store its best start. As you enter into negotiations, recognize the commercial real estate market is now a tenants' market. The landlord should be eager to accommodate you.

TRY TO ADJUST THE LEASE TERMS TO MEET YOUR NEEDS

Seek a lease that allows flexibility, with an option to renew written into the agreement. The ideal situation will be a five-year lease with the right of renewal for another five years at the end of the initial period. Recognize that a short-term lease can be more dangerous for you than a long-term lease. You can always get out of the long-term lease. With the short-term lease, however, the landlord enjoys considerable leverage once your business is up and running, wholly dependent on its location. Again, you never know how your business will fare until you open the doors. After a year, you'll know if you're in the right place.

If success arrives early, you may need to expand your store into adjoining space, or find larger facilities in the same building. Ask for right of first refusal should adjoining space become available. It's within your rights to request a radius clause, whereby the landlord agrees not to lease space to other retailers in direct competition for the same sales. Since you're starting a business, see if the landlord is amenable to a graduated payment scale, with your monthly rent increasing over time. Agree on a date when a specific increase will take effect, at least a year after you open your doors.

In today's market you can look to your landlord for help with other aspects of the start-up as well. The cost of renovation will prove one of your most expensive out-of-pocket investments. See how much of that expense your landlord will assume, or finance. It may add to your rent, but it will relieve you of some initial financial burden.

When negotiating, always keep your long-range interests in mind. You want to secure the right to assign the lease, without liability, should you decide to sell your business or close shop. Whenever an action on your part will require the landlord's consent, you want an assurance the decision will be made in a reasonable and timely fashion.

RESPECT THE LANDLORD'S NEEDS, HOWEVER

Throughout negotiations, respect the seller's or landlord's interests as well as your own. All negotiations are a process of give and take. You need space, the landlord needs to fill it. He has no guarantee of a permanent tenant until your business succeeds. Asking him to tie up his property with that uncertainty poses a risk he may want to be compensated for. You may be asked to pay more in rent in order to enjoy that option. Work toward a common ground that fairly takes into account the needs and interests, long- and short-term, of both parties.

MAKE SURE ALL THE BASES ARE COVERED

Everything that concerns you as the store owner should be expressed in the lease or contract: your responsibilities, what the landlord agrees to supply, the occupancy date, the structure of the payment schedule, how any additional expenses for utilities or maintenance will be determined, your rights regarding potential subleasing or assigning of the space to a third party, and an acceptable method for terminating the lease by either party. In the event that you and your landlord should butt heads over something related to this agreement, the contract should also spell out both parties' right to arbitrate or mediate your differences through an independent agent.

MAKE SURE YOU CONSULT YOUR ATTORNEY

Before you agree to any contract, consult your attorney. (For advice on selecting your attorney, see Chapter 9.) Legalese is a language in itself, and you need the services of an interpreter. When it comes to fine print, follow your attorney's advice . . . to the letter. Your attorney should be involved throughout the negotiation process to make sure your rights and interests are protected. Have him or her explain every clause of the contract, and any riders to it, so you know exactly what you're agreeing to. When it comes to negotiating and signing contracts, a competent business attorney is your best protection.

SIGN AS A CORPORATE OFFICER, NOT AN INDIVIDUAL

One more note about the contract. We'll discuss your options for structuring your business to your best interests in the next chapter. But at this point you should understand that it's in your best interest to sign the lease as the principal of a corporation (your business), not as an individual. Even if you structure your business in some other way, use a corporation name when signing the lease, even if the corporation exists solely for that purpose. What if your store goes bankrupt in its third month but you've signed on for a five-year lease? If you signed as an individual, you'd be liable for the rest of the rent, whereas if you signed as the principal of a corporation, your personal obligation is nil.

LEASEHOLD IMPROVEMENTS

After signing the lease, you'll be able to turn your attention to creating your store. If you think store design is a do-it-yourself project, an area where you can cut corners, forget it. Until your store's personality is established through advertising or word of mouth, its look will be your only way to convey its unique qualities to shoppers. The design will invite them in or keep them away. Approach design with an eye for economy, and your "savings" could deny you success.

DESIGN FOR SUCCESS, AND DON'T FORGET SECURITY

Effective store design may seem easy, but there's much more to it than putting products on shelves and racks. Here's another area in which it may be best to turn to outside help, at least in the initial design and setup of the showroom floor. A professional store designer brings a knowledge of the psychology of color and lighting, and understands how to direct traffic through the store. Such visual cues will help a retailer realize the maximum sales potential for his sales floor. (For advice on hiring a designer and other professional help, see Chapter 9.)

If you decide to design the store yourself, spend a lot of time in other stores exploring the details that contribute to effective design. Take notes on how your senses are stimulated as you move through the store. Recognize how color promotes a mood, and lighting directs your attention to what the store wants to promote. How are the themes of the main displays reinforced throughout the shop or department? What do you find to be the comfortable heights for racks and shelving? What types of signs make the best floor directory to products and departments?

There's a deliberate decision behind the placement of every product in a successful store. Highly profitable but low-cost impulse items can usually be found in several areas of the store, most visibly right near the front counter. A product that's much in demand is often placed in the back, compelling shoppers to walk through the store and visually sample everything else the store has to offer. Related products and accessory items are placed nearby as well as in other areas to give shoppers several opportunities to consider them.

While in the stores, also note how different retailers address security issues in the setup of the sales floor. Checkout counters, almost always staffed, typically sit where the employee has a direct line of sight to all areas of the store. Sometimes this vantage point is near the front door, or in a counter kiosk slightly elevated above the rest of the sales floor. In stores with a lot of angles, concave mirrors or video cameras serve as practical and psychological deterrents to pilferage. Security poses such a critical issue, and protection against theft and pilferage is such an important consideration, the start-up retailer should seek expert advice. Store designers bring a thorough knowledge of security issues to the projects. If you're not using one, at the very least set up a consult with a local security firm, preferably one specializing in commercial or retail accounts. You'll find them listed in the yellow pages.

For more information on store security, take a look at the following books:

- *Security for Small Businesses,* by David Berger (Butterworth-Heinemann, 1981)
- *The Small Business Security Handbook,* by James E. Keogh (Prentice-Hall, 1980)

FLEXIBLE DESIGNS WILL TRANSLATE INTO SAVINGS

Taking all these issues into consideration, you should plan a certain degree of flexibility into your store design. The first and most obvious reason is one of economics. Permanent fixtures and renovation are expensive undertakings. You don't know yet if this site will be the permanent home for your store. What you spend to improve that site will only serve you in that location. If you decide to relocate, you'll be making the same investment all over again. A modular approach to design, with portable fixtures and displays, also allows you to maintain a certain degree of freshness in the look of the place.

While shoppers expect a certain consistency in a store's look, they respond well to occasional redesign. That may be as simple as highlighting a different product in your main display area, or moving your racks to redirect floor traffic from time to time. When you redesign a store, you invite shoppers to explore the place anew, and in the process, hopefully discover some of the products they may have missed before. A flexible, modular approach to design will allow you to move displays and departments easily. It can prove less expensive in the short term, and more beneficial to the retailer over the long term. It represents one of the most sensible ways you can guarantee maximum return from a necessary investment.

SOLICIT THREE DETAILED BIDS FROM QUALIFIED CONTRACTORS

Unless you'll be handling the renovation work yourself, you'll need to supply those you hire to do the work a set of blueprints for what you want done. These plans should be detailed diagrams, with exact specifications on where work is to be done and what materials are to be used. Here's another reason to seek the help of a store designer or architect. You can't expect anyone to work from the rough sketch you scrawled on a napkin and realize your vision of the store. It's fair to neither you nor the contractor. The more specific you are about what you want done with the space, the more detailed and accurate will be the bids you receive from contractors.

Never assign construction work based on a single bid. What contractors charge, and what they try to get away with, varies greatly. Two bids are nice, three is ideal. When the bids are submitted, make sure to ask each contractor for proof she carries adequate insurance. Always ask for names of people she has done similar work for in the past. Call these references and visit their sites. After you've had the chance to review the bids and check references, give the job to the contractor you feel most comfortable with. That doesn't necessarily mean the lowest bidder. After picking one, approach the contractor about financing the work. Explain your situation as the owner of a new business. See how much the contractor will work with you, to ease your financial burden. In the final bid, the contractor should describe exactly what she will do, her fee, what materials or permits it covers, and when she will complete the work. As protection, you need to insert a penalty clause—which specifies your options if the work isn't completed on schedule—before you accept the contractor's bid. In general, don't agree to any work at an hourly rate, even when there's a ceiling on hours. You could exhaust your renovation budget and end up with a job that's only partially completed.

KEEP AN EYE ON THE WORK
WHILE IT'S BEING DONE

Try your best to be around while the construction is taking place. If you can't be there all the time, get in the habit of popping in unannounced to check on the progress of the job. When informed something is broken or worn and must be replaced, ask to see it. When the project is completed, thoroughly inspect it. Pay promptly when satisfied, and not until then. Once you've signed the check, you've surrendered your leverage, short of legal proceedings, with the contractor. When the contractor is through, you want to spend your time setting up shop, not finishing her job.

❧ 6 ❧

THE BUSINESS PLAN

Can you tell me how to get from where I am to where you are . . . without a map? Creating a success as a retailer without a business plan can prove just as challenging. I could find you, eventually, were I to spend a good part of the future wandering the planet. And success could be yours if you never commit your goals to paper. It's just that committing a plan to writing makes it so much easier to know where the store is going, and how far it has come. With a written plan you won't do so much stumbling around in the dark. You'll constantly have a sense of how the reality of your store compares with the vision that inspired it.

After you've identified a lucrative market niche, and scouted locations and real estate prices, you can get to work finalizing your business plan. In reality, you're developing aspects of the plan as you conduct the research that convinces you to open a specialty store. Now it's time to use what you've learned to outline the goals of your business and how you intend to get there.

A well thought-out business plan can be your most important resource when building your business. It's the toolbox containing all the information, inspiration, and strategy for realizing your dreams of independence. The plan maps the store's future, tracing the route you've selected to your goals. It's a journal of the process and progress that gets you there, a yardstick with which you can measure how far you've traveled on the road to retail success. Finally, the business plan serves as a compass that tells you when you've wandered off course, and directs you back onto the path that leads to your goals as a store owner.

Your plan need not take the traditional form advocated by business professionals for generations. That form was designed with professional investors in mind. It was drafted to put your business

78

in a context that a banker or venture capitalist could understand. There's no need for you to do that now, simply because, as we'll see later in this chapter, there's no way the banker or venture capitalist will lend you money to start your business. But you do need to put your plan in writing, for a variety of practical and personal reasons.

As we'll discuss, you'll be approaching others for financial support as you start your business. They may not be members of the professional investment community, but they will want to know where their money is headed, and when they should expect a return. Present them a written plan, with detailed financial analysis and projections, and they'll be a little less leery of the venture.

Whatever format you choose for the document, it should include a statement of mission—why the store exists—and demonstrate you have the credentials to make the store concept work.

The plan should demonstrate how you propose to make your specialty store a success, and what that will require in financial resources, with a detailed breakdown of financial needs, including the cost of start-up and annual operations, as well as sales projections.

On a personal level, a business plan provides a focus for you and your retail venture. This written document should serve as your business handbook, a guide to what you want your store to become, and how to get there. It should be so thorough, so comprehensive, that you can turn to it repeatedly for an update on your progress, advice on keeping the business on track, and the inspiration to forge ahead.

Let your business plan take whatever form you're most comfortable with. You may confine the plan to the pages of a notebook, or to scraps of paper loosely organized in a file folder. Some will prefer a detailed organizational chart, with a time line of activities and detailed cost analysis. Computer users may favor a typeset booklet produced with desktop publishing software, complete with supportive charts and graphs. Whatever form your plan takes, it's critical that it be a written document you can return to, to refresh your thoughts or revise your strategy. But remember you may want to share the document, or portions of it, with outsiders as you start and grow your business.

The topics you'll need to address are: your store's mission; your qualifications and retail strategy; your store's legal form; a budget detailing start-up expenses, operating costs, and capital needs; projections of income and profitability; your financial resources and outside sources of financing.

YOUR STORE'S MISSION

The foundation of any store is the philosophy underlying it. That philosophy defines a mission for the store, why it exists and whom it serves. Every entrepreneur has professional and personal reasons for going into business. Defining that mission allows you to focus your efforts as you put your philosophy into action, working for those goals.

For the owner of a tool specialty store, the mission statement might read like this: ''The Tool Shed will carry every type of carpentry tool, with a low-price guarantee, to serve the growing ranks of woodworking hobbyists. Our services will include tool repairs, educational classes for all skill levels, and custom-built reproductions of antique furniture. This will be an opportunity to put my years of carpentry experience to work as I realize my lifelong dream of running my own business.''

Another retailer might describe her store's mission this way.

''Since my grandmother taught me how to make my first quilt, I've been fascinated with quilting. I spent years making them, and years more collecting them. With my store The Patchwork Quilt I'll share my lifelong interests with quilters and those who simply appreciate their work by providing a source for everything to do with quilting, from materials, tool and patterns to authentic antique quilts from around the country.''

Although their missions differ, both statements capture the essence of the business, why these entrepreneurs are opening stores and what they hope to accomplish. Such a statement should appear at the top of your business plan to lend a focus to all the details that follow.

WRITE DOWN YOUR GOALS SO YOU CAN REFER TO THEM REGULARLY

Prosperity for you may mean escaping corporate halls to run your own business. Maybe all you want from a store is to make enough to support your current lifestyle and provide for a comfortable retirement. Maybe you want nothing short of enormous wealth and all it brings.

Each of us has personal and professional goals. Writing them down, having them there to return to, forces us to confront ourselves, and our ambitions, honestly. The business plan provides a reference, a blueprint for the activity we believe will best serve those aspirations. It should evolve with the business. As you learn from the experiences of running your retail business, you may want to set new goals or develop the store in directions you cannot now envision. Your mission should remain the same.

SPELL OUT THE THEORY UNDERLYING YOUR BUSINESS

The notebook pages filled with your responses to the questions posed in previous chapters go a long way toward defining the philosophy that brings you to retailing. Taken together, those answers define your business theory. It begins with an evaluation of your skills, experience, and the retail marketplace to develop a vision of the store you would like to open. Then that store concept enables you to identify the customers you want to reach and where you might find them.

Your business plan will benefit from a description of the store's mission: the type of retailer you want to be, the customers you hope to reach, and what your retail concept offers that's so appealing, so unique, they will want to shop with you. The description should include the products and services you will offer, your pricing structure, the customers you plan to serve, and the marketing program that will reach them.

Your credentials, commitment, and the details of your business plan will all determine how well you are able to realize your store's mission. The mission will serve your future much like the foundation that supports a building. Your philosophy should evolve as your needs identify weaknesses or opportunities inherent in your store concept. When there are cracks in the foundation, the homeowner heads for the basement to patch them. Before he adds a new wing to the house, he expands the foundation, and builds on that. That's how your mission should serve your business strategy. The core remains solid, yet adaptable to new opportunities, new endeavors.

A written mission statement can give your store that foundation and focus.

OUTLINE A STRATEGY

Once you've composed your mission statement, you begin filling in the details of how you intend to breathe life into your store. A lot of that depends on you. Define yourself, in terms of the business. Write into your business plan what you bring to the store with your experience and interests. Your qualifications, commitment, and the enthusiasm that drives you to start the store will do most to determine your retail future. With your mission and credentials established, you can concentrate on the practical aspects of your business plan.

Think of creating a retail business in terms of constructing a house. In a sense you're building a home for your dreams of financial independence. Once the foundation is in place, the floors and walls go up, and at last the roof. When you understand your mission, you begin setting the framework, the business plan, to make it a reality. Once the broad goals are accomplished, the builder concentrates on the minor projects that transform the shell of a building into something more, a home. Your business plan should establish, in logical order, specific tasks to accomplish to create a secure home for your store. It should serve as your detailed guide to everything required of you to make the store a success.

MAKE REALISTIC PLANS

It's important that your approach is realistic. You only have so much time and money. The store owner inevitably faces many unforeseen demands during the first year of operations. If you believe something will require one month to accomplish, allow yourself two.

PLAN FOR THE UNEXPECTED

Build a reserve into your schedule and budget. Events rarely adhere to the details of the most well-conceived plan. There will be schedule delays and cost overruns. Expect them. Better to find yourself with an abundance of time and money than angered at a failure in your planning.

That said, though, remember there are deadlines and financial goals that you must meet if you're to get your business off to its best start.

THINKING AHEAD WILL PUT YOU AHEAD

When drafting your plans, strive to open your store at least two months before your product category's peak selling season. Work back from there and allow yourself ample time to complete renovation and design of your space. Figure out when you'll need to place your product orders so you'll have supply on hand when consumers want the products. Remember: Always build a buffer zone into your plans. That way, when the unexpected occurs, you can right the wrongs and keep the process running without interruption.

YOUR STORE'S LEGAL FORM

You must decide on a legal form for your business. While not the most rewarding part of the process, or thrilling element of the business plan, this decision has profound implications for your business future. Your business structure determines tax obligations: how you pay them, and what types of tax breaks and deductions you're entitled to as a store owner. It also establishes the personal liability you assume in connection with your business activities.

GET PROFESSIONAL HELP IN SELECTING A LEGAL STRUCTURE FOR YOUR BUSINESS

Selecting the appropriate business structure is another area in which it's advisable to seek the advice of a business-oriented attorney or an accountant with special expertise in retailing. The experience of an expert will help determine which structure best serves your business needs and goals, as well as what the impact of local regulations might be.

A lawyer or accountant will understand your obligations in terms of business licenses, permits, and responsibilities for the payment and collection of taxes. Depending on where you live and where you locate your store, you may be required to purchase a special license, or file special applications to comply with local business tax and sales tax obligations. Such local regulations, as they affect your venture, may have a direct bearing on how you structure your company.

There's no single business structure appropriate for all retail store owners; investigate these options thoroughly with your professional adviser before deciding which structure offers the most support for your goals. Each has distinct advantages and disadvantages. As a general rule, approach the decision intent on minimizing your personal liabilities and tax obligations.

SOLE PROPRIETORSHIPS KEEP THINGS SIMPLE

The simplest form of business structure, the sole proprietorship establishes you and your company as a single entity. Your income and the company's profits are one and the same. You report your profit, after allowable business deductions, as income to the Internal Revenue Service on your personal tax form, and pay the corresponding taxes. The advantage to this business structure is its simplicity. Unless you register as another type of business, you're already operating a sole proprietorship.

Inherent in the sole proprietorship is one major disadvantage. Since owner and business are synonymous, any claims against the business amount to claims against your personal assets. If someone is injured in the store, you'll be held personally liable unless you carry adequate business insurance. If the business fails, its creditors have the right to come after your personal property in order to satisfy outstanding debts.

SIMPLE PARTNERSHIPS ARE JUST COMBINED SOLE PROPRIETORSHIPS

In its most basic form, a simple partnership operates like a sole proprietorship with two or more people involved. Each shares equally in the profits, reports it as income, and pays the appropriate taxes. And each is held fully liable for any claims against the business to collect damages or debts. If you select such a structure, it's in your best interest to have a written document defining the agreement and extent of involvement for all partners. (Taking on a partner is also a way the retail entrepreneur can finance the business, a consideration covered in Chapter 7.)

CORPORATIONS LIMIT AN OWNER'S PERSONAL LIABILITY

The corporation is usually a more savvy way for you to structure your business than a sole proprietorship or partnership. The major advantage is that it limits your personal liability to however much you've invested in the business. Your personal assets cannot be attached to any claims against the store, except for tax obligations to the federal government. This is especially important for you as a retailer, since there's a certain amount of liability inherent in any business serving the public. And if you take on partners in your business, being incorporated frees you from personal liability for their misdeeds or neglect in connection with the store.

If there are disadvantages to incorporating, they are that you'll probably require legal help to set up your corporation. You'll also need an accountant's aid when figuring taxes and for deciding how any change in the tax laws impact your business. Your tax burden, as a corporation, could be heavier, since the corporation exists as its own entity, separate from the owner. Before you can take any income from the profits of the business, the corporation must meet its own tax obligations.

S CORPORATIONS MAY OFFER THE BEST OF BOTH WORLDS

If you see merits in both sole proprietorships and corporations, structuring your retail business as an S corporation may offer the best of both worlds. An S corporation limits your personal liability, just as operating as a regular corporation will, while also allowing you to report profit or loss from the business on your personal income tax form, in many cases without paying separate federal taxes for the corporation.

Again, your interests will be best served by consulting with an attorney or accountant before deciding how to structure the business. They know the laws and their implications, and can assist in selecting the best business structure for your retail organization.

YOUR STORE'S FINANCES

Lack of funding puts an end to good ideas quicker than any other factor. That's true for small business in general and retailing in particular. In other businesses, the entrepreneur weathers slack periods with belt tightening, awaiting the promise of better days ahead. For the underfunded fledgling retailer, the belt is already as tight as it gets. Any efforts to cut costs undercuts the store's chances for success.

Starting a store is an expensive gamble on the future. In the building phase of the business—the period when the store isn't yet self-supporting—the retailer needs enough working capital to keep the store solvent as it grows toward success. A useful business plan, therefore, must include a detailed analysis of the store's expenses and financial needs and projected sales. With those figures in hand, you can set out to gather the resources required to give your store its best chance to succeed.

We haven't addressed the financial aspects of the business before this point since, until you know approximately what you'll be paying for rent, you can't pretend to accurately project your expenses. In addition, if your search for the right location is dictated primarily by cost, you'll probably end up in the wrong site. It's better to find out what the right location for your planned business costs, see if you can afford it, and change your plan if you can't, than end up with a location you can afford and hope it serves your plan. Assuming you've an idea what you must spend to be where your target customers can find you, you can now begin assessing your financial needs.

The start-up retailer faces two categories of related expenses during the first year of operations. Your start-up costs include every financial investment you must make to set up your store and prepare it for opening day. Some of these will be onetime expenditures: buying a delivery van, installing fixtures, and painting business signs, for example. Others, like inventory costs, wages, and salaries, require a substantial investment before opening, and then become ongoing expenses (or "operating expenses," explained below) once the business is in operation.

RETAIL START-UP COSTS Work Sheet

Enter the appropriate amount to determine your start-up costs. This is not a comprehensive list. Costs and items to be included will vary greatly depending on your store type. Use only as a reference; make sure your work sheet is comprehensive and covers all your applicable costs.

Deposits: _____

  Rent: _____

  Telephone: _____

  Utilities: _____

  Insurance: _____

Leasehold improvements (expenses for

  preparing the store space): _____

  Contractor's fees: _____

  Store displays and fixtures: _____

  Carpeting and/or painting: _____

  Security system: _____

Professional services: _____

  Market researcher: _____

  Attorney: _____

  Accountant: _____

  Architect: _____

  Store designer: _____

  Computer training: _____

PR or advertising agency: _____

Other professional(s): _____

Furniture/office equipment: _____

Desk, chairs: _____

Safe: _____

Typewriter: _____

Computer System and software: _____

Telephone system: _____

Copy machine: _____

Fax machine: _____

File cabinets: _____

Cash register: _____

Office supplies: _____

Other equipment: _____

Transportation (van or delivery truck): _____

Total advertising _____

Inventory: _____

Working capital for first year: _____

Other expenses: _____

TOTAL
START-UP COSTS _____

The second category of expenses to consider is the operating expenses, the month-to-month expenditures required to keep your doors open beyond opening day. The primary difference between your start-up and monthly overhead needs is that your start-up costs usually represent an out-of-pocket investment in the business. In that, they are a gamble on the future. Operating costs, however, represent monthly bills and financial obligations that must be met on a regular basis for the business's continued vitality. From day one, sales should help defray part of the ongoing expenses, and within the first year of operation, sales revenues should cover the bills or the store has serious problems.

Projecting your costs and committing the numbers to paper will help you run a smarter business and provide a gauge for measuring your store's progress. For the start-up retailer, it's best to seek professional help when figuring your numbers. The software program you select to manage your business may include a detailed model budget, as well as reference models for costs, sales, and profitability ratios. Nevertheless, it's in your best interest to have the professional help of a qualified business accountant when you first set up your plan and financial projections. He should have the expertise and experience to give you a realistic assessment of what you will need to get the business started, to keep it going, and what you should expect from sales during this critical first year.

These numbers will vary greatly, depending on what type of retailer you plan to become, the inventory you sell, and your location. Inventory costs will vary by industry, as much as commercial rents and the costs of marketing and labor do from region to region. There are, however, general categories that concern all retailers when projecting a store's budget for start-up and monthly operations as well as sales during its early history. We'll discuss these expense categories in a few pages as we review the specialty store owner's monthly and annual overhead expenditures.

Every type of store has its own specific needs, but as a guideline, you can refer to the budget and sales projections for ''A Start-up Retail Store'' included on page 106. This should help you understand how thorough you need to be in your financial planning, and the many factors you must take into account before you have a realistic idea of the funding you will need to run your business.

Your assessment of need begins with a detailed assessment of every spending requirement for start-up and then what's necessary to run the store month to month. Include everything contained in this model and anything else pertinent to your store, attaching a realistic price to each item on your list. Don't think in terms of cutting corners on spending, or about getting price breaks for the required goods and services.

Expenses like rent, utilities, and taxes will be exclusive to your location; others to your retail or market sector. In any event, don't rely on your best "guesstimates" alone when projecting costs or sales. Solicit advice from those with experience in your chosen field, or retailing in general. Check with the retail contacts you bounced your ideas off earlier, and see if any will share their breakdown of annual expenses. See if your trade group publishes any detailed analysis of the cost of doing business in your retail specialty. Take that same search to an on-line business database service and your local business library. If you selected an attorney or accountant with retail experience, seek his or her advice when compiling your estimates. Be as thorough as necessary to make sure every reasonable expense is anticipated.

Let's go through the process in detail.

YOUR START-UP INVESTMENTS

The costs required to move your store from paper to practice represent investments in your retail future. As such, these out-of-pocket expenses also demonstrate your confidence in yourself and your store concept. Consider these necessary and basic investments that give your business its best start. What they include, and the cost, depends on your ambition and the costs of doing business in your location. But projecting these costs is relatively easy as all you need to do is contact your suppliers for prices, and request bids for whatever services you require.

Projecting these costs can be relatively easy but does require a fair amount of work. It must be a thorough process if you are to have a realistic idea of what it will cost you to get your store to opening day, and then to carry it through its first year. You can learn what inventory will cost you by contacting your product suppliers or distributors; independent contractors will furnish bids for everything from store design to renovation. You must also be sure to account for every other conceivable expense—utilities, phone, computer equipment, advertising, staff salaries, etc.—discussed in the following pages. If you're in doubt, use the Start-up Costs Work Sheet as a reference for what you should include. Add up those bids and expenses, and you know exactly what it will cost to open your doors.

CALCULATING START-UP OVERHEAD

There's a lot more to overhead than monthly rent during the weeks or months before opening day. These expenses include items you must pay for just to begin working toward opening day: down payments for rent or utilities; fees for consultation with professionals; the cost of the research that convinces you of the viability of this market; the preparation of your store site. If you choose to rent your site, you can expect to provide the landlord with some form of security deposit, a dollar amount often equal to two months' rent, before you can move into the space. Local utility companies will also require a cash deposit or connect fee up front, as well. Local or county governments may stipulate you buy a special license before you can begin operation. Again, how much you spend during this period depends on where you situate your store. These costs can vary greatly from site to site, even within the same community.

PREPARING YOUR SITE

Depending on the terms of your lease, the store owner may bear the costs of preparing the store site for occupancy. Or you may need to hire a professional architect or store designer and a contractor to create the proper look and ambience for your store. Anyone who purchases a location has no choice but to make these investments. The expenses may range from simple painting and carpeting to a complete overhaul of the space to suit your retailing needs. Most store owners must buy fixtures, shelves, and counters for sales transactions and display of merchandise.

EQUIPPING YOUR BUSINESS

After the site is ready for occupancy, you need to concentrate on your working environment. Whether you purchase or lease it, you'll need a computer system with software. Then there's standard business equipment for your office like a desk, telephone system, file cabinets, lamps, chairs, copier, telephone, and fax machine. For the business of selling you'll need at least one cash register, possibly a delivery truck, store bags and other packaging, and personalized signs for the inside and outside of the store. You may also want a music or video system to create excitement on the sales floor.

STOCKING THE SHELVES WITH INVENTORY

You can't sell from empty shelves and need to fill the store. Some suppliers may be willing to help finance your order; assume for now none will. What do your competitors offer, and how do you plan on responding? Go back to your supplier contacts and ask each for advice on opening-day inventory. Keep in mind your need to open with as broad a selection of merchandise as possible. Stress your desire to be conservative financially, yet to offer full service to your customers. Take the supplier estimates and run them by your retailing contacts to minimize any inflated salesmanship.

LINING UP YOUR STAFF

If you plan on hiring staff, you'll probably need them at least two weeks before the store opens. Factor in the cost of their salaries, any benefits, payroll taxes, and the fees incurred during the hiring process (see Chapter 9). Also include the cost of any training you deem necessary to enable you or your staff to do the best job.

PRODUCT SELECTION Work Sheet

Use this work sheet as an outline for determining your inventory needs. The specialty store should be the definitive source for what it sells, and the inventory mix and pricing strategy are critical tools for establishing the store's identity. Your product selection should also be a response to what you learned about area competitors when you filled out the work sheet for Choosing Your Market earlier.

Main Product Sales Category:
The store will:
Offer everything available in this category   _____
Offer a good-better-best selection   _____
Concentrate on a selection of
   Low-   _____
   Mid-   _____
   High-priced products   _____

Based on your response to the above statement, create a listing for each supplier, its products, and the finance terms available to you. Make listings for related products and accessories you will carry as well until you achieve the inventory mix described above. It's important you also consider the minimum order requirements, turnaround time on orders, and the financial terms available from suppliers.

Product supplier(s): _____

_____

Products and price points: _____

_____

Minimum order: _____

_____

Order turnaround: _____

_____

Payment terms available to you: _____

_____

Promotional support available: _____

_____

STARTUP COSTS CHARTS

The following numbers, prepared by James Leonard, CPA, of the New York City-based accounting firm of Diamond, Wohl, Fried & Leonard, are a breakdown of the startup costs for a hypothetical small clothing boutique.

Rosario's Sweet Impressions Clothing Boutique, Inc. Startup Costs

Initial Start-Up Costs:

1. **Construction Costs**

Leasehold Improvements	$100,000
Demolition, Sprinkler, Accessories	10,000
Architectural Drawings & Design	3,000
Contingency	10,000
Total Construction Costs	$123,000

2. Furnishings & Fixtures	50,000
3. Equipment—Cash	
Registers & Computer	5,000
4. Capitalized Start-Up Costs	
Pre-Opening Rent	
(3 mos @ $4,000 ea.)	12,000
Legal	2,500
Advertising	2,500
Accounting	800
Total Capitalized Start-Up	
Costs	17,800
5. Lease—Rent Security	
(2 mos @ $4,000 ea.)	8,000
6. Security Deposit And	
Installation Charges	
(Telephone, Utilities, etc.)	1,500
7. Payroll—Sch. I	2,100
8. Inventory	40,000
Total Start-Up Costs	$247,400

Rosario's Sweet Impressions Clothing Boutique, Inc.
Startup Costs
Supporting Schedules

Schedule I

Projected Start-Up Payroll Costs	People	Monthly Salary	Months	
Owner (Manager)	1	$0	3.0	$0
Assistant Manager	1	2,000	0.5	1,000
Stock Persons	2	800	0.5	800
				1,800
Payroll Taxes		15.00%		300
Total Projected Start-Up Payroll Costs				$2,100

ADVERTISING AND PROMOTION

Your store will never again be as dependent on your advertising spending as it will on opening day. For particulars on how to give it the promotional push it deserves, turn to Chapter 13. No matter what media mix you select, make sure you allow enough of a promotional budget to ensure the people you depend on as customers hear about your store. Don't forget the cost of other forms of promotional materials like business cards, stationery, premiums, brochures, and direct mail.

YOUR MONTHLY AND ANNUAL OVERHEAD

As soon as the store doors open, you, as owner, assume responsibility for the store's overhead. It's easiest to think of these as monthly obligations or bills, but not all your financial obligations will present themselves on such a regular basis. Your inventory needs, for example, will probably rotate throughout the year through successive selling cycles or turns of merchandise. You'll know the particulars once you've been in business awhile.

For planning purposes, regard these overhead expenses as monthly obligations that remain relatively stable throughout the year. Again, where you're uncertain about making these projections, consult with your professional advisers and retail contacts. Whatever advice or statistics you rely on, your cost projections should be as realistic and honest an assessment of the cost of doing business, and your need for working capital, as you and your accountant can devise.

AT THE TOP OF THE LIST

Rent or mortgage payments and utilities rank at the top of inescapable monthly expenses. Write down your approximate rent, and a best estimate of monthly utility bills—water, gas, electric, phone, trash collection—for your chosen type of location. If you don't know what to expect, ask your landlord or another retail tenant at the site. Remember to include the total cost for any yearly business expenses that must be met on a quarterly, semiannual, or annual basis. Such things as insurance, organizational dues, license fees, maintenance contracts on any equipment or vehicles you buy or lease. Customer credit makes it more attractive to shop the store, but it will cost you money to offer it. Look at the model for expense breakdowns, and factor in an amount for every item on that list appropriate to your store, and any other special expenses you anticipate.

CALCULATE YOUR PERSONNEL COSTS

As the store owner, you probably plan on drawing your living from the business. You should have a reserve fund set aside to carry you through at least a year, but it's also important to factor in a salary for yourself as part of your overhead costs. Enter the salary that's required to support your lifestyle. You can be frugal or generous with yourself; it's your liability. Don't forget to include the cost of health insurance, and to factor in federal, state, or local taxes, and Social Security. Once again, ask your accountant for help.

If you can't get family to donate their time to the enterprise, you'll need to allow for the wages of other employees, as well. Unless you already know your staff needs, figure you'll employ the equivalent of two full-timers, at the prevailing hourly wage for store employees in your area. Speak to your accountant and other area retailers for help in coming up with that number. Remember to allow for overtime or additional workers during your peak sales season. Offering a benefits package is up to you, but it's a good idea if you want to hire and keep good people. Include a figure that reflects any paid vacation or holidays you will grant as well as the cost of a benefits package for each.

PUT SOME MONEY IN MARKETING

Your store's rate of growth and expansion this first year should reflect how much of a promotional push you throw behind this effort. Plan to spend more now and in the first two months surrounding opening day than during any comparable period in the store's future. The amount will reflect your own ambitions, the cost of advertising media in your retail market area, and the level to which you want to experiment with different media. At the extreme, you may need to invest as much as ten percent of your total operating budget this first year to get the word out about your store. (For advice on getting the most from your marketing budget, see Chapter 11.)

REVIEW THE DETAILS

Using the expense breakdown on page 95 as a guide, closely review your cost projections for start-up and overhead to make sure you've included everything. Only when you have all the relevant figures, and a final tally, can you begin to draw some critical conclusions about your needs for working capital and the store's future.

INTERPRETING THE NUMBERS

You and your accountant will interpret those numbers in different ways. For you, they clearly represent how much money you'll need to keep your business afloat for a year. You could also view it as how much income the store will need to generate the first year in order to carry it to a second year. At this early juncture, that's a foolish way to look at it. All businesses require a certain period to grow and develop before they can generate revenue at full potential. There's always an exception to the rule, but don't plan on being the lucky one. To rely on your store producing enough income to cover monthly expenses from day one amounts to setting yourself up for disaster. Better to treat the tally as a reference figure for the amount of funding you'll need to get the store through that critical first year. Consider the cost projections as indicative of the amount of funding sales must generate to carry the business through its typical yearly sales cycle. The first year for any store is one in which the business grows toward its full capacity. Your annual projections represent the sales revenue and business needs to generate under ideal conditions. During the first year, use them as a gauge for measuring the store's performance against your expectations. In twelve months you'll sample the entire sales cycle and know if your concept has real merit and appeal.

As part of your business plan, your accountant can take these numbers and work up an annual expense budget for your business. The budget entails much more than dividing your total expenses for the first year by twelve, and using that figure as your average monthly expenses. There are other expenses not directly reflected in the physical operation of the store, such as interest payments on any debts you assume to finance your business. And your expenses should grow as your business expands. An accountant with retail experience should be able to tell you what to expect in terms of escalating costs and how it will impact sales. His expertise should also help you project the store's profitability as you look ahead.

Projecting income, based on your sales expectations, poses the trickiest aspect of the store's budget. In some retail categories market research exists to demonstrate the profitability of average retailers, based on store size and the amount of time in business. Your accountant may also have experience with a store similar to yours. But there's no typical store; your location, store concept, and you are all unique. Until you've been in business for at least a year, any projections you make are, at best, guesses. Be conservative in any assumptions you make about sales when starting out, but not overly conservative. It's safe to assume the store will begin covering its expenses within the first year, a year and a half at the outset, or the store concept is flawed.

The budget included in your business plan should incorporate a five-year projection of costs and sales, and the store's profitability. You may start to profit the first month, as soon as the revenue generated by sales exceeds your monthly cost of operations. More likely it will take longer than that to build your business to the break-even point when revenue from sales covers expenses. Until that happens, you're operating in the red. When you've got money left over, and your monthly expenses are met, you're in the black, and the business is profitable. When those profits are enough to allow you to satisfy any debts incurred by you to set up the business, you'll begin to realize the full profit potential of your store.

The trends will vary from month to month, especially during this first year. Rare is the retail category with steady sales throughout the year. Some specialty dealers do as much as 80 percent of business in the fourth quarter. Sales then literally carry them through the lean months of the rest of the year. That's why it's so important to get your business up and running at least two months before your peak selling period. Be there at the beginning and you take some pressure off. You want your accountant to prepare annual projections for sales, expenses, and profits, as well as monthly breakdowns for the first five years of operations. You won't have a real sense of your business until you can review it on an annual basis, and can make year-to-year comparisons. Think of the only variable in your budget for the first year as the amount budgeted in for your salary. You can certainly live on more and, if need be, will learn to live on less. Everything else represents a necessary investment in giving the store its appropriate start.

FINANCIAL PROJECTION CHARTS

The following financial projections, also prepared by James Leonard, are for the same hypothetical clothing store used for the startup cost charts.

Rosario's Sweet Impressions Clothing Boutique, Inc. Summary of Significant Projection Assumptions

NOTE A—NATURE OF PROJECTIONS

These financial projections are based on projected sales levels and present, to the best of management's knowledge and belief, the Company's expected results of operations for the projection period. The presentations are for the purpose of establishing a proposed corporation that would own and manage a clothing store, and should not be considered to be a presentation of expected future results. Accordingly, these projections may not be useful for other purposes. The assumptions disclosed herein are those that management believes are significant to the projections.

The start–up period (including construction) is projected to go from January 1, 1993, through March 31, 1993. April 1, 1993, has been targeted for the grand opening to the public. Where possible, the projections have been rounded to the nearest hundred dollars.

NOTE B—SALES

Sales revenues are based upon statistical studies of the population in the immediate area, as well as industry averages and analyses of other stores of similar size and location.

These projections are based upon activity at a particular level for each year. Since this is a new venture that does not have an established volume, these levels will be attained gradually.

Sales revenues should be slow at first and then will vary due to seasonal fluctuations. The Projected Monthly Sales volume has been projected as follows:

	Projected Monthly Sales
April 1993	$20,000
May 1993	30,000
June 1993	30,000
July 1993	30,000
August 1993	40,000
September 1993	45,000
October 1993	45,000
November 1993	70,000
December 1993	100,000
January 1994	25,000
February 1994	35,000
March 1994	30,000
	$500,000

Note C—Cost of Sales

Cost of goods sold to the public is estimated at 55.00% of sales.

Initial purchases of merchandise must be made at a level that is sufficient to stock the shelves and provide inventory for resale. Thereafter orders are placed on a seasonal basis well in advance of when the merchandise is required to be put on the shelves. Therefore, actual purchases, which are projected as follows, may not mirror fluctuations in sales.

	Projected Monthly Purchases
March 1993 (Initial Inventory Purchases)	$40,000
April 1993	15,000
May 1993	15,000
June 1993	15,000
July 1993	20,000
August 1993	25,000
September 1993	30,000
October 1993	35,000
November 1993	50,000
December 1993	25,000
January 1994	15,000
February 1994	20,000
March 1994	30,000
	$335,000

Note D—Operating Expenses

The operating expenses are based upon industry averages and comparisons made with data available regarding retail clothing stores of similar size and location. Except for those items that have been separately stated below, the operating expenses have been projected at a fixed regular amount per month.

OFFICER'S COMPENSATION

Officer's compensation is estimated to be $2,500 per month, and is projected under the assumption that he/she is performing the basic managerial functions required to run the store. For this reason officer's compensation is included in the schedule of salaries & wages below.

SALARIES & WAGES

Salary and wages have been broken down on a monthly basis by job title as follows:

	People	Monthly Salary	←——Projected——→ Monthly Salary	Medical Insurance
Owner (Manager)	1	$2,500	$2,500	$600
Assistant Manager	1	2,000	2,000	600
Salespeople—Part-Time	2	900	1,800	0
Monthly Salaries & Wages			$6,300	$1,200

CREDIT CARD DISCOUNTS

Credit card discounts are the fees charged by the charge card companies and are projected at 2.50% of sales.

ADVERTISING

Advertising is projected at $500.00 per month except for the first three months, during which additional cost must be incurred to inform the public. Advertising during this three-month period is projected at $2,500.00 in total.

RENT

The lease on the premises is projected at $30.00 per square foot annual rent. The area of the store is projected to be 1,600 sq. ft.

PAYROLL TAXES

Payroll taxes are calculated as a percentage of all payroll, including officer's compensation and salaries & wages, at 15.00%.

Note E—Other Expenses

DEPRECIATION & AMORTIZATION

Depreciation & Amortization is calculated on a straight line basis over the following periods:

	Cost	Period in Years	Monthly Expense
Construction Costs	$123,000	31.5	$300
Furnishing & Fixtures	50,000	7.0	600
Equipment	5,000	5.0	100
Capitalized Start-Up Costs	17,800	5.0	300
Totals	$195,800		$1,300

Note F—Taxes

Taxes would be paid by the corporation on an annual basis when the return is due.

Rosario's Sweet Impressions Clothing Boutique, Inc.
Projected Statement of Income & Expenses for the 15 Months Ended March 31, 1994

	STARTUP PERIOD —————>			TOTALS STARTUP PERIOD	APR 93	MAY 93	JUN 93	JUL 93	AUG 93
	JAN 93	FEB 93	MAR 93						
TOTAL SALES	0	0	0	0	20,000	30,000	30,000	30,000	40,000
COST OF SALES:									
BEGINNING INVENTORY	0	0	0	0	40,000	44,000	42,500	41,000	44,500
PURCHASES	0	0	40,000	40,000	15,000	15,000	15,000	20,000	25,000
ENDING INVENTORY	0	0	(40,000)	(40,000)	(44,000)	(42,500)	(41,000)	(44,500)	(47,500)
TOTAL COST OF SALES	0	0	0	0	11,000	16,500	16,500	16,500	22,000
GROSS PROFIT	0	0	0	0	9,000	13,500	13,500	13,500	18,000
OPERATING EXPENSES:									
SALARIES & WAGES	0	0	1,800	1,800	6,300	6,300	6,300	6,300	6,300
CREDIT CARD CHARGES	0	0	0	0	500	800	800	800	1,000
ADVERTISING	750	750	1,000	2,500	500	500	500	500	500
SUPPLIES/BAGS/BOXES	0	0	1,500	1,500	500	500	500	500	500
BANK CHARGES	250	50	50	350	100	100	100	100	100
CARTING	0	0	100	100	250	250	250	250	250
INSURANCE	1,200	500	500	2,200	500	500	500	500	500
INSURANCE—HOSPITALIZATION	0	0	0	0	1,200	1,200	1,200	1,200	1,200
ACCOUNTING & LEGAL FEES	0	0	0	0	400	400	400	400	400
SECURITY	500	100	100	700	100	100	100	100	100
RENT	0	0	0	0	4,000	4,000	4,000	4,000	4,000
REPAIRS & MAINTENANCE	0	0	0	0	200	200	200	200	200
TELEPHONE	200	200	300	700	350	350	350	350	350
UTILITIES	500	500	500	1,500	500	500	500	500	500
PAYROLL TAXES	0	0	300	300	900	900	900	900	900
MISCELLANEOUS	1,000	1,000	1,000	3,000	500	500	500	500	500
TOTAL OPERATING EXP'S	4,400	3,100	7,150	14,650	16,800	17,100	17,100	17,100	17,300
NET PROFIT(LOSS) BEFORE OTHER EXP'S	(4,400)	(3,100)	(7,150)	(14,650)	(7,800)	(3,600)	(3,600)	(3,600)	700
OTHER EXPENSES:									
DEPRECIATION & AMORTIZATION	0	0	0	0	1,300	1,300	1,300	1,300	1,300
CORP. INCOME TAX	0	0	0	0	0	0	0	0	0
TOTAL OTHER EXPENSES	0	0	0	0	1,300	1,300	1,300	1,300	1,300
NET INCOME	(4,400)	(3,100)	(7,150)	(14,650)	(9,100)	(4,900)	(4,900)	(4,900)	(600)
CUMULATIVE NET INCOME	(4,400)	(7,500)	(14,650)	(14,650)	(23,750)	(28,650)	(33,550)	(38,450)	(39,050)

	SEPT 93	OCT 93	NOV 93	DEC 93	JAN 94	FEB 94	MAR 94	YEAR END MAR 94	TOTALS % SALES	TOTALS 15 MOS ENDED MAR 94
TOTAL SALES	45,000	45,000	70,000	100,000	25,000	35,000	30,000	500,000	100.0%	500,000
COST OF SALES:										
BEGINNING INVENTORY	47,500	52,700	62,900	74,400	44,400	45,600	46,300	40,000	8.0%	0
PURCHASES	30,000	35,000	50,000	25,000	15,000	20,000	30,000	295,000	59.0%	335,000
ENDING INVENTORY	(52,700)	(62,900)	(74,400)	(44,400)	(45,600)	(46,300)	(59,800)	(59,800)	−12.0%	(59,800)
TOTAL COST OF SALES	24,800	24,800	38,500	55,000	13,800	19,300	16,500	275,200	55.0%	275,200
GROSS PROFIT	20,200	20,200	31,500	45,000	11,200	15,700	13,500	224,800	45.0%	224,800
OPERATING EXPENSES:										
SALARIES & WAGES	6,300	6,300	6,300	6,300	6,300	6,300	6,300	75,600	15.1%	77,400
CREDIT CARD CHARGES	1,100	1,100	1,800	2,500	600	900	800	12,700	2.5%	12,700
ADVERTISING	500	500	500	500	500	500	500	6,000	1.2%	8,500
SUPPLIES/BAGS/BOXES	500	500	500	500	500	500	500	6,000	1.2%	7,500
BANK CHARGES	100	100	100	100	100	100	100	1,200	0.2%	1,550
CARTING	250	250	250	250	250	250	250	3,000	0.6%	3,100
INSURANCE	500	500	500	500	500	500	500	6,000	1.2%	8,200
INSURANCE—HOSPITALIZATION	1,200	1,200	1,200	1,200	1,200	1,200	1,200	14,400	2.9%	14,400
ACCOUNTING & LEGAL FEES	400	400	400	400	400	400	400	4,800	1.0%	4,800
SECURITY	100	100	100	100	100	100	100	1,200	0.2%	1,900
RENT	4,000	4,000	4,000	4,000	4,000	4,000	4,000	48,000	9.6%	48,000
REPAIRS & MAINTENANCE	200	200	200	200	200	200	200	2,400	0.5%	2,400
TELEPHONE	350	350	350	350	350	350	350	4,200	0.8%	4,900
UTILITIES	500	500	500	500	500	500	500	6,000	1.2%	7,500
PAYROLL TAXES	900	900	900	900	900	900	900	10,800	2.2%	11,100
MISCELLANEOUS	500	500	500	500	500	500	500	6,000	1.2%	9,000
TOTAL OPERATING EXP'S	17,400	17,400	18,100	18,800	16,900	17,200	17,100	208,300	41.7%	222,950
NET PROFIT(LOSS) BEFORE OTHER EXP'S	2,800	2,800	13,400	26,200	(5,700)	(1,500)	(3,600)	16,500	3.3%	1,850
OTHER EXPENSES:										
DEPRECIATION & AMORTIZATION	1,300	1,300	1,300	1,300	1,300	1,300	1,300	15,600	3.1%	15,600
CORP. INCOME TAX	0	0	0	0	0	0	0	0	0.0%	0
TOTAL OTHER EXPENSES	1,300	1,300	1,300	1,300	1,300	1,300	1,300	15,600	3.1%	15,600
NET INCOME	1,500	1,500	12,100	24,900	(7,000)	(2,800)	(4,900)	900	0.2%	(13,750)
CUMULATIVE NET INCOME	(37,550)	(36,050)	(23,950)	950	(6,050)	(8,850)	(13,750)	(13,750)		(13,750)

(Note: The Statement of Income & Expenses summarizes the income received and the expenses incurred by the company during a specific period of time. It is frequently called a profit & loss statement and includes not only the actual cash received and checks written during the period, but non-cash items as well such as depreciation of fixed assets and amortization of other capitalized expenses for which checks were written in previous periods.)

Rosario's Sweet Impressions Clothing Boutique, Inc.
Projected Analysis of Cashflows for the 15 Months ended March 31, 1994

	JAN 93	FEB 93	MAR 93	STARTUP PERIOD (TOTALS)	APR 93	MAY 93	JUN 93	JUL 93	AUG 93
RECEIPTS:									
SALES	0	0	0	0	20,000	30,000	30,000	30,000	40,000
WORKING CAPITAL CONTRIBUTIONS	100,000	50,000	150,000	300,000	0	0	0	0	0
TOTAL RECEIPTS	100,000	50,000	150,000	300,000	20,000	30,000	30,000	30,000	40,000
DISBURSEMENTS:									
CONSTRUCTION COSTS	41,000	41,000	41,000	123,000	0	0	0	0	0
FURNISHING & FIXTURES	0	10,000	40,000	50,000	0	0	0	0	0
EQUIPMENT	0	0	5,000	5,000	0	0	0	0	0
CAPITALIZED STARTUP COSTS	5,900	5,900	6,000	17,800	0	0	0	0	0
SECURITY DEPOSITS—RENT	8,000	0	0	8,000	0	0	0	0	0
SECURITY DEPOSITS—UTILITIES	1,500	0	0	1,500	0	0	0	0	0
PURCHASES	0	0	40,000	40,000	15,000	15,000	15,000	20,000	25,000
SALARIES & WAGES	0	0	0	0	6,300	6,300	6,300	6,300	6,300
CREDIT CARD CHARGES	0	0	0	0	500	800	800	800	1,000
ADVERTISING	1,500	1,500	2,000	5,000	500	500	500	500	500
SUPPLIES/BAGS/BOXES	1,500	1,500	2,000	5,000	500	500	500	500	500
BANK CHARGES	250	100	100	450	100	100	100	100	100
CARTING	200	200	200	600	250	250	250	250	250
INSURANCE	1,200	500	500	2,200	500	500	500	500	500
INSURANCE—HOSPITALIZATION	0	0	0	0	1,200	1,200	1,200	1,200	1,200
ACCOUNTING & LEGAL FEES	0	0	0	0	400	400	400	400	400
SECURITY	500	100	100	700	100	100	100	100	100
RENT	0	0	0	0	4,000	4,000	4,000	4,000	4,000
REPAIRS & MAINTENANCE	0	0	0	0	200	200	200	200	200
TELEPHONE	200	200	300	700	350	350	350	350	350
UTILITIES	500	500	500	1,500	500	500	500	500	500
PAYROLL TAXES	0	0	300	300	900	900	900	900	900
MISCELLANEOUS	1,000	1,000	1,000	3,000	500	500	500	500	500
TOTAL DISBURSEMENTS	63,250	62,500	139,000	264,750	31,800	32,100	32,100	37,100	42,300
CASH REQUIREMENTS:									
BEGINNING CASH	0	36,750	24,250	0	35,250	23,450	21,350	19,250	12,150
RECEIPTS	100,000	50,000	150,000	300,000	20,000	30,000	30,000	30,000	40,000
DISBURSEMENTS	63,250	62,500	139,000	264,750	31,800	32,100	32,100	37,100	42,300
ENDING CASH	36,750	24,250	35,250	35,250	23,450	21,350	19,250	12,150	9,850

	SEPT 93	OCT 93	NOV 93	DEC 93	JAN 94	FEB 94	MAR 94	YEAR END MAR 94	TOTALS 15 MOS ENDED MAR 94
RECEIPTS:									
SALES	45,000	45,000	70,000	100,000	25,000	35,000	30,000	500,000	500,000
WORKING CAPITAL CONTRIBUTIONS	0	0	0	0	0	0	0	0	300,000
TOTAL RECEIPTS	45,000	45,000	70,000	100,000	25,000	35,000	30,000	500,000	800,000
DISBURSEMENTS:									
CONSTRUCTION COSTS	0	0	0	0	0	0	0	0	123,000
FURNISHING & FIXTURES	0	0	0	0	0	0	0	0	50,000
EQUIPMENT	0	0	0	0	0	0	0	0	5,000
CAPITALIZED STARTUP COSTS	0	0	0	0	0	0	0	0	17,800
SECURITY DEPOSITS—RENT	0	0	0	0	0	0	0	0	8,000
SECURITY DEPOSITS—UTILITIES	0	0	0	0	0	0	0	0	1,500
PURCHASES	30,000	35,000	50,000	25,000	15,000	20,000	30,000	295,000	335,000
SALARIES & WAGES	6,300	6,300	6,300	6,300	6,300	6,300	6,300	75,600	75,600
CREDIT CARD CHARGES	1,100	1,100	1,800	2,500	600	900	800	12,700	12,700
ADVERTISING	500	500	500	500	500	500	500	6,000	11,000
SUPPLIES/BAGS/BOXES	500	500	500	500	500	500	500	6,000	11,000
BANK CHARGES	100	100	100	100	100	100	100	1,200	1,650
CARTING	250	250	250	250	250	250	250	3,000	3,600
INSURANCE	500	500	500	500	500	500	500	6,000	8,200
INSURANCE—HOSPITALIZATION	1,200	1,200	1,200	1,200	1,200	1,200	1,200	14,400	14,400
ACCOUNTING & LEGAL FEES	400	400	400	400	400	400	400	4,800	4,800
SECURITY	100	100	100	100	100	100	100	1,200	1,900
RENT	4,000	4,000	4,000	4,000	4,000	4,000	4,000	48,000	48,000
REPAIRS & MAINTENANCE	200	200	200	200	200	200	200	2,400	2,400
TELEPHONE	350	350	350	350	350	350	350	4,200	4,900
UTILITIES	500	500	500	500	500	500	500	6,000	7,500
PAYROLL TAXES	900	900	900	900	900	900	900	10,800	11,100
MISCELLANEOUS	500	500	500	500	500	500	500	6,000	9,000
TOTAL DISBURSEMENTS	47,400	52,400	68,100	43,800	31,900	37,200	47,100	503,300	768,050
CASH REQUIREMENTS:									
BEGINNING CASH	9,850	7,450	50	1,950	58,150	51,250	49,050	35,250	0
RECEIPTS	45,000	45,000	70,000	100,000	25,000	35,000	30,000	500,000	800,000
DISBURSEMENTS	47,400	52,400	68,100	43,800	31,900	37,200	47,100	503,300	768,050
ENDING CASH	7,450	50	1,950	58,150	51,250	49,050	31,950	31,950	31,950

SALES & COSTS PROJECTION MULTIPLIERS

The following chart can serve as a good starting point for projecting sales and costs. It shows what percentage of sales is normally spent on officers compensation, rent, taxes, interest, and advertising in a variety of different retail businesses.

| Classifications | <-------- (Percentage of Sales) --------> | | | | | Asset Turnover |
	Officers Comp.	Rent	Taxes	Interest	Adver.	
Hardware stores	5.3%	3.0%	1.9%	1.3%	1.2%	3.2 Times Per Year
Garden supplies & mobile home dealers	3.4	2.6	2.6	1.5	1.7	3.3
General merchandise stores	10.1	4.7	3.0	1.0	1.5	2.9
Grocery stores	2.2	1.9	1.5	0.5	0.7	6.4
Gasoline service stations	2.8	2.0	2.2	0.4	0.3	7.9
Apparel & accessory stores	3.8	9.0	2.4	0.8	2.3	2.4
Furniture & home furnishing stores	5.6	4.7	2.0	0.7	2.5	3.3
Eating & drinking places	4.6	7.1	4.3	1.4	2.0	3.2
Drug stores & proprietary stores	5.7	2.9	1.9	0.7	0.8	3.7
Liquor stores	2.9	2.8	1.8	0.9	0.2	4.2

RECORD YOUR PROGRESS

Comparing your actual sales figures and expenses with the numbers in your budget will give you a real sense of how your business measures up to your expectations its first year. Later you'll make these comparisons by month, quarter, and for the first year as a whole. As you do, the cyclical nature of your business will emerge and you'll be able to adjust your sales strategy to periods of special sales opportunity.

Until you reach that point when your sales revenues carry the business, you'll need working capital—or seed money. You'll need sufficient money to cover the cost of start-up and to get you to the point when the business begins to pay for itself. The budget your accountant prepares for your business plan should detail that amount, as well as the point at which you can expect positive cash flow—when sales revenues meet or exceed expenses. The numbers need to be so thorough that you can use them as a tool for convincing others to invest in your business, and for measuring performance against expectations.

If you think this has been difficult so far, just wait. The primary financial challenge to the start-up retailer is one of funding. With your plan in writing, you must now secure the financial support that will allow you to cover your store expenses this first year.

The Business Plan

To sum up, regardless of what form you choose, there are certain items that should be included in your business plan. Consider the following as a guide for what you should include:

The Business Plan

Store Name and Description: Describe the company behind your store, including business form, partners, etc.

Mission Statement:

The Market: An explanation of the product category and trends that support this store concept, including suppliers and current availability of products in your area. Include the results of any test marketing you've conducted.

The Customer: Who the customers are, where they live, and what needs your store will serve.

Your Credentials: Explain why you're the right person to run this store.

Your Strategy: Explain how your skills and store concept will enable you to respond to the needs of the market and customers described above.

Your Location: If you have a site, explain why it is the perfect location; if not, explain what you need in a location and why.

Products and Services: A detailed breakdown of what your store will offer and how it will make these goods and services available to customers, including your staffing plans.

The Promotional Push: Explain the marketing strategy you will use to convey the advantages of your store to consumers.

The Finances: This part of the plan should begin with a detailed breakdown of the cost of operation of your store, with start-up cost projections, an estimated annual budget, and sales projections for at least the first year.

Your Contribution: Explain how much you are investing in the business, and the sources.

Outside Investors: Identify who is investing and how much they are contributing, and what they expect for their money.

Need: If you are trying to attract a loan or woo other investors, use all of the above to demonstrate how much you need and why your store represents a good investment.

Conclusions: Sum up everything you've already said with confidence and enthusiasm.

For more information on business plans, take a look at the following books:

- *Business Plans That Win Venture Capital,* by Terrence B. McGarty (Wiley, 1989)
- *Crafting the Successful Business Plan,* by Erik Hyypia (Prentice-Hall, 1992)
- *The Start-up Business Plan,* by William M. Luther (Prentice-Hall, 1991)

⋘ 7 ⋙

YOUR SOURCES OF FINANCING

Once you know what your financial needs are, your burden becomes locating and securing the financial resources required to give your store a fair chance at success. Let's assume you haven't won a lottery and weren't born into wealth. You're the average, ambitious man or woman intent on doing it your way with a retail store. Your only option is to look to outside sources of funding. This search for money will take some time as you search for lenders confident enough in you and your store concept to risk an investment in it.

FORGET ABOUT INSTITUTIONAL SOURCES OF FINANCING

This is your store, so it's entirely your responsibility to raise the financing. Forget about lending institutions, like banks and venture capital firms, for now. It's not that these houses of finance don't like entrepreneurs. They just don't want to lend you money until you can demonstrate your success. When you can present a track record that shows you've weathered a few ups and downs, and can hand them sales reports that prove the greatness of your store concept, they'll be more likely to respond to your need for funding. Until then, you must first look within yourself, and your circle of family and friends, to finance your dream.

TAKE OUT A SECOND MORTGAGE AND CONVERT ASSETS INTO CASH

If you believe in your vision, you'll refinance your home mortgage for the sake of it. You'll also sell your prized collection of barbed wire and Elvis singles, the boat, and even your faithful dog—you'll need to do whatever it takes to get your dream off the ground. That's because until *you've* done everything you could and are completely at risk, no one, no matter how much they love you or how much money they have, will want to take a risk with you. You must demonstrate in deeds, as well as words, your complete devotion to the success of your business before you can ask your maiden aunt to lend you money.

Once considered a last desperate act for those overburdened with debt, the second mortgage is often a necessary step for anyone who wants to breathe life into dreams of financial independence. A second mortgage or home equity loan implies some risk on your part, in terms of increased financial burden. You'll be able to borrow a share of the difference between what your house is worth and what you still owe on your existing mortgage. With the recent decline in interest rates, many people are refinancing their homes entirely for a cash advantage and saving money on monthly payments in the process. Which way you go should depend primarily on how much money you're able to generate from other sources. But realize you probably will need to secure some of your seed capital by borrowing against your home.

Shop around for a home equity loan as you would any other bank loan. It's advisable to submit your application while you're still gainfully employed with someone else. Don't volunteer details about your plans to use the money to start a business. A new business is a risk in the eyes of the banker, and banks prefer to avoid risks.

How important is your store to you? It should mean enough that you're willing to part with anything and everything that's not absolutely necessary to your lifestyle right now. Take a good second look around your house or apartment at your prized possessions. Are they more important to you than a future of self-determination? If there's a market for your collections, or jewelry, or anything else lying around, turn those dubious assets now collecting dust into the cash you need for your store. The same goes for any IRA or Keogh accounts. The cash they can put in your hands today may mean a lot more than they ever could to you at retirement. It's a risk, but you must be willing to take it. For unless you do everything in your power to finance your store, you can't expect others to lend their support.

Only after doing everything you could on your own can you turn to Ma, Uncle Fred, third cousin Rita, good neighbor Otto, and your childhood cronies for little loans, much-needed "investments" in the business.

APPROACHING FAMILY AND FRIENDS FOR INVESTMENTS AND LOANS

You may elect to secure the necessary funding from one rich aunt or from a whole roster of acquaintances. Each approach has merits. A single financier may stay completely in the background until the store shows signs of faltering, and then become an aggressive adversary in deciding how your business should be run with her money. If cash flow ever proves a problem, it may take more work to explain your problems to many supporters. But with less at risk individually, none will apply the same kind of pressure as the single friendly lender with a lot of money at stake. Whatever combination of personal financiers you use to set up your shop, expect to get to know each much better if circumstances force you to explain why you can't make payment on the loan until next month.

When approaching friends and family as financiers of your retail dream, you should present this as an opportunity to help you as well as themselves. Share your enthusiasm about the store and what it could mean for them and you. You'll need to be attuned to what type of agreement each of these personal contacts prefers. Some will feel most comfortable making you a straight loan, to be paid back over time with interest. Others may prefer lending the money with expectations of being paid back, and a share in the future profits of the store. Deal with family and friends on a case-by-case basis, sensitive to their needs. Any agreement you reach should be in writing, even if it's just an informal letter outlining the terms: the amount of the loan, the payback plan, and what, if any, their long-term interest in the business will be.

APPROACHING PEOPLE YOU DON'T KNOW

Of course, the potential pool of funding sources you don't already personally know is much wider. It's just more difficult to identify and find moneyed individuals receptive to helping the total stranger with the start-up store. Anyone you approach to invest in or lend you money for your business will want to know how much you are bringing to the table. Before you approach outsiders, you should have at least 50 percent of your seed money secured from your personal assets and contacts. They will also want to review your business plan with its detailed analysis of projected costs, savings, and profits.

CONSIDER TAKING ON A PARTNER

One alternative the cash-poor entrepreneur should consider is taking on a partner in the store. The partner you should look for is someone who's a little older, experienced in the business you're going into, and with enough money in reserve to help you through that critical first year. He will bring insight and a financial foundation to the company. The best partner, though, is the silent partner: the individual who believes in you and your idea enough to fund your retail dream, and sit back and watch your success.

Whenever you take on a partner, there's strength in numbers. Having two ambitious skilled people at the helm of the store tends to strengthen how it's perceived by the professional community and public. It makes for a whole greater than the sum of its parts. If you decide to enter into a partnership, I strongly advise you to work up a written agreement that describes your relationship, what each partner contributes to and expects from the arrangement, and terms under which the partnership might be dissolved to your mutual satisfaction.

TAP INTO YOUR WORKING PARTNERSHIPS

The new realities of retailing dictate you treat your suppliers and service providers as partners in your business (see Chapter 9). Partners work for and with each other. Consider them as potential sources for reducing your need for working capital during the start-up phase. Suppliers may not lend you money outright, but they can finance your orders or give you inventory on a consignment basis. The same is true with contractors and other service providers. Instead of one lump payment, they may be willing to structure a payment schedule that works with your budget. You won't know what kind of flexibility is available to you from these ''partners'' until you ask.

CONSIDER RECRUITING INVESTORS

They do exist, and once you have a business plan on paper, you can make a pitch for investors. Advertise or spread the word. Usually they want equity, a share of the business and profits based on their contribution to start-up funding. For providing ten percent of that cost, an investor may expect a payback plus ten percent of profits. Think of this as selling shares in the business. Such an arrangement has legal implications that require the involvement of an attorney.

LOOK FOR ANGELS

Yet another alternative for financing exists outside the halls of finance: ''angels.'' Successes of their own making, or natural-born philanthropists, these rare and elusive individuals want to help people like you. Driven by a deep sense of altruism, or the desire to repay the community that nurtured their dreams, they make seed money available to entrepreneurs. This may be what amounts to a start-up grant either through an outright donation to the cause or a low-cost, long-term loan. If the business prospers, the angel may expect a return. If not, the angel can walk away from the endeavor knowing he tried to help someone where it counts. Finding your angel—that's a challenge! It's more likely they'll find you, so don't count on their help.

INSTITUTIONAL LENDERS

Good advice to the contrary, you may decide it's worth investigating your chances for a business loan from a local lending institution. This may prove an exercise in futility, especially if the store is your first stab at self-employment. You may have good personal credit, and a good relationship with your local loan officer, but it may not be enough to get the loan you need. Make your case, in person and on paper. If all else fails and you need the funding, consider asking for a personally guaranteed loan. It's not the best situation, but if the store really matters, you'll have little trouble living with the commitment.

Also check in with the area office of the Small Business Administration and see if you qualify for one of its guaranteed loans. The application process is thorough, and funds are limited. But you won't know if you qualify until you apply. The SBA exists to help people like yourself start businesses, and part of that support includes helping those who meet its criteria secure the necessary funding. And if the SBA officers can't help you get the loan, they will provide ample direction and resources that will prove invaluable in other aspects of starting your store.

THE TRADE-OFF

There's a definite trade-off when turning to any of these outside sources for funding. The entrepreneur who gets the money must surrender some autonomy in the process. Investors, partners, angels, and lending institutions bring their own expectations to the project, driven by their need for a return on their investment. Building a successful retail operation is a long-term project, but some expect financial rewards in the short term. That often places unwanted pressure on the entrepreneur at a time when the challenges of the start-up store will breathe enough discord into your life.

GETTING THE WORD OUT

Finding outside sources to fund your retail dream from paper to storefront takes considerable time and effort. When you decide you want to take on a partner, bring on investors, or could use the help of an angel, tell everyone you know. Request assistance from the local chamber of commerce, business development offices, the Small Business Administration, merchants' associations, local trade organizations, and any club you belong to. Business schools share a new sense of responsibility to help their graduates and the business community at large and can prove ideal networking centers. Basically, exhaust any and every conceivable channel of communicating your idea and need. And expect nothing for your efforts. That way you may be surprised, but won't be disappointed.

SELLING THE PLAN TO OUTSIDERS

Once you realize you can't secure the funds the store requires from your personal wealth, you get promoted to salesperson. Selling yourself and your idea to family and friends poses a challenge easily met. You know these people, know what excites them, and frightens them. So you know how to talk to them. And they know you, for better or worse, so they have no illusions for what and by whom their money will be spent.

When you approach strangers for funding, it's a much different game. Until they've had a chance to thoroughly review your plans, all they know is that you want some of their money. The impression you make, as much as your store concept and business plan, will win or lose their support. The entrepreneur presents himself as a person who knows what he's doing, where he wants to go with the store, and how he will get there. Everything about how you present yourself to these strangers, from the way you dress to how you field questions you have no idea how to answer, will help or hurt the financial picture.

Your enthusiasm for the store should be contagious, your confidence in yourself unshakable. It's to your benefit to submit something in writing prior to your first meeting with potential investors or lenders. A page or two defining the store concept, the market it will serve, and why the marketplace needs it will do. Also include a brief summary of your experience and interests as they relate to your ability to run the store.

Bring along a typed outline of your business goals and financial projections to your meeting; better yet, show off your business plan. Today's business standards call for a typeset document of a few pages, perhaps some supporting graphs, bound or stapled with a cover page.

Dress neatly but conservatively for the meeting. Be prepared with any and all information you've gathered while researching your market opportunities. After the formalities of introduction, explain your background, the marketplace, and how the two combine for the store concept. Answer any questions put to you directly, to the best of your ability. When you don't know an answer, lay off the bull. Promise to get back with a response, and make sure you do.

When the subject of money comes up, be completely honest and forthright about your needs, and how it will help the business. Also emphasize what you'll bring to the project in money, time, and commitment. Reiterate the optimism your research allows and do your best to address any concerns expressed. When offered criticism, consider its merits. Never take it personally or grow aggressively defensive. Remember, a professional always remains cool under pressure. The person who can't handle a little flack in a conversation promises to crumble when the inevitable business crisis presents itself. That's not the entrepreneur who wins investors to her ideas.

When the meeting is over, express sincere thanks for the other's time and interest in your idea. Hopefully your winning personality, confidence, and professionalism will allow you to leave with the promise of the funding. If not, you should have learned from the experience. Always follow up on anything promised during the interview, and comply promptly with any application requirements. When things go well, a letter of thanks is always a nice touch.

A PLANNING CROSSROADS

When you've exhausted all your financing options, you'll come to a crossroads in the planning stage of your store. If you've been able to secure adequate funding, you can get to work filling in the details of your business plan and setting them in action. You'll need to rework your budget in consideration of the payment arrangements you've made with any lenders. If, however, you cannot pull together enough resources to meet your financial goals, you have three choices: You can give up, you can start the business without enough money, or you can revise your expectations, for now.

If you're truly an entrepreneur, giving up isn't an option. That will leave only two: going into business undercapitalized, or reinventing your dream. If you're going to proceed intelligently, there really is no choice. The number one reason small businesses fail is undercapitalization. If you've projected what it will cost you to succeed, and you can't raise enough, you're in effect projecting failure.

Still, the can-do spirit of the entrepreneur often leads to a "damn the torpedoes, full speed ahead" attitude. The entrepreneur decides to gamble on her own strength and determination and intelligence being enough to carry the business over the obstacle of not having enough money. While there are people who succeed in this kind of risk-taking manner, they are few and far between. The numbers don't lie, and neither should you—especially to yourself—especially when it's your nest egg at risk. Instead, take the third option and try to reinvent your dream to fit your financial resources.

REINVENT YOUR DREAM IF YOU CAN'T FIND ENOUGH MONEY

You may want to reconsider one of the alternative routes for testing your store concept suggested in the last chapter. If you've already done that and found your idea a winner, perhaps you can expand the scope of that retail experiment. Use this setback to your advantage and cultivate increased demand for your products. Consider doubling the amount of inventory you carry in the booth or kiosk, or set up two ministores in different locations around your area. The added exposure can only broaden your customer base. If you're truly an entrepreneur, you won't give up; you'll turn adversity into opportunity.

On the other hand, if your experiments brought you limited success, and your best efforts failed to generate the financial support to get your business off the ground, it's time to step back and reevaluate the store concept.

Consider the experience of the visionary behind Hub Central, specialist in automobile hubcaps. He recognized his business opportunity one afternoon driving home along one of his busy home city's neglected byways. What did he see? A lot of potholes, a lot of cars hitting them, and a lot losing their hubcaps. What start-up inventory he couldn't collect from the road shoulder, he purchased at area junkyards. He started in an open-air market conveniently situated across from the city's strip of auto parts stores.

Some of his customers were the disgruntled drivers who lost wheel covers during their daily commute. Most, though, turned out to be car collectors and restorers looking for vintage caps for their vintage cars. They also inquired about other parts: chrome fenders, trim, and hood ornaments. After a few months he realized there weren't enough people who needed hubcaps to justify his retail existence. Hub Central became The Chrome Palace, and quickly outgrew the flea market to become the source in the state for vintage auto trim *and* hubcaps.

That may seem a highly specialized example, but it demonstrates the kind of thinking that should guide you in reinventing your store if you must. You may have the right idea for the wrong audience, or be approaching a valid market with a flawed strategy. Review all your notes about the theory behind your store, searching for the opportunities you may have missed or overlooked the first time around. Rethink the concept, and begin experimenting again.

For more information on financing your specialty store, take a look at the following books:

- *Finding Money for Your Small Business,* by Max Fallek (Dearborn, 1994)
- *Free Money: For Small Businesses & Entrepreneurs,* by Laurie Blum (Wiley, 1988)
- *Getting Money: A Getting-into-Business Guide* (International Self Counsel Press, 1991)
- *Raising Start-up Capital for Your Firm,* by Gustav Berle (Wiley, 1990)
- *Start-Up Money: How to Finance Your New Small Business,* by Michael McKeever (Nolo, 1986)
- *Starting on a Shoestring: Building a Business Without a Bankroll,* by Arnold S. Goldstein (Wiley, 1991)
- *The Radical New Road to Wealth: How to Raise Venture Capital for a New Business,* by A. David Silver (International Wealth, 1990)
- *The Bootstrap Entrepreneur,* by Steven C. Bursten (Nelson, 1993)

⟨⟩ 8 ⟨⟩

YOUR PRE-OPENING CHECKLIST AND SELECTING INVENTORY

I f you were fortunate enough to win sufficient financial endorsement for the store concept, or if you've reinvented your dream to fit your budget, you should waste no time in putting your plan into action. Before embarking on your quest for funding, you compiled a list of everything required to put your store in operation. Now organize those needs into a logical progression of manageable events.

TARGET OPENING DAY AND DRAW UP A CHECKLIST

For now, your concern should be working toward one deadline: Opening Day. Your first reference point in setting up the schedule of activity is the date when renovation work will be completed and you can occupy the space. Try to set opening day for at least a month from that date. You can always open your doors before the event, if things work to your advantage. You may also push it back a little if something slows the schedule. The important thing right now is to set a target date, a fixed deadline you plan to meet.

Next take your expenses list and compile a checklist of whatever you must do in order to acquire those goods or services. Make this as detailed a list as necessary. You'll later experience a tremendous sense of satisfaction crossing completed tasks off the list.

Sign the lease, hire the contractor, and let the renovation work proceed. If you decide to do the work yourself, push your opening day back at least two weeks, preferably a month, immediately. That's because you should be using the time the premises is being readied for occupation to handle other start-up activities. Like arranging for telephone service. Purchasing fixtures and displays. Developing and approving a store logo. Ordering business signs and business cards. Investigating and deciding on a computer/ inventory management system. Installing a security system. Setting up displays. Loading shelves. Training staff. Planning pre-opening day advertising and promotion. And inviting dignitaries and the media.

These activities will vary, depending on the type of store, your space needs, and how you plan to reach your audience. But every checklist should be a detailed accounting of everything that must be done, broken down by the month, week, even day leading up to the big event. Let's look at the two major items likely to be on that checklist: inventory and personnel.

SETTING UP YOUR INVENTORY

Your store is all about what it sells. From your earlier contact with suppliers you should already know what kind of turnaround they can give on orders, and the terms available to you. As soon as you give the contractor the go-ahead to start work on the store, get out your inventory lists of what you plan to sell. Organize it by source, manufacturer, distributor, or individual and by product category. Get in touch with your sales contacts. Tell them your target opening day, and when you expect to be ready to take delivery of the products. Ask if they'll take your order now and hold the goods at the warehouse. This is a good idea if you're entering any high-demand category as product shortages do develop. If you haven't already worked out the terms of sale, now is the time to handle that as well. (We'll discuss inventory selection more thoroughly in a few pages.)

Finally, request information about any upcoming advertising programs, promotional campaigns, or co-op requirements. Request your contact mail you anything that's available, immediately. The material may help with your promotional plans.

Before you're ready to take delivery on the goods, you must prepare the space for them in two areas of your store: on the sales floor and in the warehouse. If shelving isn't part of the renovation project, determine your needs and order what's necessary. The same for display racks and other floor fixtures. You want to be ready as soon as the goods arrive.

Next, for your pricing responsibilities. Unless you plan on your store being one where the customer who must ask cost has no business coming in, every item needs to be ticketed with your selling price. First, ask your suppliers if they will supply pre-ticketed merchandise. Some do, for a fee. If not, it's your responsibility to go through this rather labor-intensive process. How you handle this should be based on whether or not you'll be using a computer system for sales and inventory management (see Chapter 10).

The most difficult part of setting up a computerized system is entering all the products you sell into that system. Even if you decide to use bar coding for product ID and price information, you or an employee must enter a price and description for every SKU (stock-keeping unit) in the store, as well as the number of each item you have on hand. It makes the most sense to set up this system when you take your first shipment of products. The person who enters this information should be one who'll continue to work on the system. If you need to hire additional help, you want this done before opening day. If you have an employee do the bulk of this data entry, just make sure you or another family member learns the computer system and its operation. If not, you'll face major headaches if that employee ever opts out of your retail dream for greener pastures.

TRAINING YOUR PERSONNEL, INCLUDING YOURSELF

If yours will be a "ma and pa" shop, take the time now to make sure Ma and Pa know everything they need to know about running the business. This may mean extensive self-education using how-to books, enrolling in a business seminar, or taking advantage of supplier-sponsored training programs. Learn all you can before you open your doors. Study time will prove more elusive once you're in business.

Training should reflect each person's responsibilities in the business. If you're the entire staff, that's easy—you're responsible for everything and therefore must learn everything. Get out your trusty notebook and compile a detailed list of responsibilities related to the long-term and day-to-day operations of your business. Next, divide those responsibilities, based on the number of staffers and their respective strengths and interests. Compile another list of any areas where there's a gap in knowledge. These should guide you in your self-education process or serve as the basis for the job descriptions of any outside help you need to hire.

There will be more on developing job descriptions and hiring employees in the next chapter. For now, suffice it to say that your checklist must provide you with time to find, interview, and hire any employees. The target hiring date should be at least two weeks before you'll need their services. The want ads should appear in local newspapers at least two weeks before that. Allow time for interviews, too. Remember to coordinate your hiring plans with any training programs you want prospective employees to participate in.

YOUR YEARLY CALENDAR

You can't expect to make all your decisions before you open the door. A large part of retailing is responding to developments in the market and fine-tuning the business to address them. But you should, to the extent possible, draw up a yearly calendar for your activities. If you wait until those customers start coming in the store do to your planning, you'll find it's impossible to carve out the time. Just make sure that it provides you with some opportunities to review and plan.

ADD YOUR ADVERTISING SCHEDULE
TO THE CALENDAR

Achieving the right promotional mix often involves a great deal of hit and miss. Take out your calendar and assign different modes of advertising to each month during the first two quarters. You may spend more on newspaper in May, and radio in June, for example, while retaining a mix of other media. Identify four major calendar events for major sales promotions, aside from your principal selling season, to serve as the basis for in-store sales. Identify two weekends on opposite ends of the year for creating your own sales events. You may want to experiment with related products and services too. If so, assign these trial months as well. (We'll get into a great deal of detail about all these promotional techniques and devices later in Chapter 13.)

ADD REGULAR PLANNING AND REVIEW MEETINGS TO THE CALENDAR

Plan ahead for weekly, monthly, and quarterly meetings and reviews of all business activity at the store, including sales trends, customer profiles, buying patterns, and advertising impact. Assign a day for these beginning with the next week. For instance, schedule meetings for every Tuesday morning; the third Tuesday of each month could be for a monthly review, while the second Tuesday of the new quarter could be for evaluating the previous quarter.

ADD EVERY STAFFER'S RESPONSIBILITIES TO THE CALENDAR

Then compile a list of all responsibilities that must be handled on a weekly and monthly basis: placing advertising, ordering new inventory, paying rent and utilities, etc. Assign each to the appropriate day of the week or month.

If you're computerized, it will be a big help in drawing up this calendar. But no matter how you prepare it, remember that it will grow as you learn more about running the store, and expand the scope of its operations.

The value of having a business plan, a pre-opening checklist, and a yearly calendar is that, taken together, they define your responsibilities and aspirations and allow you to measure how well reality compares with your vision behind the store. What you do with what's written in these three documents determines your future as a retail entrepreneur. Carefully drafted and regularly scrutinized, they'll provide you an ongoing guide to ensure your store, in practice, lives up to the ambitious plans behind it.

SELECTING INVENTORY

A store is known by what it sells as well as by who's selling it. Once you decide what type of store you want to open, and where to pursue that dream, you get down to the nuts and bolts of acquiring the stock you'll sell. As the store owner and operator, the visionary behind this specialty store, selecting the right inventory mix is one of the most critical decisions you will make. A store is what it sells, and selection is what sets the specialty store apart from its competitors. Your decision to open the shop is based on the opportunities you see in the market, opportunities to give consumers a selection of merchandise, backed by service, not available anywhere else. The research that went into your decision to open this particular type of shop equips you alone with the insight to make the right decisions on selecting merchandise. Everything else about the business depends on what you decide will fill your store's shelves. Retailing giants employ buyers and product managers who take care of the selection and purchasing of products. As the owner/operator of the specialty store, it's your call, from start to finish.

Selecting inventory is easy; selecting the right inventory poses much more of a challenge. You must know the products, and what your competitors are doing, and devise an appropriate response. Product selection is all about positioning. It's one thing to stock every item in a category; it's quite another to selectively choose those products that enhance your reputation.

That's something you won't accomplish by mixing and matching from among the brochures and catalogs salespeople drop by your office. It's your responsibility to see and handle products before you sell them. Early on, trust your own judgment only, to separate the good from the bad, the cheap from the quality, for the selection that best defines your vision of your store.

MAKE IT YOUR BUSINESS TO ATTEND
TRADE SHOWS

One of the best forums for accomplishing this is at trade shows. Every industry hosts a convention at least once a year. There you'll find everybody who pretends to be anybody in that business showing their wares. Retail trade shows, and the many exhibits that fill their aisles, serve product suppliers in two ways. They use their exhibits as showcases for products they already sell. They also take them as an opportunity to announce or introduce new products. Based on the reaction of retailers like you, and the amount of orders they receive, the suppliers decide which products actually make it to market.

All retailers should try to attend at least one industry convention a year, especially during the planning and developing stages of their businesses. If you've doubts on which to attend, contact the appropriate trade group, publication, or other retailers in your business. The trade show presents the ideal opportunity to get to know your suppliers and develop a sense of where your business is headed. Apart from the cost of travel, hotel, and whatever other indulgences you pursue, the trade show provides a cost-effective way to see everyone and everything you need to under one roof. Spend the time wandering the aisles, browsing the exhibits, sampling new products, collecting literature, and making contacts. The education will prove invaluable when you're back in the store, fine-tuning your strategy.

ATTEND AS MANY DEALER MEETINGS
AS YOU CAN

In many industries the largest suppliers sponsor dealer meetings. Some hold national events, others host theirs on a regional or state-by-state basis, depending on the number of retailers in an area. Usually attending these events is by invitation only. Suppliers use their dealer meetings like closed-door trade shows for the introduction of new products, to outline the marketing and promotional strategy behind them, and to get feedback from the dealer network about company products and policies. Like larger.

industry gatherings, these meetings give dealers the chance to get together with peers and exchange ideas, opinions, and perceptions about your retail market.

IF NECESSARY, REQUEST IN-STORE DEMONSTRATIONS

If you can't attend these meetings, you can always request your sales contacts bring the manufacturer's new products to you for an in-store demonstration. Most will eagerly accommodate you. If you do opt for such a meeting, try to arrange it so that as many as possible of your store personnel can sit in on the demonstration. If you decide to stock the product, this demonstration will serve as sales training for the staff. The only difference between the store demonstration and the trade or dealer meetings is that you'll see a more limited selection of product. There may also be more pressure on you to place an order at the close of the meeting. Always think things through before ordering product. There's too much money you'll be tying up with your decision to leave it to impulse.

MAKE SURE YOU KNOW YOUR MARKET

It's critical for the future of your business that you know the market—that means the products you don't sell as well as those you do. Being on the front lines of retailing means knowing what's coming in a few months so you can adjust your strategy to maximize opportunities as they present themselves. Ignoring what's happening in your market, to the point where customers start to tell you what's going on in your specialty, invites them to take their business elsewhere.

There's another aspect to the front line in retail that will enlighten the savvy retailer. It's your market as revealed there in the showroom and sales receipts. That's where the trends will show themselves, and where you'll see them emerge. Retail success follows careful planning and acting on the right hunches. You need to develop a sense of what people will want and then offer them enough choice to pursue their options and individuality.

The successful retailer learns when and how to respond to sales activity in the store. To accomplish that, use your computer system to identify the trend, and effective promotion to fan a spark of interest into a full flame.

So how do you do it? Track what's happening in your sales reports. Talk to customers, at the cash register and at the service desk. Find out why they select what they buy, and what features or functions turn the decision. At the service desk, ask what's right and wrong with the product. When you hear similar responses on any matter, any demand, consider it an emerging trend. It either means opportunity or a potential problem that must be addressed.

DEVELOP A SALES PSYCHOLOGY TO GO ALONG WITH YOUR INVENTORY SELECTION

Part of the psychology of retailing requires that you always offer shoppers a choice in what they buy. The simplest way to go about it is to look for a good/better/best selection of any product you stock, at successively higher prices. Pricing alone will not imply the advantages, however. The shopper must recognize the worth of the added cost in the quality, features, or product performance. Some always want the best, others only the best buy. Letting your customers determine what's right for them is an important part of the purchasing process.

Everyone wants a fair deal. How you and your customers define that may be entirely different. For the customer it may mean the lowest cost; for the retailer, a reasonable profit on the sale. In fiercely competitive product categories, where it's either sold at a low price or it isn't sold at all, you must look for other ways to sweeten the sale and shore up profits. That may mean setting up a rack of candy bars near the cash register, for a low-price, high-markup impulse sale. No matter what else you sell, a share of your customers will respond to the availability of food at the cash register.

While that will certainly add to profits, it will be to your greater benefit to concentrate on the accessory and impulse items that go with the mainstays of your specialty. Many retailers regard accessories as a key to profitability. In general, accessory items are not prone to price competition. They're usually inexpensive enough to make it easy for the shopper to make the purchase, often on impulse. Comparatively inexpensive though these products may be, the profits from accessory sales quickly add up for the dealer. Deciding which accessory and impulse products to push depends entirely on your retail specialty. These are definitely products that shoppers expect to find in the small specialty store.

When selecting products for your main product categories, and when reviewing them at trade shows, think in terms of the total experience of users of that product. Accessories typically add to buyers' enjoyment of a product, allowing them to do more with it.

Take your cue from specialty stores that depend on accessory sales. Consider camera stores, for instance. When selecting inventory, the camera store owner thinks in terms of the total photographic experience. The core business may be selling cameras, but that's not where the profits are. The camera dealer makes as much, if not more, from the accessories he carries: bags, lenses, tripods, film, filters, how-to books, picture frames, photo albums, film, and batteries. The camera dealer tries to stock everything and anything related to use of that camera.

That's what a good specialty store is: a one-stop shop for everything related to a particular category, product, interest or experience. In achieving that, you can never settle on a product mix. You need to constantly seek out the new products that will enhance the enjoyment and use of the main products you sell.

Experiment. Regardless of the background you bring to the store, the first year in business serves as an education in your retail specialty. Learn from your suppliers and customers. Test new ideas, services, and products in your search for the mix that will distinguish your store from its competitors.

Of course, the strategy you choose must offer financial rewards. In many retail categories it's the other things you sell—the accessories and impulse items—that float the business. Cameras can be found just about anywhere. All stores carry at least a sampling of current models. But few of those same stores carry the accessories that promote total enjoyment and usage of that camera. People head to the specialty store for those extras.

As the retail specialist, it's these other things you offer, the extras that no one else stocks, that strengthen your presence in the market. The best specialty store is the shopper's source and resource for everything she needs or needs to know about a class of product.

Selecting inventory, then, is not a onetime deal, but an ongoing responsibility. If you do it well, develop your expertise, know every product from every supplier, stick with quality, and develop a selection that distinguishes your store, shoppers will respond.

For more information on inventory, take a look at the following books:

- *How to Control & Reduce Inventory,* by Burton E. Lipman (Bell, 1988)
- *Procurement & Inventory Ordering Tables,* by Jerry Banks and Charles L. Hohenstein, Jr. (Franklin, 1977)
- *Recent Developments in Inventory Theory,* by Moshe F. Friedman (Pergamon, 1981)

YOUR PRE-OPENING CHECKLIST

Use this work sheet as a guide for setting up your pre-opening checklist. Be as thorough as possible in your list, accounting for every activity you must complete before you're ready to open your doors. Enter a deadline for each and also the date that project is completed. Allow some flexibility in case you are unable to complete all projects by opening day. If necessary, you can open your doors on your target date, or push that day back, but hold your grand opening celebration later, when everything is in place.

TARGET OPENING DATE:

Project	Target Date	Date Completed
Occupy Space	_____	_____
Utilities Hookup	_____	_____
Store Design	_____	_____
Store Renovation	_____	_____
Install Security System	_____	_____
Purchase Fixtures/Displays	_____	_____
Purchase Office Furniture	_____	_____
Set Up Sales/Office/Warehouse Space	_____	_____
Order Computer System	_____	_____
Design Logo	_____	_____
Order Signs/Stationary/Bags	_____	_____
Purchase Delivery Truck	_____	_____
Install Signs	_____	_____
Order Inventory:	_____	_____
Supplier	_____	_____
Supplier	_____	_____
Supplier	_____	_____
Staffing:	_____	_____
Place Ad	_____	_____
Interviews	_____	_____
Hire for Office	_____	_____
Hire for Sales Floor	_____	_____
Hire for Stockroom	_____	_____
Employee Training	_____	_____
Computer Training	_____	_____
Ticket/Set Out Merchandise	_____	_____
Promotion:	_____	_____
Send Store Opening Release	_____	_____
Print Ads	_____	_____
TV Ads	_____	_____
Radio Ads	_____	_____
Send Invitations for Opening	_____	_____
Follow-up Calls	_____	_____

9

BUILDING YOUR TEAM

Until now, you've probably thought of your store as your own. The product of your imagination and ambition, it's your ticket to a better and more rewarding life. But you're not the only one who stands to gain from this endeavor. The store may be your business, but plenty of others hope it means opportunity for them, as well. Your plans to enter business breathe a little more vitality into the local economy. The money you spend starting up and then running your store will find its way into and around other businesses, through the hands of everyone you purchase products or services from or hire to help run your store.

That's why, as an entrepreneur, the owner of the small business, you'll become a valued and respected member of the community. The town fathers and mothers may not rename Main Street in you honor, but they'll appreciate your contribution nonetheless. Even if you don't hire a single staff member, you'll make a positive contribution to the overall employment picture. As a purchaser of products, you'll be helping the salesman and the factory worker. As a seeker of services, you'll employ the expertise of people whose income depends on clients like you. Your store means new opportunity for everyone whose products, services, and support help bring the dreams of your own store to life. You're both the benefactor and beneficiary of these relationships.

When you think of it in those terms, there's much more riding on your business than your future. Everyone you work with shares in your success or frustration, to some degree. All have an interest in seeing you prosper. Certainly you'll encounter some who want nothing more than to take you for all they can get. Those opportunists represent the exception, not the rule. Like you, most of the people you'll be dealing with have a dream they want to pursue.

A career offers its own rewards, but it's also a means to an end. You've accepted responsibility for your own career; financial independence is your goal. Others may envy that freedom and confidence, but they'll also respect you for it. No matter what role they play, how minor or major their contributions, they demand the same respect from you.

Building the team that will bring your store success begins with developing that sense of respect for others; for the individuals you deal with and for their contributions to your enterprise.

THE TEAM EFFORT

Every commercial venture amounts to a team effort. Where would suppliers be without the store owner? Where would the retailer be without the newspaper that carries its advertising? What could your employees do without the opportunity to work in your store? Each of these contacts draws something from the business and contributes something to its successes. While assisting you, they progress toward their own personal goals.

You'll have the freedom to select some members of your team. Others, you'll have no choice over: you'll be forced to learn to get along with them. You won't be able to hire the guy who makes deliveries from your suppliers, nor your sales contacts. You'll need to develop a polite, professional relationship with these people, if nothing more. And you won't get to choose your customers, either. They'll choose you. Sure, you've an idea of who they are, in terms of interests, but you know nothing of their personalities. They could be gracious and demanding, and polite and rude, all in the same visit to your store. They're team members too: essential ones who'll carry your dreams to daylight. You'll learn, if you don't already know, that it's much easier to get along with people than not to. A grudge gets heavy after a while. You won't need the headaches. Running the store will present enough.

SEEK EXPERIENCE FIRST

That said, there are things you can do to ensure the team members you do choose are the most qualified for the jobs you want accomplished. When turning outside, for business counseling or to build store staff, always look first for someone with retail experience. It's easier to instruct the attorney with a roster of store clients about the peculiarities of selling garden tools than it is to instruct the recent law school graduate on the special concerns of the store owner. So, no matter who you're hiring or contracting with, seek someone who's familiar with the industry you're entering. That's retailing. You may sell shoes, you may sell shawls, but the industry is retailing.

MAKE SURE TO CHECK REFERENCES

And always, always, always check references. If the guy at your cash register lost his last store job for sticky fingers, you're to blame when cash receipts start coming up short. It's your mistake when the systems manager's "extensive computer background" is as much as a video game endows, and the computer crashes, hourly. You're at fault when all you get from a two-thousand-dollar market research project is confirmation that people do buy clocks, not who's doing the buying, what they want, or where they prefer to do their shopping. In the long run you'll save time and money defining your needs and expectations, and probing the background of anyone you intend to employ. See work samples before making a decision. Forget checking personal references—we've all put in a good word for a friend. But pursue professional references: That's the easiest way to make sure the person you're considering, be it for a job or consultation, possesses the skills and experience that address your present need. If you can't go that far to protect your interests, you alone are to blame if your team member disappoints.

Your retail team operates in several spheres. There are those invisible members providing everyday services that keep the business running, a circle of professionals who remain in the background of the business. Rarely are these individuals "on staff"; you'll contract for their services as needed. Then there are the visible people who actually work in the store.

YOUR "BACK ROOM" STAFF

In the course of setting up and then running your store, you'll employ the services of a variety of skilled professionals who never actually join your staff. They work on contract or by the project in the background, in the back room, so to speak. Invisible to the public, they'll play an active role in guiding you to the right business decisions. When and whether you need their assistance is your call. If you're an avid reader and a quick study, you may get by without their help. Be aware of your limitations, however. A lot of what the people in your "back room" bring to your concept is the insight gained only through experience. They know their respective businesses as they relate to your business. They're the experts in their fields. Your strengths and opportunity spring from specialization. Anyone who understands the merits of specialization should understand the good sense it makes to hire other specialists when their help is needed.

TALK THE TALK EVEN IF YOU CAN'T WALK THE WALK

Every profession has its own language, and professionals respond best to those who talk in their terms. You'll get more from providers of professional services if you invest some time learning to speak their language. Know what a clause is before presenting your lawyer with a contract, for example. All you need do is spend some time with a business or legal guidebook before your consultations. When you're being billed for a professional's service by the hour, you don't need to pay for a basic education you could have gotten on your own.

YOU'LL NEED SOME LEGAL ASSISTANCE

Your attorney may prove one of the most expensive team members to bring on board, but she's the one who could save you the most money in the long run. No matter where you live, an attorney's services may seem excessively expensive. But when questions of legality or liability are raised, the expense is an investment in your protection. Some entrepreneurs turn to an attorney only as a last resort, when threatened with legal action or sued for damages. Others seek advice early on, consulting with a lawyer about every legal consideration that goes with starting a business. It makes good business sense to consult with an attorney (or her paralegal assistant) whenever you question your own judgment of the law.

Unless you've a legal background yourself, it's wise to have an attorney review any contract you're considering signing. A legal professional can help you through the entire development process, aiding with everything from making sure your store's name and logo won't infringe on any trademark, to handling the necessary paperwork to establish your business structure. And if you ever get sued, it's best to get guidance from someone with whom you've already established a professional relationship.

Once you decide you need an attorney, locating one is a relatively simple procedure. But finding the right one to represent your store takes a little work. First, request leads from friends, business acquaintances, and local retailers. Remember: Your first choice is an attorney who specializes in business and corporate law, who has retailer clients. Ask each candidate how long she has been practicing law, what her hourly fees are, and how they're applied. It's usually to your benefit to take your business to the attorney who has the most experience. The older attorney, with years of practice, can provide more valuable advice than an attorney with a year or two of experience. Insight follows experience; the more one has, the more one can offer.

YOU'LL NEED HELP WITH THE BOOKS

Unless you're planning to add an accountant to your permanent staff, you'll need to contract for the services of one, at the very least to help prepare your tax returns. As with the lawyer, hiring an accountant will likely save you money in the long run. Especially since accountants usually charge less than lawyers for their services and they have a greater direct influence on your finances.

How involved you want your accountant to be in your business depends on how much of the bookkeeping you want to keep in-house. Some retailers turn all their financial records and the year's receipts over to their accountants at tax time. Others invite the accountants in monthly for regular updates of the books and an evaluation of the store's financial health. A good accountant can spot the early signs of trouble or opportunity. She can function as your financial conscience, prodding you to make the right strategic response to what the numbers say. When it comes tax time, a good accountant can prove protector of your personal fortune.

Here again, you're looking for a professional with a retail background first, and general business background second. Ask other retailers who they use. Any retailer's recommendations should be your first choice and your preference. Call each candidate and again ask about her specialty, years of experience, and rates. Ask what computer software she uses, and if she can recommend a bookkeeping or accounting program. This is important because within a few years, every retail business should be fully automated. The savvy accountants are already there; it makes them work smarter and their job easier. Explain your store and its projected sales volume. Inquire about how the accountant prefers to handle business, and what kind of reports she'll be able to provide. Finally inquire about any special tax considerations you should make when setting up your business. The thoroughness of the response should separate the accountant you want handling your finances from the rest of the pack.

During your first year, expect to rely on your accountant more than at any other time in your store's future. There are two reasons for this. First, you want your accountant to help compile your numbers, set up your budget and record-keeping system, help make sales projections, and then interpret your numbers so you know what's going on in your business. At the very least, you should have the accountant in every quarter this first year, if not every month, for a financial assessment of your progress. Throughout this first year, consider the accountant your personal professor of finance. Learn as much as you can from him on every aspect of your store's finances, from how to track profits and losses, and respond to these trends, to knowing when you're extending too much credit to your customers. The education will help you manage the store's finances in years to come, but you'll always want your accountant's help come tax time.

YOU'LL NEED A BANKER, EVEN IF SHE WON'T LEND YOU MONEY YET

The banker is a professional you must cultivate to support your cause over time. While bankers work for their lending institutions first, they can help an independent businessperson to the extent the institution's own interests will be served. Banks are in the business of making money through effective money management. The banker with whom you establish some sort of personal relationship will work harder to help you. Friends—professional and personal—always get the extra effort. Think of your banker as the pinch hitter who sits on the bench for most of the game, but is ready when needed. You need to think and plan ahead. That means cultivating a relationship now, so that your banker's lending power will be available to you when it's required to expand your business. You're establishing a relationship with a banker now so later in your game, when your strategy requires more funding, you'll have someone you can count on for help.

You actually start that process when you apply for your first loan for the business. No lending institutions will gamble on a start-up business without some sort of personal guarantee or collateral. But even if it's actually you, not the business, who's borrowing the money, that first loan application is an important part of your long-term strategy. It's where the banker first gets to know you and what your business is about. You're making an impression, one you should build on as your business grows. Open your business accounts at that bank, and keep a dialogue going with your banker. Use polite conversation as an opportunity to keep your banker posted on your store's progress. You'll realize the benefits of this subtle approach later when you sit down to discuss funding needs.

YOU MAY NEED TO HIRE CONSULTANTS

An attorney, accountant, and banker are the three professionals every store owner needs in his or her corner at some point in the history of the store. Depending on your goals, budget, and scheduling, there are many other types of professionals you may need to employ. Most of these, like you, want to make their own way through the world. They hire themselves out for projects in areas in which they've developed an expertise. Many of these people call themselves consultants, a title bandied about a little too much these days. Some unscrupulous individuals use it as a ruse to get money for services in which they possess no special skills. That's why it's especially important for you to do a background and reference check, and review completed projects, before contracting the help of any self-described consultant.

That said, the professionals with valued services to offer during one phase of your business range from retail architects to advertising copywriters. If your budget allows, you may also contract the services of a researcher while investigating your market; an artist to design your logo and marquee; or a store designer for help with your floor plan.

Consider your insurance broker as much a consultant as a member of your back room staff. Before you open your doors, you'll need to consult with the broker to determine what type of insurance you need to protect your business interests. Throughout the year you'll continue to consult with him whenever there are claims, or when you make changes in your store that require a change in coverage. Every year you'll seek the broker's help in working up a new insurance package and submitting it for bids from insurers. Although you may only be in contact with your insurance broker a few times each year, you will continue to consult with him for years to come.

Deal with every consultant as you would with a contractor. Be as specific as possible when outlining your needs. Expect a detailed project proposal defining the project, what it will cost, and when it will be completed.

When seeking these individuals, request recommendations from other retailers first. Get the names of references, and ask each about his or her satisfaction with the service before you make any commitment to the consultant. Consultants charge by the hour or project, and don't come cheap. No one but you can make sure you're getting what you expect for your money.

YOU'LL NEED TO WORK WITH SALESPEOPLE

You'll be doing the calling on most of the outside professionals you'll be dealing with as store owner. You'll also be fielding calls from professional salespeople. Any sales activity implies competition. You'll find most salespeople eager to please so they can get your order. Pleasing you is their only advantage. There's only so much a salesperson working on staff for a supplier can do for you. Developing a good rapport as part of your professional relationship will help you realize the full benefits of that service.

In other categories, the salespeople's ability to serve depends on how much autonomy they have in their businesses. Consider your insurance needs, for example. The house broker, working for one underwriter, can only offer you as good an insurance package as the company provides. The independent agent, on the other hand, can shop around for you, vendor to vendor, and put together a package that's best for your business. You need to take this into account when deciding whom to entrust with your business. The salesperson who can do the best job for you is always the one with the most options.

STAFFING YOUR STORE

The team members discussed until now contribute to your success, but remain forever in the background. The comparatively few players visible to the buying public—the store staff—directly shape perceptions about your store, what it sells, and the service it offers. A strong staff has members who complement one another. A good staff can provide critical support to you. They can share and assume responsibilities to allow you to concentrate on managing the business. Hiring staff is a strategic process; the wrong person can easily upset the balance of your entire operation. But the right person, in the right position, strengthens everything about your store.

That's why determining your staffing should be regarded as a critical process. Of course, if yours will be a one-person shop, your staffing decisions are already made. But there does come a time when every retailer needs help, even if it's only help to meet the demands of the holiday rush. A larger operation may grow to the point where too much of the owner's time is taken up with minor details, and not enough in making decisions, creating a need for an assistant manager. Or your present ambitions may be such that you can't think of even opening the doors without a staff. Every hiring decision, whatever the timing or circumstance, begins with a thorough, realistic assessment of needs.

If you followed the advice of the last chapter and developed a list of activities and responsibilities, you should already have an idea of where you need help. Most small retailers need employees who can handle varied chores around the store. The person you hire for stockroom clerk will need to help at the cash register when the crowds gather. You may want a sales clerk who can think creatively when it comes to setting up a monthly display. Regardless of how they function, all members of your staff should be outgoing, articulate, and eager to learn.

WHERE DO YOU NEED THE HELP?

Entrepreneurs typically have a problem surrendering responsibility and decision making. Never will that be more difficult than when you're starting the business. Try to put those anxieties aside for now. Unless you're planning a major retail venture—thousands of items sold from thousands of square feet—your staffing needs are simple. You need unskilled support personnel for sales, the stockroom, and at the cash register. One person may be enough to handle all the duties in a small store. A larger operation may need one for each area. In the largest retail operations, the owner requires middle managers, responsible for specific areas like advertising, purchasing, and office management.

For you, it's best to think in terms of minimum needs. Hiring employees adds significantly to your financial burdens, and during the start-up phase it's important to keep these to a minimum. Still, these early hires will be the heart of your staff; as your business grows, they'll assume greater responsibility. And make no mistake about it: Staffing needs will increase with sales growth. But take your time. Staffing decisions, after your start-up staffing, should always be made in response to what's happening in your business, not in anticipation of it.

Review your notes on the breakdown of activities and responsibilities that go with your store. Begin to develop a profile of your needs. First on the list should be the more mundane tasks that go with retailing, the tedious details that could prevent you from attending to more important things: unloading boxes and packing shelves, applying merchandise tickets, making deliveries, and sitting at the cash register. Next add the responsibilities you don't really enjoy or for which you don't feel especially qualified; things like designing an ad, rearranging displays, or perhaps taking and filling telephone orders. Finally, outline the areas in which you'd like to develop your store, once its sales base is established.

Your list describes your employment needs. How many people and whom you hire depend on the size of your operation and the length of that list of responsibilities. In larger organizations, staffs have historically been built, like a pyramid, with the owner on top, middle-level managers handling specific areas of responsibility below, and a large number of support staff on the bottom. That's changing today, as people realize pyramid structures are expensive and inefficient. Instead, most corporations are trying to create diamond-shaped structures, with very few people on both the top and bottom, and with a mid level that's essentially self-directed and self-supporting.

For you, this debate over structure is really academic . . . for now. Your only goal should be to enter into business with as lean an organization as will support the store. Your business partner or spouse can be trusted to remain in the business for the duration—or at least they won't pull out without notice. For the people you hire, though, this is more a job than a career, at least at this point. All the business offers is promise; there are no guarantees. If something goes wrong, they could pull out. If you trust them with too much of your management, when they leave you'll be faced with a situation that threatens the business. Keep the hires outside your immediate circle to a minimum, until you simply can't run the business without them.

DETERMINING YOUR STAFFING NEEDS
Chart

Use this chart to help determine your staffing needs. First check off the jobs or responsibilities that apply to your store. After you've reviewed the entire list, assign specific tasks to personnel. These can be you, another family member, or unnamed employees you will need to hire. Of course, the size of your staff depends on the size of your operation. A large store will need dedicated employees for many of these tasks, while employees of the smaller store can handle multiple responsibilities. Be sure and include any jobs not listed below that pertain to your store.

General Areas of Responsibility: _____

Stock/Warehouse: _____

   Tracking Inventory   _____

   **Unloading Deliveries and Stocking
    Shelves**   _____

   Processing Orders   _____

   Applying Merchandise Tickets   _____

   Packing/Processing Orders   _____

   Shipping and Receiving   _____

   Deliveries   _____

Sales Floor: _____

   Set up/Maintain Displays   _____

Stock Shelves and Racks   ———————

Cash Register   ———————

Assist Customers   ———————

Track Ad/Promotion Response   ———————

Process Service Orders   ———————

Handle Complaints   ———————

Qualify Customers   ———————

Sell Products   ———————

Office: ———————

Balance Books   ———————

Payroll   ———————

Pay Taxes for Business and Employees   ———————

Place Orders   ———————

Pay Bills   ———————

Collect Bills   ———————

Run Computer System   ———————

Handle Phones   ———————

Store Management: ———————

Open and Shut Store   ———————

Set Work Schedules   _____

Develop and Place Advertising   _____

Plan Promotions and PR   _____

Determine Inventory Mix   _____

Deal with Complaints   _____

Talk with Salespeople and Reps   _____

Track Competitors   _____

Track Sales   _____

Plan Expansion   _____

Cover Expenses   _____

Hire and Fire Staff   _____

SHOULD YOUR EMPLOYEES BE FULL- OR PART-TIMERS?

Once you've an idea of what positions you need to fill, your attention should turn to when you want those employees around. For the larger retail operation, the schedule will likely require several full-timers. For the small store owner, it's best to think in terms of part-time help first, with the option of expanding hours as business grows. Since retailing is one of those businesses that generates most of its sales in the hours when the rest of the population is off work—evenings and weekends—scheduling can pose an issue when hiring. Even the employer of part-time help may need to split the schedule among a couple of workers to ensure help is available when most needed.

You'll learn exactly when that is after the store is in business a few weeks. Still, there are some assumptions you can safely make about when you'll need help before you open the doors. Unless you've selected a location in the heart of the business district, expect to be busiest on weekends. For the downtown store, the busy hours include the lunch period and early evening when people get off work. Traffic in all stores tends to build toward the end of the week, as people cash their paychecks.

There may be other factors affecting shopping habits that you'll discover after you've been in business awhile. For example: The area's major employer may pay its employees on the first and fifteenth of the month; or a local nursery school may bring droves of young mothers into the area every Tuesday and Thursday morning. Your scheduling needs and assignments should evolve as a response to when the most shoppers can be found in the store. It's best to hire someone part-time, with flexible hours, who's willing to put in more time and take on more responsibility as the business expands.

FINDING STAFF

Were it only as easy to find such people as it is to describe them. The hiring cycle is a hassle, both for you and for the applicants who suffer the application and interview process. The quicker it's done with, the better, for all concerned. But hiring is not a responsibility you should rush to complete. Shortcuts do exist, however: You can solicit the help of an employment agency or look to hire from your circle of family and friends. The former costs you money; the latter can prove to be a source of ongoing headaches.

If you decide to go the agency route, expect to pay a finder's fee. You'll probably end up interviewing many of the same candidates you would have attracted with your own ad in the paper. But if you do solicit an employment agency's help, be as specific as possible when describing your needs, including the type of person you want. For example: a mature worker with some retail experience, or a student interested in working evenings and weekends. Set definite time periods during which you'll be available for interviews, so you're not constantly interrupted in the course of your day.

RETAIL HIRING IS A CHALLENGE

Finding and retaining a qualified staff has always been a challenge for retailers. The problem may owe as much to retailers' own attitudes as to any circumstance of the market. Frustrated by their past hiring experiences, many retailers come to regard their labor pool as one of transients. With that attitude, they see little cause or call to offer those they employ anything more than the minimum wage. This approach becomes a self-fulfilling prophecy. Sure, it has worked in the past and may continue to serve some retailers in the future. But remember what we've already discussed: the new realities of the marketplace, and the opportunities for the specialty retailer.

Tomorrow's shoppers will want a certain familiarity in their shopping experiences. Familiar faces in the store aisles go with that. That means you must work hard to attract and retain staff. And that means you must promise employment that offers opportunities to grow, personally and economically. The standard option, one that has always worked for retailers of large-ticket items, is to offer a commission on sales. If the opportunity to make more money won't inspire staffers to do better for the store, nothing will. Retailers of all products, including you, now need to adapt this incentive plan to their businesses. And when you do, you'll also need to come up with something extra for employees who never close a deal, like the cashier and stockroom clerk. To stay with the job, they'll want a profit-sharing plan: a stake in the business their best efforts help build.

This could take many forms: an accrual fund of 1 percent of all sales, a share of each quarter's total dollar volume, an investment package of some type, or an incentive program that rewards all staff people for their contributions to a job well done. The critical difference between past and future is that any employee you want to keep will want some form of vested interest in your store's success. That kind of incentive promotes the effort that encourages all to contribute to a shared success.

If you'll depend on your staff, and you need to keep them, you'll learn to adapt to each individual employee. Treat each as part of your team and part of your family. Remember their birthdays and anniversaries, and make a big deal about them and their successes. Understand the special scheduling needs of the young mother. Reward the guy who's spending a couple of evenings a week at night college to improve his skills. You may start as strangers, but if you treat your employees with respect and recognize their contributions, you'll end up with friends who are eager members of a team that shares your goals.

THERE ARE PROS AND CONS TO HIRING FAMILY

Sometimes there's just as much challenge in deciding who *not* to bring on staff. If you're able to meet staffing needs with family members, you can consider yourself blessed, if your family shares your interest in the business. The major problem with a staff of family members is that any tensions that exist at home will carry over to the store, and vice versa. Your teenage son's shaved head and pierced nose might not make you too happy, and it certainly won't wow shoppers either. If there's one person in the family who loves to bicker, and constantly probes for new ways to get under everybody's skin, tactfully discourage him from joining the family business.

The other problem with hiring family members is an issue also raised when you hire friends: money. Your friends and family, especially extended family, usually expect more of a share in your prosperity than the person hired off the street. Thinking you're doing well while they're getting a paltry wage breeds resentment. Unless addressed with more money from your pocket, resentment festers and eventually explodes. That's not healthy in a business where customers respond to happy, friendly faces.

But if yours is a supportive family, the benefits of staffing the store from the gene pool far outweigh the risks. For one thing, the family business is a shared enterprise; what benefits one, benefits all. If each person's livelihood depends on the venture, he or she will share in its success and will work harder to carry your retail dream to its potential. And your family has already worked out its politics for survival. Everyone knows one another's personality; how to motivate it and how to get around it. Family members also have well-developed modes of communication, verbal and nonverbal. A nod or look to your spouse says as much as a ten-minute conversation with a stranger.

Finally, you can plan a future built on the skills of individual family members. If you think in terms of long-term responsibilities for the people whose strengths you know, you can nurture them, through training and education, to benefit the business. Sometimes one family member is designated the future decision maker, and how well family members deal with the politics of The Anointed One will decide the fate of the next generation of the family-run business.

When hiring immediate family, don't think solely in terms of your long-term strategy. Take the short-term view as well. If your spouse or child has a good job, it's probably best to retain it for now. He or she can always quit when your business absolutely requires the help. During the first year especially, you may need to lean on those other income sources while nurturing the store to its sales potential. Cut too small a pie into too many pieces and everyone goes hungry.

HIRING FRIENDS IS EVEN RISKIER THAN HIRING FAMILY

If you and your friends really wanted to be in business together, you'd be partners. Hiring friends is a bad idea for all the reasons you might hesitate to hire family members, and then some. Employment implies authority. Yet your friends are your equals. Even if you're a nice, easygoing, understanding individual, your friends will resent it when you tell them do a better job. Friendship mars the employer/employee relationship from the outset. Better to develop new friends on the job than bring your existing friends into the process. Unless you're offering your friends a career opportunity, the chance to realize their potential, they'll come to resent your success and their ''inadequate'' compensation. If you value the friendship, keep it out of the workplace.

That said, if a friend desperately needs a job, you can take a chance. But first, thoroughly explain your reservations and how much you value the friendship. Try to make it a temporary arrangement until your friend finds other employment. The situation may still present difficulties, but you've done your best to minimize problems and protect the friendship.

ADVERTISING FOR EMPLOYEES

Even with everything we've said about the dangers of hiring family and friends, your immediate circle still constitutes one of the best places to turn for recommendations on who to hire. Make no promises to your contacts, just let them know you're accepting applications for positions that may open up at the store. Hiring a contact's son or niece poses the same dangers as hiring the friend, but there are far fewer problems when you hire a friend's neighbor's kid. As names trickle in, ask the people to comply with the same application procedures as everyone else. Talk to them when you can, and unless they seem perfectly qualified for the job, tell them you plan to interview more people.

THERE'S NOTHING WRONG WITH STEALING STAFFERS FROM OTHER RETAILERS

If, during your tour of other retailers and competitors, you met someone you consider the ideal employee, take your search directly to that person. Contact her at home or as she's leaving work and ask if she's interested in changing jobs for more opportunity. If you get a yes, ask what she makes, how satisfied she is with her current job, and what she's looking for in terms of salary and responsibilities from you. Take this conversation as an opportunity to negotiate an agreement, or at least to arrange for a meeting as soon as possible. If the candidate isn't interested, leave on good terms. She may come around to the idea once she sees your success. Ask if she knows of anyone else with a similar background who might be interested in the position, and follow up on any recommendation.

TRY TO TARGET YOUR CLASSIFIED ADVERTISING

Unless you've an unusually large network of contacts, you'll probably be forced to advertise to meet your staffing needs. A classified ad that appears in your local paper should attract enough candidates to let you selectively fill the position. If you're looking for a particular type of person—the college student or senior citizen—avoid the newspaper and run the ad where you can best reach your target audience: the classified section of a local school's student newspaper, or a publication targeting the area's mature market. You may also take your search to where these people congregate. Describe the opening on an index card or sheet of paper and pin it to the bulletin board in the student lounge or in the area's community center.

With that form of advertisement, there's room to go into details about your business and the position. The best a classified ad will do is summarize the job offer. Work on your ad before you contact the paper, so you know it will read exactly as you want it to. Start with a one-word job title that best describes the main responsibility of the job: cashier or salesperson, for example. Next mention whether it's a full- or part-time position. Then describe the store by type: shoe store, sporting goods, etc. After that, list the other responsibilities involved, benefits offered, and mention if this job offers opportunity for advancement. Always close the job description with a mention that retail experience is preferred. If you've already set a wage for the position, and will pay no more, list that. The number will screen some candidates out of the interview cycle. When advertising for a managerial position, ask that applicants *mail* or fax in resumes, preferably to a post office box or to a box number at the newspaper. Most other positions can be filled through an interview alone. For these, close the ad with your telephone number in bold, and when during the day to call.

A word about wording: The normal procedure on classified ads is to charge by the word or individual letters, with a slight break in the rates depending on how often the ad appears. If you're running an ad in a major metropolitan newspaper with a large circulation, even a small ad can prove expensive. As a response, the pages of the classifieds are filled with cryptic messages that say a lot in very few words. Read through the classifieds and you'll quickly gain a sense of how to get the most from your ad for the least money. Some newspapers even have telephone sales staff in their classified departments who can offer help in minimizing words.

THE INTERVIEW

Before the ad appears, decide when you'll do the interviewing: what day and what hours. It should be in the business week following the last appearance of the ad. Work up a schedule on paper, figuring each candidate will take up twenty minutes of interview time. As you take the calls, fill in the blanks, using the space for brief notes about what you learn about each candidate during your telephone conversation.

THAT INITIAL CONVERSATION IS ROUND ONE OF THE INTERVIEW PROCESS

Treat these initial telephone calls as your first round of interviewing. Listen to how well the callers express themselves. Do they strike you as cheerful, outgoing, optimistic? If you detect nervousness, don't let it put you off. Some people regard job hunting as one of life's traumas. Ask about the callers' backgrounds and experiences as they relate to the job description. Take the names and numbers of those with no appropriate skills, explaining for now you're looking for people with more experience. If they persist, give them the interview: An unwillingness to take no for an answer is a positive trait in a retail salesperson.

Schedule interviews for anyone else who seems qualified, telling each what time you'll conduct the interview. Ask them to come by at least ten minutes early to fill out a job application. Repeat when you'll meet them, and the request. These instructions comprise an important test of punctuality and the candidate's ability to follow instructions.

For positions that require the candidates to send in resumes, the procedure is pretty much the same. Before you make the calls,

though, read each reśumé, looking for experience, skills, and interests that match your current needs. Note the appearance of the
reśumé, its layout and wording. A good reśumé tells you the person has good organizational and communications skills.

On the day of the interviews, make sure you've an ample supply
of pens, chairs, and something hard for the candidates to write
on. Also have ready a copy of a detailed job description for each
applicant, including responsibilities, hours, benefits, holidays, vacation days, and opportunities for advancement. Preferably you'll
be meeting the applicants at the store site. If you'll be the only
one there that day, it's no problem. Otherwise set up an area with
some semblance of privacy for the interview.

REMEMBER THERE ARE THINGS YOU CAN'T ASK CANDIDATES

The state and federal governments, in an effort to protect the
rights of the individual and promote equal opportunity for all
citizens, impose severe limits on the type of information that may
be sought during the employment interview process. These anti-
discrimination laws vary by state. It's your responsibility to seek
guidance from your state's equal opportunity office or department
of civil rights. Failure to do so, or to fully comply with the guidelines, opens you up to lawsuits and penalties if any candidate
takes you to court and proves your hiring decision was based on
anything but merit and qualifications.

As a general rule, you've no right to inquire about an applicant's race, sex, religion, place of birth, marital status, or age.
Nor may you ask any questions from which you'll be able to infer
this information. For instance, you can ask a candidate if she's a
United States citizen, but not where she was born or what citizenship she holds. It's permissible to ask her if she's over eighteen,
but not how long she has been married. Developing an application
in compliance with all applicable laws can prove a time-consum-
ing process. That's why it's probably in your best interests to use
a standardized job application form, available in most business
supply stores. If you can't find one, request a sample application
from your state's Department of Labor. When you purchase the

application form from an office supplier, it's still your responsibility to make sure the form adheres to local regulations. Also make sure it allows space for the names and numbers of professional references.

SOME THINGS CAN ONLY BE LEARNED FROM A FACE-TO-FACE MEETING

Prepare a candidate evaluation sheet for your use during the interview. The list should include what's important to you and cover five broad areas (discussed below): appearance, attitude, communications skills, experience, and ambition, with space for additional comments at the bottom of the page. The ideal interview amounts to a conversation in which you and the candidate learn about each other, and about how well the applicant matches what you need in an employee. It should be informal enough that you both feel comfortable, but not too relaxed.

As soon as the candidate submits the completed application form, present the job description you've prepared. Use the time required for the applicant to review the job description to review the application. You'll know right away if this person is literate and organized.

Pay more attention to the thoroughness with which the application form is completed than the style of the person's handwriting. If anything about the responses on the application poses a concern, mark it and refer back to it during the interview. It's important for you to keep the applicant talking as much as possible, so it's a good idea to have a list of prepared questions to explore the applicant's background and ambitions. This approach also provides a framework for comparing all applicants on the same basis in order to identify the best candidate for the job.

The questions should vary with each employment opportunity. In general, they should explore the applicant's skills, interest in the store's specialty, and career attitudes in relation to the responsibilities of the job. Again, retailing experience is always your first preference, followed by knowledge of, and interest in, the store's specialty. You can teach an enthusiastic candidate the art of selling products he already knows and enjoys. But you're better off taking someone who already knows how to sell, and teaching him what there is to know about your product specialty.

EVALUATE EACH CANDIDATE IN THE FIVE BROAD AREAS

- Appearance: A job interview is an event in every person's life; we all dress for it. That may mean putting on the torn T-shirt and worn shoes that say, "I don't want your damn job." Or it may mean donning a dress suit because you're eager to please, even if it only means $4.25 an hour. Appearance counts in retail, and it's as important in the store clerk as in the floor design. Appropriate grooming, neatness, and cleanliness are essential qualities for store personnel. Consider the visual impression the candidate makes in terms of how that will play with the store's ideal type of customer. If you decide this is the right candidate in the wrong outfit, you can always institute some form of dress code in the shop.

- Attitude: Everyone is a little nervous early on in an interview, so discount that. But what else can you discern about attitude? Did she show up ten minutes early, as directed, to fill out that application? If she didn't, did she offer an apology and a reasonable excuse? Cut short the interview of any candidate who doesn't. She's careless and forgetful, the kind of employee who'll leave the day's receipts on the car roof as she hurries off to the bank. When you met, were you greeted with a smile and a handshake, or a shrug and a shuffle? Does she volunteer information to keep the conversation going, or is the interview more like pulling teeth? A positive attitude, and an outgoing but not aggressive manner, are appealing traits in store personnel.

- Communications Skills: You've already spoken to these people on the phone. How does that compare with conversing with them in person? Shoppers respond to the person who looks them in the eye, speaks directly, and provides as detailed a response as the query requires. You should too. Listen to how each applicant speaks, for both the tone and content of what is said. A store needs a person who comes across as both friendly and informed, and whose speech is easily understood.

- Experience: Inquire about the jobs listed on the application, asking what the candidate liked and didn't like about each job. Be wary of anyone with several jobs during a relatively short period. Ask for an explanation. If every boss was a jerk, you don't want to join that club. Wrap up the interview. Allow the candidate the chance to explain any lengthy gaps in employment history. Focus on the jobs that draw an enthusiastic report, as they reveal what she enjoys doing and where she'll apply her skills. Let the candidate explain how prior experience and interests will fulfill the requirements of this job description.

- Ambition: When you ask people to describe what they want to do with their lives, you provide an opportunity for them to define themselves. So ask, and listen closely to what each says. This is a window on the entire personality. Be realistic if the answers don't completely match your expectations for this position. Unless the person is applying for a managerial position, all you're offering is a job in a store. That's not a career move for most. Put your ego aside and question the honesty and sincerity of anyone who tells you all he wants from life is to work for someone like you in a store like yours.

IT'S IMPORTANT TO BRING CLOSURE TO EACH INTERVIEW

After you've reviewed the application and gone through your prepared questions, fill in any gaps in what you need to know. Then it's time to wind down the interview. Encourage the candidate to ask questions: He can reveal a lot about how he views this job. Answer thoroughly. This is also your opportunity to explain any policies of yours that might affect the person's decision to take the job. Reiterate your expectations of the employee, including work hours. Explain any special scheduling needs, such as weekend or evening hours. Also, outline any special policies of yours now, as they relate to the employee: a probation period, a dress code, drug usage on the job, excessive lateness or absences. Never hire anyone on the spot, at least not when you've others coming in for an interview. Ask your preferred candidates when they'll be available, and how much notice they must give their present employer. Ask if it's okay for you to contact their present or previous employers for references. If they say no, abide by their request, but ask for other sources at previous jobs. Tell each when you expect to fill the job and that you'll get in touch if it's his or hers. Never promise to let applicants know either way. It's something you'll never get around to doing, and it builds ill will.

MAKE SURE TO CHECK CANDIDATES' REFERENCES

After you've had the chance to review the applications and notes from all your candidate interviews, narrow the list to the top three. Make a point of contacting as many of their references as possible. When you check a reference, inquire about the working relationship between the contact and job applicant. Ask yes-or-no questions that touch on the candidate's attitude, performance, ability to follow instructions, and how well the employee fulfilled responsibilities. Finally, ask if the contact would rehire the candidate if he had the opportunity.

THE HIRE

Balance what the references tell you with your impressions from the application, résumé, and interview. Decide who gets the offer first. Contact the candidate. If she's not at home, leave a message where you can be reached. Once you have the candidate on the phone, tell her how impressed you were with the interview and references, and that you'd like her to come work for you. Give a starting date and the starting wage, and advise her how long the probation or training period lasts before she'll be eligible for a raise.

WHAT IF THEY HESITATE TO ACCEPT YOUR OFFER?

She'll either tell you yes on the spot or request time to consider the offer. Making a job offer is a binding contract as soon as the applicant says yes to your terms. If she requests time to consider the offer, you're committed to the offer for the duration of a period of time you both agree to. Give her a day, two at the most, and an hour by which you expect an answer. If she doesn't get back to you by then, she has effectively turned down the job, and you can make the offer to the next candidate. If she refuses your offer, request an explanation. Ask if there's something you can do to make the job a more attractive package to either her or another candidate. If all of your top three candidates turn you down for similar reasons, rethink your offer. There's something you're not doing right. People should be anxious to come work for you.

ALWAYS KEEP YOUR HIRING OPTIONS OPEN

When someone accepts, don't forget your other top candidates. Calling them would prove a major disappointment if you're only telephoning to tell them someone else got the job. Rather, drop them a brief note in the mail, thanking them for coming in, and explaining that a person with more experience was hired. Say that you'll keep them in mind for future openings. Do this with all the top candidates uncovered in your search. They'll appreciate you for it, and the next time you need to expand your staff, you'll have a head start. All it will then take is a call to see if they're still interested in working at your store. If they are, you've escaped the hassles of the hiring cycle.

One of the real secrets to building the right team for your store is to continually think long-term as you work short-term. If you're ambitious, the store is merely your starting point. As you grow the business, your employment needs will grow with it. By collecting the names of likely candidates early on, you develop a reserve for the future. That will make building your team much easier.

Look for the people who share your commitment to the customer, who exhibit the enthusiasm about life that translates into excitement about what they sell. Remember, retailing in the 21st Century is all about making the shopping experience as convenient and pleasant as possible for your customers. Your staff, like yourself, must recognize the customer as king.

10

YOUR ELECTRONIC EMPLOYEES

E very store needs some personnel to run the business. How you handle these staffing needs depends on the size of your store and your own ambition and resources. But whether your retail dreams fill a nook in the corner of the local mall or an entire building on the downtown landscape, your business will benefit from the technology you employ during setup and throughout its operation.

The ceaseless evolution of communications and information technology offers today's retailer a range of "electronic employees" for strengthening business performance. Once employed, they'll enable you to work harder and smarter, and, if desired, serve a much broader market area. They'll also help you keep track of each of your customers' preferences in style or color, spot trends as they emerge, and take orders after hours, or at the shopper's convenience. These are basic requirements for a specialty shop to survive in the information age.

Still, they only hint at how you'll benefit from technology in the future. You can begin to realize some of these advantages today, almost as soon as you invest in the equipment. What follows should be regarded as suggestions rather than a list of the technology you must have in place from opening day. These are tools for modern retailing. If your start-up budget is tight, though, the cost of technology will limit what you can use. Accept that an investment in any technology that strengthens your retail strategy saves money in the short term, and enables you to make more money over the long term.

The products discussed in this chapter are not luxuries; they're the building blocks for retail success in the next century.

THE FAX MACHINE

A fax machine is already as basic to the office as the telephone. If your store sells anything more than the morning paper, the business will benefit from a modest investment in a fax machine. In an age that thrives on instant access to information, the fax sets up a communications link with anyone, anywhere, anytime. You wouldn't think of telephoning a supplier at midnight when you finally finish your inventory check to place next month's order. You can fax it in, though. That same convenience applies to your customers. They can place orders with you around the clock, or when your voice phone is busy, by fax.

As valuable as the fax is for ordering, it's a uniquely useful tool for transferring printed information whenever it's needed. Suppose your distributor is out of stock of the product you order, but suggests something similar. As soon as you're off the phone, you can be reading the specification sheets on that item, sent via fax. And think of the promotional possibilities. Suppose your store's specialty is industrial cleaning supplies. Your latest stock check reveals you've overordered and have an abundance of Brand Z vacuum cleaner bags sitting on your shelves. You've got to unload them, and free up those inventory dollars. You work up a special deal, and distribute it via fax to customers who are big users of that particular bag. They take advantage of the deal, ordering by fax. Within two days you've reduced the inventory to the appropriate level.

In the smaller office with limited needs, the fax can also do double duty as a copy machine. You wouldn't want to run off hundreds of sales flyers with it, but when you need one or two copies in a hurry, the fax machine's copying capabilities serve well.

Before you head out to purchase your fax, determine how it'll be used. Then decide how many phone lines you'll need installed in your shop. You're already paying the phone company to have one phone installed; there's no reason to pay for another service call. If your fax usage will be limited to business management chores—correspondence with suppliers, placing orders, and the like—you can probably get by without a dedicated fax line. If you use the Call Waiting feature on that line, make sure you can disable Call Waiting service or you'll lose your fax transmissions whenever another call comes in. On the other hand, if you plan to publish or promote your fax number, and encourage customers to use it to reach the store, you'll need a separate line for the fax machine.

SELECTING A FAX MACHINE THAT'S RIGHT FOR YOU

Even the most inexpensive fax machines offer more features than the retailer is likely to need. If you plan on using the fax as a promotional tool, announcing special sales to a select group of customers, look for "broadcast" capability. Faxes with this can be set to automatically dial a list of fax numbers and transmit a document to each, unattended. Models with a "delayed calling" feature let the user set the time to make these calls, say, after hours when the phone rates drop. A built-in memory is a valuable feature if you'll rely on the fax as an electronic order taker. Should the machine run out of paper, it'll store any received documents in memory until it's reloaded with paper. Without a memory, you stand to lose the orders.

The main decision you must make is whether to buy a plain-paper or thermal-paper fax machine. This is where the price breaks occur. Most fax machines use special heat-sensitive "thermal" paper. These cost far less than plain-paper fax machines, although prices on the latter continue to fall. Plain-paper faxes deliver a higher-quality document, are easier to load, and work with regular paper. If you decide to go with a less expensive thermal fax model, make sure it has a built-in automatic paper cutter. Without it, you'll spend a lot of aggravating time with scissors cutting up documents and orders.

THE RETAIL COMPUTER

Wouldn't you instantly hire someone who could identify every customer by name, address, buying habits, and number of visits to the store; manage your inventory; handle all your bookkeeping; pay the bills; and track trends in the store, right down to what hour of the week you're selling the most squeegees? Then invest in a computer system. Even if yours will be a one-person shop, you need a computer system now and for the future. With the right combination of hardware and software, a computer system will help you be more effective in at least two broad areas of responsibility: information management and inventory management.

KNOW YOUR COMPUTER BASICS

Computer mavens can skip through this and move on to the next heading. But for the novice and uninitiated, here's a brief rundown of the computer terminology that will help you through your search for the right system.

A computer is *hardware*. The computer *keyboard* is what you type on; it's laid out like a typewriter. A *mouse* is a pointing device that allows you to manipulate the cursor around the screen as you run an application. The *cursor* indicates on the screen where you are in the document you're working on.

The program, or application, is *software*. If you think of the hardware as a record player, the software is the record. But software does much more. It allows the computer to perform specific tasks the software is written to accomplish. *Word-processing* software transforms the computer into an electronic typewriter and more. A *spreadsheet* program offers the software equivalent of a financial spreadsheet, with report, graphics, and interpretive functions built in. A *database* is a file of information, called data, that can be organized by category or an attribute.

Software is sold on computer media: either a *floppy disk* or *CD-ROM* as of this writing. Floppy disks are a form of magnetic media, while a CD-ROM, which holds hundreds of times more information, is a laser-based technology. Software sold on disk may also be loaded and stored on the computer's *hard drive,* a large-capacity disk. Hard drives may be internal—built into the machine—or external—connected by cable to one of the computer ports. The storage capacity of a hard drive is measured in *megabytes* or *gigabytes*. For simplicity's sake, think of one megabyte as equal to the amount of information stored on one floppy disk. One thousand megabytes equal one gigabyte.

A *port* is where you connect other devices to the computer, by plugging their cables into the port. These devices are called *peripherals,* of which printers are the most commonly used. Several types of printers can be connected to the computer. A *dot matrix printer* is a low-cost unit that produces serviceable quality text for most purposes. A *laser printer* produces much higher-quality images. Laser output represents today's business standard for official correspondence. Another peripheral, the *modem,* enables the computer to communicate with another computer over telephone lines.

Taken together, hardware, peripherals, and software comprise a computer system.

THE COMPUTER IS A TOOL FOR INFORMATION MANAGEMENT . . . AND MORE

As a tool for information management, the computer frees the retailer from many of the lesser chores that go with being in charge. In the process it also delivers the power to accomplish things once considered too labor-intensive for the individual store owner to accomplish. Consider your need to know customers as an example. In the past, everything a store owner knew of customers, their likes and buying habits, was kept in that gray filing cabinet in the head. With the right computer system, you become master at the science of knowing each shopper.

You can use database software to create a detailed profile of every customer. The first time a shopper comes into the store, you or your clerk enters what you deem appropriate information into your database. For example: name, address, phone number, family members and ages, the purchase, and how that customer learned about the store. Next time the customer makes a purchase, you pull up that file on-screen and enter the new information. The process is the same for every customer in your store.

In two months you have instant access to a profile of what's selling, who's buying, and which advertising generates the most response. You know how wide an area the store is serving, and, if needed, which day of the week, and the hour of the day, you're selling the most products, by category. And that's only how the system helps track customers.

Software enables you to balance your books, track profits per department and item, and pay the bills without lifting a pen to your checkbook. You can use the system to set up your business plan and annual budget, project realistic goals based on past performance, and compare year-to-year sales growth by category or product. Then, with a laser printer and desktop publishing software, you can produce professional-quality ads, brochures, newsletters, or promotional posters in-house!

THE COMPUTER IS A TOOL FOR INVENTORY MANAGEMENT . . . AND MORE

The system also brings features and functions that streamline inventory management. If, when you take delivery on a product, you assign it a code number, you can track its history from arrival to when it moves out the door. Use the system as your electronic cashier, and up-to-the-minute information on every item in your inventory is there at your fingertips: your cost, selling price, an item description, supplier, number in stock, whatever you decide it will help to know. Connected with a bar code reader and software, the process is even simpler once the bar code label is affixed to the product. (Some of the more progressive suppliers will now handle this chore at their warehouse, before they ship the goods!) The customer selects the item, steps up to the counter. All your clerk does is pass the magic wand over the code. Even as the sales receipt is being printed, the system updates information on inventory levels and the day's sales. The inventory management system can be set to alert you when stock is dangerously low, or point out a sudden surge in sales that means opportunity. Sound enticing? It should. Today, a computer system makes good retail sense.

DETERMINING YOUR NEEDS

Selecting the right system for your store demands time. It's not a decision to rush. A computer system is a relatively expensive investment. If not carefully thought out, it can prove a frustrating waste of your limited resources. The search begins with an honest evaluation of your own computer skills, then your needs. If you've been working on a computer system for years, and are comfortable with the platform, you're already ahead in the game. You don't need any convincing on how a computer can help manage a business.

Assuming you're satisfied with the system you presently use, your search comes down to deciding which software best addresses your needs. You may even be proficient enough to modify some off-the-shelf database, accounting, or business management software to your particular needs. The practice is definitely not recommended for the novice computer user, however. There's enough to learning your system without fiddling around with software. Novices should concentrate their search on software packages that specifically address retail management in your history and product category. More on that in a moment.

WHAT IF YOU'RE NEW TO THE WORLD OF COMPUTERS?

If you're entirely new to computers, selecting the best system begins with the software. You may think of computers in terms of hardware, but the software is the key that unlocks all the power for you. The computer will only prove as useful a tool as the software allows. At this writing, many software programs are available in different versions for different operating platforms. Some are published only in versions for one type of machine. A few years from now, compatibility won't be an issue. We're not there yet, though. The software you decide best services your needs will dictate which hardware you buy. You can purchase an integrated package of software, hardware, and technical support from a single vendor, but it's not always the most cost-effective way to go about it.

More likely than not, there's already a software program on the market for your particular needs, specific to your retail industry. Over the past decade many entrepreneurs made careers for themselves developing software programs for every conceivable application, including retail management. If you browse the smaller ads and classifieds in the back of the trade magazines, you'll probably come up with the names of a few of these programs.

BEFORE YOU BUY, MAKE SURE TO SPEAK WITH THE REAL EXPERTS

Before you contact any computer dealer or manufacturer, and your name gets in the hands of a salesperson, talk to other retailers in your business about what programs they use. Take notes on what they tell you—they're the real experts. You stand to benefit from what they share about their experience with the software and how it helps manage stores. You'll find the satisfied ones pretty chatty. People take pride talking about how much they've been able to accomplish with their computers.

You need to know the name of the program they use, how long they've had it, and what computer hardware they run on it. Get the names of the program(s) used for information and inventory management, and the name and number of the vendor and publisher. Ask all if they're completely satisfied with what they use, and if they would recommend it. Always inquire about other programs used in the past. If they used any others, why did they switch? Some of those programs may still be on the market, and the retailers may provide you with good reasons to avoid them.

Next, contact your industry trade group or the appropriate retail organizations. Inquire if they've tested any software, and if so, could they recommend any particular program. Some trade groups publish software guides, with reviews of what's currently being sold. Request or purchase a copy. Your next best bet is to ask for the names of industry contacts well versed in the available software. Another source for leads should be the trade magazines specific to your retail category. Contact the editors, ask if they've done any software reviews, and request copies. Again, ask for contacts who know the software.

With all these calls, you're looking for recommendations. If you keep hearing good things about the same program, it's probably worth investigating first. Contact the publisher and ask for some information, including a demonstration disk if one is available. If you've searched this far and still come up empty, it may be that no one has written management software for your retail category. Start the search anew, this time concentrating on general retail management programs.

YOU COULD ENLIST A HIRED HAND IN YOUR SEARCH FOR THE RIGHT SYSTEM

You can proceed along these lines, or turn for outside help at this point. If the idea of the search overwhelms you, avoid the process by soliciting the help of a computer systems consultant. Computer consultants go by a variety of titles, including developers, systems integrators, business "automators," and value-added resellers. What each will do is sit down and talk with you to determine your computer needs. Then, based on that conference, they'll recommend a "turnkey" system of hardware and software. It's usually a system they'd like to sell you, by the way. That's why, with computer consultants, as with insurance agents, your interests are best served by the individual who represents several companies' products. That way you're more likely to end up with a recommendation that's best for you, not the consultant.

MAKE SURE TO BE SPECIFIC IN OUTLINING YOUR NEEDS

Whether you hire a consultant or go it alone, be as specific as possible when determining your computer needs. That makes selection of a computer system another project for your now dog-eared and tattered notebook. Think in terms of how you work now, and how you want the computer to help you work smarter.

Start with information management. Write down every responsibility with which you think the computer will help you do a better job: accounting, bookkeeping, scheduling, record keeping, payroll, taxes, billing, correspondence, mailings, etc.

Then turn your attention to inventory. Would you like an electronic cash register that automatically adjusts inventory levels? What about tracking transactions from delivery to shipment, processing orders, and monitoring sales trends at the cash register?

Finally, write down the things that will help you know and reach your market better: a breakdown of your customers by zip code, the ability to produce reports on buying trends and monthly activity, automated mailings, and the potential to produce all advertising materials in-house.

DETERMINING YOUR COMPUTER NEEDS
Work Sheet

As you fill out this work sheet, your answers will help you determine what you need in a computer system. Think in terms of how a computer system might make your job easier. Later you can use the form as a guide for finding the software program or programs that address your needs. If you don't already own a computer, your choice of software will dictate your hardware requirements. Place a check mark next to everything you would like to accomplish with your computer system. Be sure to add anything not on this general list.

Set up and maintain supplier files _____
Set up and maintain customer files _____
Track sales trends by product and category _____
Track activity by time period(s) _____
Track ad/promotion response _____
Track orders _____
Generate sales and trends reports _____
Electronic cash register _____
Instantly update inventory availability _____
**Profile customers by zip code, interests, or
    other criteria** _____
Automatic billing _____
Generate mailing lists or labels _____
**Produce ads, newsletters, or other
    promotional materials** _____
Write and send correspondence _____
Balance the books _____
Financial analysis and projections _____
Handle payroll _____
Calculate and file taxes electronically _____
Scheduling _____
Other: _____

COMPARE YOUR NEEDS TO THE FEATURES OF THE PRODUCTS ON THE MARKET

Your list in hand, contact the consultant or begin calling on software publishers for information on their programs. Compare the features of the programs against your needs, narrowing down the selection to the closest match. Note the recommended hardware configuration, as it relates to upgrading your system or as a shopping guide. And ask for the price of each program and what it includes.

A program can seem deceptively inexpensive if you must pay for training and technical support. These services can prove as important as the software itself. During your learning curve you can spend a lot of time on the phone with tech support.

Never buy a specialty software application without seeing it in operation and talking to present users. If a particular program seems to meet your needs, ask for a demonstration by a company representative, and get the names of retailers using that program. Call for their critiques, and if possible, drop by and see the system in operation.

Only when you've settled on the software should you begin considering your hardware purchase. That's an easy process when there's already a machine on your desk or if you've hired the computer consultant for a turnkey system. If not, and your software of choice is available in more than one format, ask the publisher which computer platform is recommended. If they make no recommendation, you're on your own.

SELECTING THE HARDWARE

As it's sold, a computer hardware system actually consists of several basic components and, depending on need, several more peripherals. The basics include the central processing unit (CPU), which is the brain of the machine; the monitor or screen; the hard drive; and the keyboard. Attached to that CPU may be a mouse for manipulating the cursor around the screen, a modem for communicating with another computer, a printer, and supplementary

disk or CD-ROM drives. The basic recommended hardware configuration for managing a business by computer today includes a
CPU, monitor, hard drive, CD-ROM drive, keyboard, mouse, and
laser printer.

If you aren't directed to a particular hardware platform, you've
a couple of choices to consider. Most small store owners will
find their needs adequately served by either of the two personal
computer formats available in the marketplace: the Macintosh
equipment currently made and manufactured by Apple Computer,
and the much broader selection of IBM PCs and compatible machines from many other computer makers.

The success of the Macintosh owes much to the ease of use
of its operating system. Users of the Macintosh have no need to
learn any codes or letter commands in order to run the system.
They direct its activities by clicking on icons—graphic electronic
buttons on the screen. This advantage has been countered in the
PC world with an operating system called Windows from Mi-
crosoft, which facilitates the ease of operation in a comparable
way. Whatever the hardware format, any new user can expect to
master the basics of operation in a very short amount of time.

MAKE SURE TO SHOP AROUND BEFORE BUYING

If there's no computer consultant on contract, it's worth your
while to spend time shopping around for the hardware. Computer
hardware is a hotly contested market, prone to fierce price competition. Typically the computer is sold as a package of the basic
system configuration described above. Most ads will mention the
size of the monitor; a name or number identifying the micropro-
cessor that drives the computer; the amount of RAM (internal
memory) standard with the machine, measured in megabytes; the
size of the hard drive, again measured in megabytes; any expansion boards included with the system; and its overall expansion
capabilities. All of this is important, and as a general rule, the
higher the numbers, the better your buy.

But take note: One of the most frustrating things about the
computer market is the pace at which new innovation appears.
Microprocessors continue to get more powerful, driving new ca-

pabilities that require more RAM and greater storage capability if they're to be utilized. Computers evolve so fast that any machine you buy today will seem obsolete when compared with the capabilities of machines offered at the same price point two years from now.

IT MAY MAKE MORE SENSE TO LEASE RATHER THAN BUY HARDWARE

That's one reason why leasing equipment may make more sense for the start-up retailer than outright purchase of the hardware. Leasing offers advantages, especially if you planned on financing your system anyway. A lease arrangement allows you to trade up to a better system when you decide you need it. Most leases include service contracts as well, so you never need worry about doing without your computer if repairs are necessary. Leasing is also a good way to sample the system before making an investment. There are companies that specialize in leasing hardware. Some companies that market software also lease hardware as part of the software sale. If you're looking for the best in a computer system, both today and tomorrow, leasing is an option that warrants your close consideration.

GET THE BEST SYSTEM YOU CAN AFFORD

Whichever way you go, get the best system your budget allows. Computer technology moves so rapidly, you'll extend the usable life of the hardware by buying the most powerful computer you can presently afford. Even if you can't conceive of filling a two-hundred-megabyte hard drive, you will, and then you'll want even more space. Look for the system that offers the most expansion options in terms of RAM upgrades, expansion slots, and ports for connection with other devices.

LOOK AT THE SUPPORT AFTER THE SALE

A one-year warranty with a toll-free number to reach the publisher should be regarded as a basic right by anyone purchasing hardware. With software, you need to investigate technical support and the company's policy on upgrades. Software publishers continually improve their programs, and remove the bugs, as a response to what they hear from customers. Before buying, ask how far the publisher is from the next version of the program, and what it will cost for the upgrade. It should be free or offered to the new buyer at a substantial discount.

The new buyer should also be entitled to a period of free technical support. It takes time to master a program—manuals are not always as informative as they should be—and you'll have questions about running the software. As a registered user who spent hundreds or thousands of dollars for a software solution, you shouldn't need to run up your phone bill to figure out how to get the program to print your reports.

Take advantage of training. If you aren't already proficient on the computer, take advantage of any offer of training thrown your way. Your store is a highly specialized business, and the software that will allow you to run it more effectively should be just as sophisticated. Time spent sitting down with an instructor is time well spent. It's much easier to learn how to navigate through an application, and get it to do what you want, once you've watched someone else run the program. Depending on the publisher, you may or may not pay extra for the training. Even if you must, it will prove money well spent.

Have at least two employees receive such training. If you're the whole business, that won't be necessary. But the store owner with staff should make sure he or another family member and an employee are fully trained on how to run the system and software.

GET A SYSTEM IN PLACE AS SOON AS POSSIBLE

Install your system as soon as you decide the business is a go. The sooner you have the computer system, the more it can do for you. As an organizational tool, the computer system will help with every phase of planning, setting up the business, compiling costs, and projecting sales goals. The more you use it, the easier it is to use. The easier it is to use, the greater the benefit.

ALLOW YOURSELF THE TIME NEEDED TO MASTER THE SYSTEM

Even with training, there's a definite learning curve for hardware and software. It will take time to set up the system that serves all your needs, even as a start-up operation. Trying to rush the process will only breed frustration. That frustration could prevent you from gaining all you can from the system.

The time required to learn and master your computer system depends on what level of computer skills you bring to the project. If you've been working on a computer for years, you'll have the system running as soon as you learn the nuances of the software. A computer novice will need to allow extra time, weeks at least, in order to get comfortable with the operation of hardware and software. All users will only begin to discover the full power of the system after using it to manage the business a few months.

DON'T BE AFRAID TO EXPERIMENT

Once you've mastered the basics of running the software, try to devise new ways of using it to gain added insight into the business. Try all kinds of reports, from day-to-day sales performance to seasonal trends by category. Your computer hardware has many more capabilities than the software that runs your business allows. Sample your options. You could invest in a desktop publishing program and try your hand at designing ads. You could even use presentation software to dazzle the banker when you go in with your loan request.

SPEAK WITH OTHER COMPUTER USERS

When you make your purchase, ask the seller or publisher for the names of other users of the system. Talk with them about what they've learned about the hardware and software. Some suppliers promote users' groups for the interchange of ideas. There should be such a group in your area. It could prove a good resource when it comes to troubleshooting or exploring the capabilities of your machine.

TAKE THE LONG VIEW ON
TECHNOLOGY

Start thinking of your computer system as an electronic assistant manager, and you'll get the most from it in the years ahead. Your system, and its contributions, can grow with your retail business. The system can teach you about your business and guide you to the right decisions. Consider the computer as something at the core of your long-term strategy for expanding your market.

You may, for example, eventually decide to distribute a store catalog on CD-ROM, complete with color photos, video, and descriptions of the selection available in your store. If your customers are scattered over a wide area, and sophisticated enough, on-line sales and service may eventually figure in your plans. Already some telecommunications networks carry advertising and conduct sales for specialty retailers in select categories.

These networks represent an entirely new sales outlet for the specialty retailer. The promised "information superhighway" will be as pervasive as today's telephone network. On-line services will enable specialty retailers to serve the electronic neighborhood mentioned in Chapter 4. Consumers will have electronic access to stores in another city or another state. This is already happening through Prodigy, CompuServe, and America Online. A few specialty retailers already use these services to sell to customers throughout the country. As more homes connect to the services and make the computer connection, people will become increasingly reliant on shopping by modem, checking the on-line service for listings of the latest sales, and browsing the catalogs of retailers connected to the service.

The computer can provide you with yet another chance to differentiate your store from its competitors. Many retail specialists now employ field sales forces, calling on customer accounts where they live or work. Equip them with laptop computers and they can work as effectively as if they were in the showroom. Your representative can make a presentation at the client's site, and connect to the office to place the order. Or he can check on the account's payment history and the status of the last order. Large businesses already employ computers in this way; in tomorrow's competitive retail market, the winners will be those who also tap the full potential of mobile computing.

Computers and related information technologies are now fixtures of the commercial landscape. Together, they'll fuel an evolution that promises to change retailing as well as all other aspects of our lives. The store you start today and the retail business you operate tomorrow may sell the same products but differ tremendously in structure: how you sell and distribute products, and how the customers access you.

Consider the promise of the computer technology already seen in point-of-purchase technology. Touch screens and interactive video can already guide a shopper through an electronic version of the store, right to the Peg-Board with the selected item. A digital mirror allows women to try out different hairstyles or mascara, even eye color, before deciding what to buy. Tomorrow's customer may be able to try on a jacket that doesn't exist, in a choice of colors, or road test a car and the smoothness of the ride from an electronic simulator in his own living room.

The full power of technology belongs to those who understand it. Understanding follows familiarity. You simply cannot afford to be without a computer. It's the tool of the present with the most to contribute to building your store's future.

❧ 11 ❧

WORKING RELATIONSHIPS AND RESPONSIBILITIES

Every store depends on the owner's ability to establish solid working relationships with everyone the business depends on: suppliers of products and services, staff, and shoppers. As we move into the 21st Century, these relationships will take on more of an aura of multiple partnerships, cooperative ventures that function to the best interests of all involved. You'll be your customer's partner in that you'll accept it as your responsibility to make sure she gets exactly what's right for her. As a partner to your supplier, you'll do all you can to get its products into the hands of consumers. In return for your effort, you'll expect the loyalty and support basic to any partnership.

You *are* your business. Certainly the team that surrounds you, inside and outside the store, contributes to your success. Were it not for your own dreams and aspirations, though, there would be no store, no team, and no retail career for you and those you employ.

It's not enough to build your team, you must get along with them and inspire them as well. Be prepared to lead and, when it's beneficial, to follow.

Obviously you already crave the responsibility of entrepreneurship, in all its forms. Retailing stands as one of the more competitive industries in this or any era. You've charged yourself with beating the odds, with making your ideas work in a business arena that historically witnesses more defeats than victories. As long as you wield your responsibilities in ways that will allow you to make the most of each working relationship, success will prove easier to grasp and hold.

FRONT MAN ON THE FRONT LINE

Your biggest responsibility is to make sure what the public sees in you is likable. All types of relationships and perceptions rest on that foundation. Recall the neighborhood stores of your youth. What do you remember most about those places? More likely than not, when you think of the store, the owner comes to mind: his personality, accent, laughter, or frown. The successful store owner is virtually inseparable from the store. The two create an identity, a unified whole. A store may change hands and be regarded as the same store. But with each new owner, the business assumes a new identity, a reflection of the owner's personality.

That's something lost to the larger stores, the impersonal places that seem to dominate so much of modern retailing. Some retail chains try to reclaim this identity through advertising, using the company founder as a spokesperson espousing the store philosophy. Noble as the attempt may be, it's just not the same as walking in and seeing that person stacking shelves or standing behind the register. That's the kind of personal connection, the sense of one-on-one contact, that makes shopping the small store so special. People want to see and hear from the expert, the front man or woman who *is* the store.

Personality is part of the appeal of the specialty store in today's market. Every successful store provides an experience for the shopper, separate from the buying process. If the store owner is obsessed with 1960s memorabilia, his shop called My Back Pages could be an emporium for all that defines a shared experience to a select age group: the records, posters, clothing, colors, and paraphernalia evoking that time. The people who visit the store expect the owner to know and be eager to share everything they'd want to know about every item in the store. It's your enthusiasm for what you sell, and your caring manner, that wins shoppers over so they want to return. You, the store owner, become the symbol, the front man, for the store and all it sells.

To a certain degree, that identity lends itself to nonstore selling as well. What matters most there is creating an aura around yourself as the expert. Don't provide mail-order customers with a catalog that simply lists products and prices; tell the story behind the merchandise. How did you find those one-of-a-kind items you're promoting? Why did you select these particular flowers for the Happy Birthday arrangement shoppers can send anywhere? In the store, the retailer's identity is built through interaction with customers. In catalogs or promotional material, it's the words and pictures used, and stories you tell, that create an identity for the store. Your enthusiasm for what you sell—be it about great prices or great features—and your eagerness to share it motivate the shopper to place an order.

As a small store owner, you've no choice but to become the front person for all you sell. That means you'll need to go out and drum up interest and awareness, tell the world of consumers your wonderful news and what it can mean for them. To the shopper you must be the recognized spokesperson for the products and services found in your store. Think again of those neighborhood shopkeepers of your youth. What did you like about them and their stores? That's who and what you want to be to your customers, no matter what your retail specialty: friendly, caring, fair, and eager to share your knowledge and passion with any who care to listen. Whether you sell from the mall or mailbox, to get to the top of the heap, you'll need to use your personality to foster an identity for the store.

PROVIDING QUALITY SERVICE

As discussed in Chapter 8, one of the most important decisions the specialty store owner/operator must make is selecting the right inventory. The selection available at your store needs to establish your store as consumers' best source for what you sell.

This same philosophy holds for service. When you think of service, the first things that come to mind are delivery, gift wrapping, mail order, and the like. These are services customers expect, and should be considered basic to every store. What sets your store apart are the services that specifically complement your core business. These are the services that draw people to the store and make them loyal customers. Every time you get someone into the store, your service should increase the odds for a sale.

LOOK FOR SERVICES THAT COMPLEMENT YOUR CORE BUSINESS

As part of your planning chores, think in terms of offering services that lend themselves to your basic business. If what you sell ever wears out or wears down, offering a repair service is an obvious idea. But unless you have the expertise and time, opening a service department increases your operating costs by adding another staff person and equipping the department. So consider contracting with someone to provide the repair service, as needed, in the beginning. Then when the repair business builds, you can add that person, or someone just as qualified, to your staff.

If your specialty item does not warrant repairs, consider the merits of offering some form of consultation services. The apparel shop could help individuals plan a complete, personalized fall wardrobe, by appointment, for example. Anyone who deals in antiques or collectibles could use an appraisal or restoration service as a lure for attracting more shoppers. Another possibility is a search service. For a nominal fee, plus the profit on the sale that hopefully results, the retailer could track down that rare item through contacts in the field.

Any service you offer should: pay for itself, provide a way to bring customers into the store, and make buyers more familiar with your business. Sooner or later, anyone who makes repeated trips through the store will buy something. Over time, a good service program wins converts to the store and contributes to profits. The right service can prove a useful tool for building business early on, and establishing the store with the audience you want to reach. The danger, though, is to overinvest in the service early on, or to devote your talents to too many things. If you decide a service department will help your store, start with the basics and build from there, always looking for the services that will enhance your reputation with shoppers. Think of the service as a traffic builder more than a moneymaker at first, and use it to your advantage.

The store exists to sell products. Accessories and services provide you with the means of attracting more customers and adding to your profits. The three should work together, to enable you to build the reputation that will carry the store to success. In everything you do, in every process and product, your must always anticipate change. Markets evolve over time, fads and fancies ebb and flow. The successful store owner has the right products and services when people need them, even as he works to anticipate their next want.

SPOTTING AND RESPONDING TO TRENDS

Once you open the store, everything you need to know is at your disposal. You can talk to suppliers and customers. You can see what one group is selling and the other buying. The challenge is to figure out how to make that knowledge work for your store. In the beginning, deciphering the trends and coming up with an appropriate response will pose a challenge not easily mastered. Master it, you must, though, if you're to boost sales. If you find you're selling more lawn chairs on Thursday nights as people think ahead to the weekend, maybe Thursday is a good night to experiment. Move the chairs to the front of the store, where people can see them as they walk past. You need to learn to respond like that, to revise your strategy in response to what observation and instinct tell you. Recognize the potential before it's a trend, and promote it into a trend.

Not all trends will deliver as anticipated. It's also your responsibility as store owner to remain open-minded enough to recognize your miscues and minimize their impact. Retailing is a yearly cycle of "turns": turning over inventory, selling what you have in stock, so you can place new orders for the next round of products. If you had the same goods in the store year-round, people would soon tire of the shopping experience. Part of the appeal of visiting stores, and browsing through catalogs, is to see what's new. It's your job as store owner to make sure the old moves out of the showroom to make way for the new.

You alone are responsible for knowing what's doing well and what's not moving. And when something is languishing on shelves, you must figure out how to move it. Sometimes all that's required is a modest price cut; sometimes nothing short of a closeout will get rid of the stuff. Never leap directly from one extreme to the other. Pricing reductions should be gradual, in steps. If you go about it any other way, you're telling your customers the goods carried an inflated price from the start.

DEALING WITH EMPLOYEES

Were it not enough to worry about meeting your many expenses, you had to go and hire someone else, someone who depends on the paycheck you promise to provide. As an employer, your foremost responsibility is an economic one. You must generate the money to cover salaries, taxes, and whatever benefits you decide to offer your staff.

That's the easier part of the task. Being a good boss asks a lot more than covering payroll—although that can be pretty tough at times. As the boss, you're the decision maker, the coach of your team. Standing at the helm of your business, you alone provide the direction that will allow the team you've assembled to realize your goals. There's an implied obligation to set a good example, and inspire each employee to develop and realize his or her individual potential in the process.

How you act is as important as what you say. The successful retailer enjoys dealing with people, within and without the organization. You set an example for employees in the way you deal with customers and how you handle suppliers. Your responsibility as the employer means providing the leadership that defines the organization and how it's perceived by those outside it. The leader inspires employees to use their talents so they can contribute their most to the organization.

YOU MUST PROVIDE EMPLOYEES WITH INCENTIVES

If you're fortunate enough to attract a staff of people you want to retain, you must offer more opportunity to them than the starting wage. Real opportunity carries incentives to grow into positions of responsibility, to prove themselves, and receive recognition for all they add to your success.

One of the important tools of that process is an incentive program for employees. Incentives provide people with tangible rewards for their efforts. They tell the employee that you value his contribution to the store's business. Incentives inspire people to give that extra bit of themselves, to apply the effort that will win them rewards.

If there's one incentive that motivates everyone, it's money. Everyone will work harder for the promise of higher pay. Any raise in salary should always be accompanied by added responsibility and a title change where appropriate. It adds to the value of the reward and tells the employee and others the increase is earned recognition for a job well done.

There are other forms of incentives that can be used to inspire your staff to achieve. You may, for example, offer prizes such as products, trips, or other rewards for performance. These work especially well when you challenge individuals or the entire staff to meet or exceed a sales goal during a set period of time. Even when opening the store, choose a category or item to promote to boost sales and traffic. Challenge the staff by setting sales goals for the promotion. If your goal is met, everyone shares in some special reward, with the biggest contributor receiving special recognition for the effort. How you structure your program, the goals and prizes, will depend on your sales category. Incentives—be they the promise of a prize, promotion, or cash—always motivate people.

Inspiring your staff is another of your responsibilities, as store owner and leader of your staff. Employees will respond eagerly to leadership when there's some tangible reward in it for them. An inspired employee is one who works harder, for himself and for the store. Employees like that can make your job a little easier.

SET EMPLOYEE POLICIES

You'll need to establish employee policy before you build your staff. Basically, the policy should describe everything you want your employees to know and understand about working for you.

What you include in that policy is your decision, but it's in the best interest of you and your employees to put together some form of written policy. Your employee "manual" need only be a typewritten page or two, if that's all it takes, but it should be written down. That way you won't waver from it, and your employees will have something they can refer back to if questions ever arise. If you ever need to fire someone for poor job performance or inappropriate behavior, it will be more easily accomplished when you have a written document defining where the violation of the terms of employment occurred.

Every written employee policy should begin with a statement that your business is an equal opportunity employer and will not discriminate on the basis of race, color, religion, age, etc. Then get into the details that most concern your workers: hours, responsibilities, and wages. The written policy should also spell out anything special about the job, such as scheduling requirements or the requirement that all employees work evenings and weekends. If the store has a dress code, the employee policy is where you define it. Include your requirements in terms of employees' personal hygiene, general appearance, and attitude. The same for your policy on drug or alcohol abuse on the job. Unfortunate as it may be, these are issues of the modern workplace. You need to let employees know how you intend to deal with such behavior.

The store policy manual should also address any security concerns that are yours as the store owner and employer. If you will require employees for certain positions to be bonded, put it in writing. The same for your policies regarding any form of theft while on the job. As a measure to protect yourself, the employee policy guidelines should state what infractions you will treat as grounds for immediate dismissal from your staff. Theft on the job, in any form; an abusive attitude toward customers, co-workers, or management; and two instances of absence without explanation are all grounds for terminating the working relationship.

Ask your attorney if there are any self-protective statements you should include in the employee manual. For instance, if your store operates in an extremely competitive business in a competitive market, losing your top salesman to the competition could hurt your business. You may stipulate that anyone who accepts certain positions at your store agrees not to work for a direct competitor for a stated period of time from the last day under your employment. It might also be important to establish that any records and business documents a staff person develops while employed by you remain your property. Just think of what could happen if you don't do this. Let's say you invest two months' salary paying someone to compile a list of leads and accounts in the area. If you leave yourself unprotected, that person could leave and take that list with him, to the benefit of the competitor who lured him away.

Conversely, if business suffers and you must let someone go, you should state the store policy on dismissals for anything other than cause. Two weeks' notice or two weeks' pay from day of dismissal seems the norm for full-time employees. The policy should also state what you expect of employees when they quit. Again, two weeks' notice, with a letter of resignation, seems a fair request.

Whatever benefits program you offer employees should also be explained in detail in the policy manual. This includes a list of paid holidays, personal days, allowable sick days, and paid vacation periods. If you'll be providing health benefits, or offer a plan your employees can buy into, their obligations and options should be described as well. The same goes for any pension or profit-sharing plan.

As for wages, while you certainly won't want to list them, you do want to explain your policy regarding them in the manual. If you'll be paying sales commissions, explain your system for compiling those funds. You may wish to establish a probationary period for new hires, after which they'll automatically be considered for permanent employee status. It's a good idea to establish a framework for periodic salary review for all employees, say, every six to twelve months from date of hire.

A lot of this will seem petty—until you fall victim to your own good intentions. Writing an employee policy, and distributing a copy to all employees, is one of the few ways you have to ensure there are no misunderstandings in your relationships with staff. It's your responsibility to make sure all employees receive a copy when they join your staff. You might as well have them sign something to the effect that they've received and read it. That way there can be no arguing later on about what was promised or intended.

YOU'RE RESPONSIBLE TO TRAIN YOUR EMPLOYEES

Along with your responsibility to pay a salary and live up to terms of your employee policy, you've an implied obligation to train the people you hire. That doesn't mean you must pay them to attend special classes or seminars. It means you must help them develop the skills that will enable them to do the best job possible while employed by you. The employee who receives ongoing training is one who learns to enjoy the job more and who works harder for the good of the store. Employees who profit from the extra training can be trusted with more responsibility. For your business to grow, you'll need their assistance. Alone, you can only carry the business so far. There are several ways to provide training right from the start. The simplest measure is to share what you know as you learn about the business. Use regularly scheduled meetings as a forum to explain what you're doing and why, and to solicit opinions. Make sure the trade journals you read for insight get circulated among your staff. Before the store opens, invite representatives from your suppliers in to talk about their products and the secrets of selling them. Continue to do that on a regular basis as new products and sales techniques become available. Pay employees one hour each week to visit other stores and see how they're handling products. Have them share what they learn at your next meeting.

Throughout all this training, encourage your staff to start thinking like retailers themselves, to understand why retailers do things the way they do, and how those things influence business. Training, like an education, is never complete. But if you handle it properly, your employees will eventually come to you with ideas on how to improve the store's sales performance. Then you'll be in position to start reaping the rewards of your emphasis on training.

YOU'LL NEED TO DEAL WITH
PROBLEM EMPLOYEES

Sooner or later he shows up in every company, every business, and every store. He's the guy, or gal, who just doesn't live up to your expectations when hired. It may be a bad attitude, tardiness, laziness, or just plain nastiness, but for one or some combination of these reasons, the arrangement isn't working out, for him or for you. Everyone deserves a second chance, unless, of course, he has knowingly committed one of the infractions that constitute grounds for immediate dismissal outlined in the employee policy manual.

It's the correctable mistakes, the little infractions—occasional lateness, long lunches—that warrant a second chance. Grant that employee an opportunity to correct the error, but make it clear failure to do so means termination. It's best to take care of these minor issues in a closed-door meeting, one on one. Don't reprimand the employee, merely suggest you're not completely happy with the way things are going. Explain what bothers you and how you'd like it corrected. The employee worth keeping will take the hint.

If the infraction is a little more serious, say, the person is habitually late or has trouble taking direction, the situation warrants a stern reprimand. How you deal with these employees is your own decision. It's often best, however, to put someone like this on some form of probation for a set period of time. If the problem is not corrected, the relationship ends. This should be spelled out in a dated letter from you to the employee.

When you sense an employee may be emotionally or psychologically unstable, it's in your interest to have another person nearby during the meeting. Should your discussion draw an emotional reaction or protest, call the other person into the room, as your witness.

When you have a serious problem with any staff person, one chance is all he deserves, and all you can afford. When you do find yourself forced to fire someone, always spell out the reason in a brief letter, as well as informing him in person. Then cut your losses and get him out of the place as soon as possible. If you must, give two weeks' severance pay and be rid of him. It's far preferable to having him stick around, causing residual stress and strain.

In your career as the employer, you can expect to do your share of firing. There will also come the time when you'll be on the receiving end of a resignation. Before you accept this, ask if there's something you could do to make the individual stay. If it's a reasonable request from a valued employee, fulfill it. It's almost always cheaper to retain an employee than to find and train a new one. When the employee is firm on resigning, accept it graciously, but always leave the door open for a return. You'll lose an employee but retain a friend and maybe gain a customer. And whatever the circumstance of departure, hold no grudges: Remember all the jobs along the trail that led to your decision to become a retail entrepreneur.

DEALING WITH SUPPLIERS

Your relationship with the suppliers of the products you sell should be regarded as one of mutual benefit and mutual dependence. Treat them as partners, eager for your success. Suppliers depend on people like you to handle their products as much as you rely on suppliers for something to sell. In theory, this should foster a certain sense of equality, with neither party dominating the business relationship. That holds in your dealings with the smaller firms that are most dependent on outlets like yours in their distribution network. When you move into the more competitive fields, where the same or very similar products of corporate suppliers are marketed through the full spectrum of retail stores, the equal footing starts to erode.

MAKE SURE YOU'RE BEING TREATED FAIRLY

Many big suppliers still treat their dealer network equally and fairly. But just as many give special deals to the big guys, the multistore chains that order in quantity. This can create severe problems for the smaller store owner who hopes to compete with

that large dealer. When you buy three of something, and the discounter buys three thousand, he's going to get a price break. It's
not uncommon to hear an independent retailer complain that a
discount store's selling price is below his wholesale price. Most
manufacturers will do their best to deny such practices exist, but
the numbers tell a much different story.

The retail entrepreneur certainly cannot avoid the problem by
ignoring those suppliers. No matter what type of store you open,
there are probably some products you simply must have to retain
an identity as a legitimate source in that category. Some of these
are the same products you'll find in every type of retail outlet.
But there are steps you can take to minimize the impact of these
policies on your business.

Start by speaking with your suppliers honestly from day one
about your expectations. Remember who works for whom here;
without you, the supplier has no way to move product. Some will
prefer the business of discounters. The ones you want to buy
from are those who understand how the specialty dealer helps
strengthen perceptions of their line. Anyone you plan on supporting should earn your business, in the same way you must win the
loyalty of your customers. The manufacturer and distributor
should be willing to do all within reason to earn your business.

If you allow the situation to evolve in the other direction, in
which you become completely dependent on them, putting yourself at their mercy, you've put the store at risk. Any supplier who
dictates terms, with a take-it-or-leave-it attitude, is one who'll
quickly abandon the specialty store owner as soon as a larger
account comes along, or who'll sell to that larger account as well
as you.

So one of your first questions to suppliers, even before inquir-
ing about the terms they offer on orders, should be a request for
an explanation of the distribution policy. Your best bets are the
companies that practice controlled or limited distribution. Such
companies limit the number of retailers handling their products
as a way to minimize competitive pricing and ensure profitability
for the retailer. You should always ask the supplier what other
stores in your immediate area are carrying its products, as well,
and what are the company's future distribution plans.

MAKE SURE YOUR SALES EFFORTS ARE BEING SUPPORTED

Next, inquire about the manufacturer's advertising and promotional spending. With major suppliers you should expect a certain amount of national print and broadcast advertising to generate brand awareness and interest. You also need to know how the manufacturer will help promote products in the local market. Inquire about advertising support or promotional materials for in-store use, and promotional campaigns aimed at consumers, as well as in-store incentive programs. Also ask about the manufacturer's training program: It's an important element of their support for the dealer network. A good supplier will provide training on a regular basis, and whenever an entirely new product comes to market.

UNDERSTAND FULLY THE ORDERING, RETURN, AND REPAIR POLICIES

Of course, you need to know the supplier's order policy before making any dollar commitments. First, you must know if there's a minimum order requirement. Often terms or financing on an order will be tied to the size of the order: Order ten and you have ninety days to pay, while it's cash on delivery if you order one or two. Ask about the supplier's entire ordering program, including pricing policy and turnaround times. When starting out, you may not qualify for any special programs, but being aware of what's available can help you plan for the future growth of your business.

It's imperative to find out every supplier's policy on repairs, exchanges, and warranty protection. These are areas in which you'll be dealing directly with the customer. If that customer is not completely satisfied, you're the one whose business will be hurt. Get specific information so you know what your responsibilities are.

Most products carry some form of warranty. How is it applied, and is there a service center in the immediate area? Consider the frustration of the customer who takes something home, finds the product broken right out of the box, and returns to the store assuming he's entitled to an exchange. But you aren't authorized to give them an exchange, you must send that shiny new product in for repair. Such a policy will lose that customer for you, for good.

Or suppose you get a batch of defective shirts, but the supplier's exchange policy is credit toward your next order. What good is that if you paid for the merchandise and are so dissatisfied with the supplier that you'll never order from him again? You'll lose the money and the shirts. These are issues to thoroughly discuss with potential suppliers before granting them your business. Your store's reputation may one day depend on how well you protect your interests in these areas.

GET ALL PROMISES IN WRITING

If your supplier's representative makes any special promises to you, such as exclusive retail right to the product in your area, request the promise be put in writing. What goes on in conversation is hearsay, a matter of interpretation. Salesmen have been known to say whatever it takes to close the deal. A written promise, however, is a business obligation. If nothing else, your request for a written confirmation ("for your files") will prove your strength and will impact future dealings with those who make promises to win your business.

Your discussions with suppliers should help decide which ones you want to patronize. Your relationship with your suppliers, if properly developed, will prove a strategic alliance for growing your business. Without trust in each other's intentions, it's a relationship that will serve neither party for long.

Be open and honest about your business plans with your suppliers, and expect the same candid respect. It's important to establish an honest, open relationship up front. If the supplier ever lets you down or compromises your business with its practices, you'll want to be able to reiterate the promises made to you, and hold your suppliers accountable to them. Should they fail to live up to their promises, and protect your business, you must always be prepared to walk away from the relationship.

DON'T BECOME OVERLY DEPENDENT ON ONE SUPPLIER

For this reason it's critical you never become so dependent on any single supplier or source for merchandise that your store's vitality depends on that source. That's an invitation for disaster. Any change in the supplier's business, any shift in their distribution policy, could have a negative impact on your store's performance. Suppliers, like stores, come and go. Their strategies evolve with their needs. Some have been known to use the small store owner to establish their lines, and then quickly abandon those retailers once larger accounts come calling. The fate of your store should not be tied to that of any single supplier. So by offering your customers a choice in what you sell, by category and product, you're also protecting your livelihood. Work for the mix from several suppliers that reflects the diversity of the marketplace.

ALWAYS LOOK OUT FOR YOUR OWN INTERESTS FIRST

In your dealings with suppliers you should be forthright and friendly, but aggressively pursuing the best deal for your store, from a combination of suppliers. Buy from more than one supplier in any category you handle, but place the most business with those who offer you the most favorable terms, the best products, and the best marketing support. Assume nothing, long-term: Always be prepared to walk away from the supplier who fails to live up to his promises to you. When you've concerns about your supplier's policy or practices, make them known immediately. Failure to do so is your mistake; failure to respond is theirs.

From the outset, you must make it obvious to the supplier's representative that he and his company need to *earn* your business. Make reasonable demands, for support, better terms on orders, training, whatever it is the supplier can do for you. You may not get everything you request, but without asking, you'll get nothing at all.

Look out for your interests. Never take for granted any promise or stated policy that isn't in writing. Track all your competitors to see how they handle the merchandise you stock. Is their pricing, even on special promotions, in line with your costs? Any significant discrepancy between your cost and their actual selling price warrants an explanation from your sales representative. Also, watch the advertising other retailers put behind products you stock. Some of it is paid for by the supplier. Are you getting the same support, or are they helping the competition gain a sales advantage?

As for the products themselves, you should accept nothing short of quality from your suppliers. When there's a problem, they should assume full responsibility for correcting it. To the consumer, a defective product reflects on the store first, and then the supplier. You may lose the customer to dissatisfaction, but the supplier can still sell them a product at another location. You have a right to demand quality, and an obligation to abandon those suppliers who consistently fail to deliver it. Excessive returns on a company's products for poor workmanship should prompt you to reconsider your relationship.

IN RETURN, OFFER GOOD SUPPLIERS SUPPORT, INFORMATION, AND ADVICE

Dealing with suppliers is not entirely a one-way street. You assume certain obligations as part of the relationship. For one, any items you stock deserve to be displayed, promoted, and supported on the sales floor. Don't look entirely to the manufacturer's efforts to create sell-through; how a product is handled on the sales floor contributes much to its sales performance. Remember: Most purchase decisions are made at the point of sale.

The retailer is in a much better position than any supplier to know what is happening in the market. You should be willing to share this insight with your suppliers. If may take weeks for the manufacturer to wade through sales reports before they know a particular color or style is flying off shelves while another collects dust. You know that the day you restock those shelves or read your sales report. This is vital information to the supplier. Pass it on to your suppliers, and you'll both benefit.

In the same way, if you know your customers, you know what they want. People will tell you how a product could be improved, what features are important to them, or why they favor one model over another. Keep this information to yourself, and you're hurting your prospects for increased sales.

Your dealings with suppliers should be exactly what the word implies: a deal. You get and you give. Each party should benefit from the arrangement, under the terms of your agreement. You need your suppliers' products; they need you to sell them. It's a fair deal as long as it works to the benefit of the store and supplier.

BUILDING LONG-TERM RELATIONSHIPS

When you're just starting your store, you'll be very dependent on the working relationships you establish with your staff, suppliers, and the other members of your team. Their contributions in effort and expertise can provide the foundation for success with your store. Recognize and appreciate that help, for without it, your store cannot prosper.

Later on, success will enable you to give as much in return. Remember that obligation, be it to your employees, suppliers, or anyone else you work with. The long-term relationships that will carry your business are built on honesty in your dealings and your expectations. Understand where others are coming from, respect their right to protect and promote their own interests, and work together for the common good. Help those you work with to develop their talents, recognize their needs and wants, and do your best to help them fulfill them.

The best working relationships are those that allow everyone a share in the success. For your employees, your success should represent a chance to increase their own earnings and further their careers. For suppliers, it means a larger market for their products, and the prosperity that follows. For you, it means the satisfaction of making your own career. The relationships that support that success over the long term operate in a big circle: What you get from others allows you to give something back; the more they help you, the more you're able to help them.

For more information on general business management, take a look at the following books:

- *Small Business Management Fundamentals,* by Dan Steinhoff and John F. Burgess (McGraw, 1993)
- *Small Time Operator: How to Start Your Own Small Business, Keep Your Books, Pay Your Taxes & Stay Out of Trouble,* by Bernard Kamoroff (Bell Springs, 1988)
- *The Essentials of Small Business Management,* by Thomas W. Zimmerer and Norman M. Scarborough (Macmillan, 1993)

❧ 12 ❧
KNOW WHOM YOU SERVE

F or the 21st Century retailer, it won't be enough to know the customer group you're serving. You must know whom you serve, on an individual basis: their personal likes and dislikes, preferences in colors and styles, whom they buy for besides themselves, and why they've decided to shop at your store. A lot of this can be gleaned from a customer database, but it's the personal touch you and your staff add that will win shoppers to your store.

When that first person steps up to your cash register to make a purchase, you'll begin learning who your customers are. Until then, you're operating on a theory of whom your store will serve and where they can be found.

Granted, your customer profile is drawn from careful research, but it's still only an educated guess. More likely than not, you'll find those who patronize your store very similar to, yet very different from, your expectations. After all, the specialty store is a response to one aspect of the consumer's life, one among many areas of interest or need. As you'll discover soon after opening, there's much more to the individuals who comprise your customer base.

Whether yours is a neighborhood store or a mail-order specialty house, you'll be dealing with a succession of individuals, with unique tastes, demands, and expectations. Some will become regular shoppers, your core group of supporters; others, occasional "browsers" who check in now and then for a look at what's new. A few you'll serve but once. Whoever the customers, regard each instance of dealing with them as your only opportunity to win them over to your cause. Miss these opportunities and you'll eventually find you've undermined the business you worked so hard to create.

As store owner, it's up to you to make the business appealing to a broad range of customer types. To be the best at retail, you must be a supportive, service-oriented adviser to every individual customer. That means different things to different people. To some you'll need to be the knowledgeable source. For others you'll be a sounding board. Still others may look on you as a consultant, even a confidant. All, however, will look for you to be the reliable and trusted merchant, caring and concerned, ever smiling and friendly.

We all have lousy days. Your customers may want to share theirs with you, but they don't want to hear about yours. It's not always easy, but you must smile and be polite even on the worst of days. Maintaining good relationships with your customers is a dance of perceptions. People respond to people on a personal level. Whether in your showroom or over the phone, the friendly voice and the kind word will build loyalty. By the same turn, a gruff attitude, a curt response, or anything that approaches rudeness will spoil the relationship.

Remember all we've said about it being the team that brings you your success? Well, your customers should be considered part of that team as well. Failure to win them to your cause can prove the biggest obstacle to your store's success.

THE SILENT SALESMEN

Your customers will never join your staff. They may never understand the fundamentals of retailing. Yet they work for you—or against you—from opening day on. The people who shop your store serve as its volunteer ambassadors of good will or ill will, depending on their shopping experiences with you. They may not realize how much they can help or hurt your store, but you should.

People talk, and people listen. A word of praise from shoppers is the best endorsement any retailer can receive. Consider the implications of the alternative. Someone has a problem with your sales or service, it's not addressed to satisfaction, and he leaves the place huffing and puffing with anger. What do you think will be the first words from his lips when the store is mentioned or someone expresses a need to buy what you sell? If he says anything, he certainly won't be singing your praises. That kind of perception feeds on itself; it grows and grows. A friend tells a friend, who tells a friend. The next thing you know, your big sale is a big bust.

Such a downward spiral happens to retailers who don't pay enough attention to how the store is perceived by shoppers. That's why someone coined that phrase "The customer is always right." Think of it not as a cliché, but as the mantra for retail success. It accurately describes a secret of successful selling, and how much of tomorrow's business depends on today's transactions. The happy customer returns to the store; the unhappy customer keeps friends and family away.

HOW TO SATISFY YOUR CUSTOMERS

What does it take to satisfy the customer? Whatever it takes, within reason. You should be as accommodating as you need to be in order to ensure the reputation and continued profitability of the store. Most customers will be satisfied with a fair price for a quality product, a friendly attitude, sound advice, and quick and competent service. Some will prove much more demanding, always pressing for extras, the better deal at the lower price. Deal with all customers on the same terms. In today's market, people have other places to shop if all they want is a lower price. Once you start making deals, you're telling them your prices were inflated to begin with.

People shop the small store for expertise and convenience. Haggling over price isn't part of that process. Many shoppers simply don't want that hassle. They'd rather shop at a place where they know the price that's offered is the selling price, and that they'll get the same treatment as everyone else. When shoppers enjoy your experience and leave the store satisfied with the treatment they receive, they'll spread the word. Everyone wants to be the first with good news. Make the shopping experience rewarding for your customers, and they'll soon be selling for the store without even realizing it.

GETTING TO KNOW THEM

To make the most of your relationships with customers, you need to know as much as possible about them. You must open your doors with a thorough understanding of why certain people should shop there. Once they do, you need to know who they really are. Such knowledge is important if you want to build your business beyond the start-up phase. When you know as much as you can about your customers—their likes, dislikes, and interests—you can revise your sales strategy to get the most from the relationship. If you learn many of your customers share an interest indirectly related to your core business, it may be worth experimenting with a venture into that arena. For example: a specialist in foreign language publications, videos, and recordings could try offering vacation packages to some of the countries her wares relate to.

Getting to know your store regulars should prove a relatively easy process. These are people who'll frequent the store on a regular basis, and with whom you'll get pretty familiar. As you get to know and trust each other, you can turn to these special customers for honest opinions on what you're doing in the store and how well you're addressing their needs. You want to do what you can to strengthen such relationships. They can prove a real asset. Invitation-only events, like special sales or previews of a new season's merchandise, help promote further loyalty and a sense of belonging for these store customers. Of course, you'll also want to include your biggest supporters, in terms of dollars, whenever you host a special event.

Here's where the computer system discussed earlier can really help. Along with the many ways a computer system helps manage information and inventory, it's your best tool for developing a detailed profile of your customers and their purchasing activity. Sure, with a keen memory you could store some of that information in your head, but few of us are blessed with a memory capable of recalling every customer and every sale. It's much easier and more efficient to write and update that history at the cash register every time the customer makes a buy. But beyond revealing who they are, the purchase, and what brings them to the store, there's little information most shoppers will share while standing at the cash register.

CONSIDER CONDUCTING A CUSTOMER SURVEY

Why not provide a short form to fill out, with the promise of some reward or prize for doing so? If you do, you'll soon be able to compile details about your audience that will enable you to run a much more responsive operation. The "reward" can be something as simple as joining the store mailing list, a free pen or some other inexpensive premium, or entry in a drawing for a giveaway of merchandise. The important thing is to make that incentive lucrative enough that a good share of customers will voluntarily fill out the form. Keep the questionnaire brief and to the point and you'll draw even more responses. The information provided, once entered into your database, will prove more valuable than anything you're giving away.

The information you request should reflect what you need to know to fine-tune your retail strategy. Get the names and ages of anyone else living in the customer's home. Find out what types of publications and TV shows the family watches, and when. Provide a list of hobbies or activities for them to check off.

Ask about shopping habits. What day of the week do they do most shopping, and what hours of that day? Do they ever shop from home, use coupons, or respond to ads that provide for a certain discount? Where do they get their information on what they buy: from what they read, hear from friends, or store personnel? What's most important to them in a store: price, selection, service?

Ask specifics about shopping your store as well. Which departments did they visit? Find out how they learned of the store. What products and services interest them? What else would they like to see you carry? Would they recommend your store to a friend? Finally, provide space for suggestions on how you could improve the store.

Once enough customers respond to this offer, you'll have an abundance of useful insight. It will tell you about the store as it stands today, and where it needs to be tomorrow. All this information will prove invaluable for fine-tuning your strategy as the business evolves. When you know who has children, for instance, you know who you need to reach with a special sale. When you know what your customers read and watch, you've a better idea where to put your advertising dollars. If most customers indicate they shop Friday nights, you might want to try some Friday night specials. Finally, the suggestions submitted on the forms may point you toward something or some opportunity you overlooked while setting up the business.

The information compiled in such a consumer survey can be of interest to others with products to sell and services to promote. Depending on your market area and store specialty, you could eventually create a customer database of thousands of names. The more names, the more valuable the list to you and others. Start compiling information on your customers from the day you open your doors.

Later you may decide to sell or trade your list to others, like a major supplier. If you even consider such a practice, you should request permission from customers before sharing the information about them with a third party. Your loyal customer may suddenly rethink her relationship with your store if she learns you supplied her name and number to the telemarketer who just interrupted dinner. Many resent the practice of passing along information given with implied trust.

As much as you learn about your customers from the database, that information can also help you identify other people you want to reach. When you want to expand your market beyond the immediate area, you may want to purchase a mailing list or database. If, for instance, your customer database reveals the typical shopper in your store hails from a two-income household with children under twelve, and the family enjoys boating, camping, and outdoor activities, you could buy a list of the names and addresses of just such families by whatever geographic breakdown suits your strategy. Sources for these lists can be found under the ''direct marketing'' and ''mailing list'' headings of the Yellow Pages in larger cities, or in the national toll-free 800 directory published by AT&T. If you don't have a copy, check with your local library.

The problem with using a purchased list, as well as selling or trading your own database, is that the practice may backfire. Many consumers already feel so inundated and resentful of all their junk mail, and the unwanted calls from telemarketers, that they've learned to loathe the messengers.

REMEMBER YOUR CUSTOMERS ARE ALL INDIVIDUALS

Your customer database paints a broad-brush picture of your audience. Be careful not to spend so much time gazing at that forest, you fail to see the trees. Although you can draw general conclusions about your clientele from a database, remember it's a compilation of individual shoppers. All strategic ambitions aside, retail success is earned or lost, in the store or over the phone, one shopper at a time, through one-on-one contact. Regardless of what conclusions you draw from the profile of your audience, what matters most is what each individual customer concludes about your store. That's a product of his or her shopping experience with your retail business. It's in your best interest to make it as pleasurable an endeavor as possible.

When you use alternate means of sales—mail, fax, or phone orders—the person who takes or receives the order must follow through on any request made by the customer. A friendly voice on the phone is a necessity, but it won't compensate for being put on terminal hold. People use these alternate means of purchase because they offer a quick solution for buying. Disappoint them, and the store loses the customers.

The perceptions of in-store shoppers begin to be shaped as soon as they enter the store. Everyone on staff should be well trained in welcoming shoppers and making them feel comfortable. All that's required is good manners. Anyone who enters should be acknowledged with a smile, a friendly nod, or a simple greeting. Always ask if the customer needs help. If he does, oblige as best you can. If you're serving another customer, direct him to his area of interest, summon someone else to help him, or promise to be with him shortly.

When the customer refuses the offer of help, or explains she's "just looking," back off and let her proceed on her own. Some people detest the assistance of an eager salesperson. Stalking that shopper through the store, ever ready to leap to her assistance, is a mistake. That smothers her, and makes her eager to escape even if she entered intending to make a purchase. It's also the kind of experience that may make her hesitate to return. When she needs help, she'll request it. Just make sure there's always someone on hand to provide it. And that employee is eager to please.

LEARN HOW TO QUALIFY BUYERS

One of the secrets to successful selling is qualifying the customer—determining what he or she wants, and can afford. It removes a lot of the guesswork from the sales process, to the benefit of store personnel and shopper. With a few questions early on in the conversation, the sharp salesperson can learn what the customer wants, the features or functions considered important, and which products to show that customer. No matter what your store sells, qualify the customer as soon as you converse with her.

Ask the customer what product she's looking for; if she has a particular model, size, or style in mind; who'll be using the product; how it will be used; and if she already has an idea of what she wants to spend. With the answers, you or your salesperson will be able to direct the shopper to the appropriate products. Good customer relations ensure the customer ends up with what's right for her, nothing more and nothing less. To sell that, you must first define the customer's need through the qualifying process.

Once you do qualify the customer, never show her a particular model, stressing this is exactly what she needs—even if it is. Selection is an important part of the purchasing process. People want to decide for themselves how to spend their money. That decision may be based entirely on what you tell them, but most prefer to make it for themselves. Offering a choice between this and that, even if it's no real choice, let's the shopper feel more in control of the purchase process. If it ends up being the wrong choice, the shopper has no one but herself to blame for the mistake.

Good verbal communications skills are especially important when it comes to helping shoppers through this process. Store staffers need to understand what people mean when they describe their wants, and be able to convey the benefits of a variety of products to them. Your attitude, as well as articulation, count. Many shoppers back off as soon as they sense pressure from a salesperson to buy a particular item.

Overblown advertising claims and product hype have made us a nation of cynical shoppers. As soon as people detect anything less than honesty from a salesperson, they sour on the shopping experience, and their resistance goes up. Honesty is what shoppers expect in their dealings. As much as they expect it, they'll rave about it when they find it. They're in the store to fill a need; they don't want to complicate the process with worries as to whether the salesperson is there to assist them or just to get at their wallet.

SETTING CUSTOMER POLICY

The significance customers assign to honest dealings with reputable retailers requires you to establish policies for customer relations. This is as important as your store's employee policy, and for many of the same reasons. Your customer policy helps define what you want your store to be, with implications for both your marketing and business plans.

Customer policy tells customers what to expect in their dealings with your store. It also provides a frame of reference for the appropriate behavior and practices by store personnel. Customer policy impacts a wide area of business. Some of it should be defined in writing and provided to customers, and some should be a matter of understanding between staff and owner.

Everyone who works for you should thoroughly understand how you want your customers treated. Here, as the store owner, you lead by example. Demonstrate what's appropriate behavior by your interactions with shoppers. If your staff can't take the hint, try role-playing at your staff meetings until they get it right. Everyone should be friendly when dealing with customers, whether in person or over the telephone. Your showroom staff may view their job as selling, but shoppers prefer the low-key assistance of informed consultants. When the customers approach with a question, respond immediately or refer them to someone

more knowledgeable. No sale is complete until a satisfied customer leaves the store. Follow-through means accompanying that
buyer to the cash register and making sure he leaves with everything required to enjoy his purchase. Ever get home with a new
radio, only to find the batteries weren't included? Then you know
the sense of frustration you want your customers to avoid.

Customer policy also entails those things you do that promote
store identity in the minds of shoppers. Advertising in every
Thursday's paper gets your message out. It's part of your media
strategy but also tells shoppers that's where they need to look to
find out what's on sale at the store. The merit of such set policies,
which benefit both store and shoppers, carries over to the showroom as well. All stores should maintain designated areas for
discounted items, closeouts, featured products of the month, and
new arrivals. Regular shoppers will learn to check these areas as
soon as they enter the store. Sometimes they'll visit the store only
for that reason.

PUT IT IN WRITING AND UP ON THE WALL

There are other matters of customer relations in which your
interests are best served by a written statement, posted and easily
visible to all customers. Some signs should greet customers right
at the door, so there can be no mistake about your policy. "Break
it and you buy it" is one warning many retailers who sell fragile
merchandise use as a friendly reminder for customers to be careful
handling the products.

When theft is a concern, a sign inside the entrance should in-
form shoppers how you intend to deal with it. A little humor
doesn't hurt in such a sensitive area. For instance, there's one
popular sign that, rather than saying, "All Shoplifters Will Be
Prosecuted," says, "All Shoplifters Will Be Eaten." Just the sign
is enough to deter some potential thieves. Some retailers minimize
the temptation by having customers check bags and packages at
the front, upon entering.

These security issues pose a touchy area in customer relations.
You want to watch your customers, yet you don't want them to
realize they're being watched and feel uncomfortable. Regardless,

when you strongly suspect someone intends to lift merchandise or is doing so, follow him through the store. Don't accuse anyone until he's exited the store: Until someone leaves the premises with concealed merchandise, he can claim he intended to pay for it. It's your responsibility to instruct employees how to deal with shoplifters. Failure to do so raises the possibility you could one day find yourself on the wrong end of a lawsuit.

Certain store policies need to be posted right near the cash register, where they won't escape notice by your shoppers. If you won't accept out-of-town checks, payroll checks, or third-party checks, put it in writing for all to see. A statement of store policy on hot checks helps protect your interests and avoids headaches. Post the fee you'll impose for any checks returned for insufficient funds and it'll dissuade some from buying beyond their means.

A statement of store policy on refunds, returns, and exchanges should also be where all can see it. The sign should state what proof you require, as well as a time limit for your return policy. Some retailers state, "All sales final." Others, "No cash for returns." You'll need to decide your own return policy; but whatever it is, it should be posted.

If you offer delivery service, it's a good idea to work out a time for the delivery with the customer, and have her tell you who'll be authorized to accept the delivery. Believe it or not, there are a few people who'll claim they never received something that was delivered, and refuse to pay for it. Your only proof is a signed receipt.

HANDLING RETURNS

You'll find the majority of your customers to be honest people who want nothing more than a fair deal. Then there are those few who won't be satisfied until they feel they've pulled one over on you. Usually they show up at the service desk, with a complaint or request for a return that simply isn't justified. For the independent store owner, handling returns can prove a perplexing problem, as consumer expectations are often an outgrowth of their experience with mass merchandisers. Many of these merchants pursue a "no questions asked" policy on refunds and exchanges. They're able to do it because they know they can send the merchandise back to the source for full credit. They get that blanket support from suppliers eager to stay in their good graces so they can continue selling them large amounts of products.

The harsh reality is that you probably won't be able to provide that same service to your customers. Usually you won't be able to get that same cooperation from the supplier. Your return policy should reflect the support available to you from your suppliers—no more and no less. Anything more can end up costing you money. That forces you to thoroughly evaluate the warranty and service support a manufacturer puts behind its products, before setting your own policy.

When the shopper is standing in your store with a defective product, it's your problem. If you aren't entitled to a liberal instant exchange policy, you need to develop an arrangement that's fair to the store and its customers. If you sell any sort of equipment, it's good to set up a "loaner" program while a product is in for repair. That way the customer never need be without a product, and won't fault the store for the wait.

With other items you need to use your judgment about when it's appropriate to accept the return and make an exchange or refund. A shirt or dress that's obviously worn is one you won't be able to sell. Unless it's falling apart after one or two wears, it's no fault of yours the customer decided, long after the purchase, it wasn't the right style. Shoddy merchandise is something the store owner must assume responsibility for, but refuse to exchange merchandise damaged through obvious abuse or neglect by the customer.

Occasionally you'll face customers who want to bully you into submission with questionable returns or exchange. They show up at the busiest time of day, loudly announce how dissatisfied they are, and demand to speak with the manager. Oblige, and usher them to the quietest corner of the store for consultation. Try to reason with them. If you know you'll be taking a loss by accepting the item, explain that you're not authorized to do so. Tell them to speak with your sales rep, or let them know when you expect the next sales call. If they persist, and you sense the commotion is hurting business, consider which is the lesser of the evils. If necessary, make the refund just to be rid of them. Better that small loss than the noisy disruption of a promising business day.

In your career as the store owner, you'll find plenty of opportunity to deal with all types of people. You'll sell to your ideal customer, as well as people who do not yet figure in your market profile. Some customers, you'll learn to like, others to tolerate. To all of them, you're a service provider, the reliable source for a set group of products. Good customer relations requires nothing more than it takes to be a good neighbor. Treat people with respect, recognize their individuality, provide a quality product backed by service, and let them know you appreciate their business. They'll thank you for it with their continued support.

❧ 13 ❧

THE PROMOTIONAL PUSH

After you've completed your planning, hiring, training, purchasing, and setting up, an even greater challenge awaits you: the promotional push.

The push is actually a three-pronged marketing program entailing advertising, promotion, and public relations. For the moment, think of the three as separate but equally important facets of a cohesive whole. Your efforts in each of the areas impact the effectiveness of the others. They also set the pace and parameters of your success.

The promotional push will make or break your store. It's critical to your future as a specialty retailer that you understand the dynamics of an effective marketing program, and how to take full advantage of the advertising and promotional vehicles available to you. This chapter outlines those options so you can effectively plan your promotions for opening day and beyond. First we'll review the important role a marketing program plays in specialty retailing. Then the discussion turns to promotions, advertising, and public relations, the three components of an effective campaign. In the final section of the chapter, the options available to you in each of these areas are discussed in detail, with suggestions for utilizing each as you develop your own promotional strategy.

Letting the world know who, what, and where you are, and why you're in business, delivers that final ingredient that sparks your careful planning and good intentions to life. If *you* don't tell people about your store, no one else will. A marketing program is what generates interest and excitement about your store. By defining and describing the store for the buying public, you'll give it a reason to visit and buy. Some people will come out of curiosity, intrigued by your marketing. Some will come of necessity because they know, courtesy of your marketing efforts, they can fulfill a need at your store. Without a well-conceived marketing strategy, you could sit idle, waiting for the occasional shopper to stumble through the doors. You'll welcome such business for sure, but the trade you need, the shoppers who'll support your retail career, turn to your store for a purpose. Some customers will initially wander in off the streets, curious to check out the new store on the block. However, your store's success depends on how effective you are in convincing the people you've already identified as your target customers to visit the shop, and to keep them coming back. You provide them that reason through the various activities of your promotional push. As you build your store's reputation, reaching this group should be the main goal of your marketing strategy. Retailing without a thoroughly thought-out marketing strategy is akin to a shot in the dark. You may hit a mark just by being there, but the odds are you will miss your target. Your target audience, the shoppers you plan to serve with your retail venture, are a select group with the spending power and interest to guarantee a success with what you're selling.

An effective promotional campaign makes these people want to get up and buy from you. When your message reaches them, they should recognize why they need your store and come running. First they must receive your message. There's no best way to get it to them. An effective marketing program encompasses everything you can use to get your store's name before the buying public. Visibility and awareness go hand in hand with retail prosperity. Without the former, you won't reach the latter.

The problem and challenge facing you is that every businessperson realizes the importance of an aggressive marketing program. There are millions of messages out there, all vying for John and Jane Shopper's limited attention. The marketing challenge you've assumed with your retail venture is to come up with a message that cuts through this advertising fog, reaching the people you consider your preferred clients. That means in today's market, the promotional push must reach both wide and near. If you're to be successful, you must use whatever means are freely available to tell the world about the store, and then spend to generate buying interest out of that awareness from the select few.

The alternative is . . . Well, there is no alternative. To fail at marketing is to fail at retail. It's that simple and that final. What if you open the store and nobody shows up? Ignore your promotional push, and you'll find out.

Your entire retail venture depends on how well you meet this marketing challenge. Your campaign, or strategy, warrants as much of your time and attention as everything else about your business, including the business plan. There's a basic difference to the function of the business plan and the marketing strategy, though. The business plan is about successive goals, a conceptual road map of where you want to take your business. When you reach one goal, you set your sights on the next. Your marketing strategy is all about the process of getting there. It's the itinerary of what you must do to move from business goal to goal. If the plan is a map, then your marketing strategy guides you to where to fuel up. Miss enough of those stops and you ain't going nowhere.

You wouldn't trust a travel itinerary to memory; if you did, you'd probably miss a stop. That's why it's important to develop your marketing strategy into a written document. Committing your plans to paper will help you organize the varied activities the effort requires. Later you can measure your successes and misses against these plans, and revise your strategy accordingly.

THE THREE ELEMENTS OF MARKETING

Before you begin writing your marketing plan, thoroughly consider the three aspects of your promotional push—advertising, promotion, and public relations—their functions, and their implications.

ADVERTISING IS WHERE YOU'LL SPEND MOST OF YOUR MONEY

Advertising poses the toughest challenge in the marketing strategy. It's the one component that requires you to spend significant amounts of money, with no guarantee of a return. And for any advertising campaign to be effective, it must appear frequently and consistently to ensure your message will reach your audience. There's no such thing as free advertising. You can come up with ways to generate free publicity or create promotions at no real cost. But advertising is going to cost you every time you use it. The problem is that you won't know what you're getting until the money is spent. There's an old adage that only half of all advertising is effective, but that no one knows which half it is. After you've been in business a while, you'll know which advertising media work for you, and which don't. Getting there and gaining that insight is a costly process of trial and error.

PROMOTION MEANS DEVELOPING TRAFFIC

Promotion, on the other hand, won't cost you nearly as much as advertising. It has more to do with developing a reputation for you and your business, and creating excitement around the store. The bottom line is still generating sales, but with promotion you can be a little freer in what you do. Effectively handled, promotion spotlights the store and what you're selling by giving people a reason to come to the store, and reason to buy once there. With advertising you deliver a message to the consumer through the medium of choice. Promotion fills that message with activity and excitement that help create the awareness that makes people want to visit the store.

PUBLIC RELATIONS CREATES FAVORABLE IMPRESSIONS

Public relations, the third component of the marketing troika, keeps your store name before the public in a positive way. It's advertising you don't pay for, and free publicity for your promotions. You should use public relations as an indirect form of advertising and promotion to create favorable perceptions of you and your store. By intent, public relations should reach a much wider audience than advertising and promotions. Good PR will have a residual effect on business, so you won't be able to gauge its impact within a week or a month. When people think well of you as an individual, they'll admire what you're doing in your business. That good will benefit the store. When the public knows you as an active, caring member of the community, some will go out of their way to support the store.

PUTTING THE THREE ELEMENTS TOGETHER

We'll get into specifics of using these components of a marketing program shortly. For now, start thinking in terms of how you want to present your business to the buying public. Consider what you need to accomplish in these areas. No matter what you sell, you want to tap every public relations avenue available to you to create awareness of the store. Approach promotions as a way to provide shoppers with an incentive that compels them to buy from you. Finally, you'll reinforce the awareness you create with these tools with advertising to reach the people you've already identified as your core customers.

In an effective marketing program these three components reinforce and contribute to the effectiveness of one another. The savvy retailer uses PR to get the name out there, devises an in-store promotional event or some other activity as a motivator, and then invests in advertising to tell the right customer why he should shop at the store. The mechanics of an effective marketing program are far more complex, but all entail awareness, activity, and motivation.

Awareness is the building block of the entire effort. Shoppers must know where you are and what you sell before they can even consider visiting the store. You generate awareness with everything you do related to the store, from hanging a sign to making an appearance on the local talk show to discuss the new season's merchandise. Building awareness requires that you keep your name before the public through every means available, from printing your logo on shopping bags to donating prizes in the store name to the local charity drive.

The promotional activity is more directly related to the business of selling. Your responsibilities, as business promoter, require that you conceive of and create ways to interest the buying public in the store and what it sells. That encompasses everything from how you display merchandise in your showroom to participating in off-site business opportunities like trade shows for consumers. Sales events, in-store demonstrations, giveaways, contests, and previews all give shoppers a reason to visit your store.

Unless the shopper is made aware of what you're doing, though, these will all prove fruitless efforts. You motivate through your public relations and advertising efforts. PR helps tell people, "I'm here, this is what I sell, come check it out." Advertising carries a specific message developed to stimulate sales. That message can be general—"Just arrived, a limited selection of the newest styles"—or specific—"Tomorrow only, 10 percent off everything in the store." The message may also be carried to only a select group of buyers through direct mail. However and to whomever it is communicated, you want that message to inspire purchase activity.

HOW MUCH DO YOU NEED TO SPEND?

On average, established retailers spend less than 5 percent of their annual operating budget for marketing activities. Most of that amounts to an investment in some form of advertising, followed by promotions, and finally public relations. Since you're just starting up operations, you should plan to spend much more, at least twice what the established retailer invests in marketing activities.

All successful promotional activities contribute an ongoing benefit to business. The longer you're in business, the better known the store. As the store develops a reputation as a source for what it sells, your marketing responsibilities will ease. You'll still need to do all you can to keep the store's name before the public, but you can concentrate your promotional push on motivating shoppers into the store.

As the owner of a start-up, however, you've nothing to build on. To your potential customers, your business is a blank page. The store enjoys no reputation; shoppers don't yet know what to expect from the business. Your first marketing challenge is making people aware you're there and explaining what you offer. This requires a combination of all three elements. Essentially you must use these tools to jump-start the business. A week before opening, your store shows promise; after opening day, it must deliver sales. You want your marketing activity to allow you to hit the ground running, so you're seeing sales from day one. Therefore, during this make-or-break first year, plan to spend more for marketing activities, proportionate to your other expenditures, than at any other time in your business.

If you followed the advice on developing your business plan outlined in Chapter Six, you already have a good idea of what you can spend. If not, you need to come up with, and commit to, a first-year marketing budget. Be liberal: As the year unfolds, you may see the need to spend more. Don't even think about spending less. When the economy gets soft and sales activity slows, advertising is one of the first areas many retailers look to, to reduce costs. For the start-up retail entrepreneur, that would be folly. The initial and most important challenge for you, as owner, is to make people aware of the store in a way that motivates them to buy. Everything else about your business depends on it.

DEVELOPING YOUR MARKETING PROGRAM

Your marketing program will evolve over time as you measure the effectiveness of the different options available to you. This is one of those learning endeavors in retailing that represents an expensive but very necessary education for you. There are no set solutions. Every market, every product, and every audience requires its own marketing strategy. But there should be a purposeful plan behind all you do. It's simply too expensive an undertaking to go about haphazardly. Review all you've written about what you're selling, who your customers are, and who will be your suppliers. Start thinking about what you can do to bring the three together in your store.

Then set to work devising a comprehensive marketing program you can use for your promotional push. As mentioned earlier, put it in writing.

Your marketing program will be a product of your budget, how much you can afford to spend on promotions for opening day and throughout the year ahead. Whatever you spend, you should be measuring the effectiveness of each advertising and promotional vehicle as you use it. Your plan should enable you to track the results of each as you try to identify your best media mix. (See the form included in this chapter.) As your business grows, you'll want to return to this plan and measure the effectiveness of each component against your expectations. Right now your plan must be made from guesswork, hunches about how to get most from the conventional marketing tools. As your store grows into its success, you'll want to refine it into a science of knowing exactly what you must do to get shoppers into your store, in every season.

PLANNING AND TRACKING YOUR PROMOTIONAL PUSH Work Sheet

Use this form as a model for developing your promotional push and tracking the results. You need to maintain a log of what promotional vehicles you use, when, and cost, and the results. In order to track results, your staff must be trained to ask all customers how they heard about the store, and keep a tally of their responses. Coupons, flyers, or direct mail pieces that invite customers to bring the document for a discount or special offer are helpful for tracking results as well.

The Promotional Push

PUBLIC RELATIONS RELEASE

Sent to:	Date	Date Used	Responses
_____	_____	_____	_____
_____	_____	_____	_____

PROMOTIONS

Event:	Date	How Advertised	Cost Responses	Sale	Giveaway
_____	____	_____	_____	_____	_____
_____	____	_____	_____	_____	_____

ADVERTISING

Vehicle/Medium	Date	Frequency/ Schedule Cost	Responses
Newspaper	_____	_____	_____
Radio	_____	_____	_____
TV	_____	_____	_____
Cable TV	_____	_____	_____
Billboard	_____	_____	_____
Direct Mail	_____	_____	_____

Initially there's only one promotional event on your itinerary: Opening Day. Before your store actually opens its door, your marketing goal is to create as much excitement as you can around this event. The new store in town always garners attention simply because it is new. That's a promotional opportunity available only once; use it to create as much awareness as possible. At the same time, you must think beyond that and develop a long-term promotional push that will pull shoppers into the store throughout the first year. Throw your full marketing support behind opening day, and plan to follow it up, consistently, week by week, as you investigate the impact of the various marketing tools available to you. Remember: There's no combination that will work for every store in every market. You'll learn from your mistakes and successes over time.

Once you develop a better understanding of each concept and marketing element, you can devise an overall marketing strategy. An effective promotional campaign incorporates the strengths of all three components to reach the widest possible audience. Consider public relations your vehicle for generating free publicity about your store's arrival, what's unique about it and why shoppers should care. Promotions create events that give people a reason to visit the store or buy from you. Advertising carries the message of PR and promotions, but you pay for it. As you develop your strategy, you always want to look for ways to get maximum bang for every promotional buck you spend. Look for ways to accomplish the most with the least spending as you develop a strategy in the main components of your advertising effort.

LEARN TO USE YOUR MONEY TWICE

There's no way to avoid the costs of a marketing program. The dollars spent represent a vital and necessary investment. And this is an expenditure more critical now than at any time in the store's history. Yet there's no tangible result from the investment. Spend for inventory that doesn't sell and you get credit; spend your money frivolously for advertising that doesn't work and call it a loss. With the need to experiment as you work toward that winning promotional mix, you want to make sure you're getting the most benefit from every dollar spent. In effect, you want to go about the process so that you use your money twice.

USE SHOPPING BAGS AS TRAVELING BILLBOARDS

Take something as basic as the store bag as an example. Every store needs bags for merchandise. There's no way around that; it's a necessary expense. You can save a little money buying generic paper or plastic bags, or you could spend a little more and have the store name and logo imprinted on every bag. That amounts to money well spent. Not only do you have the bags you need, but every bag that leaves your store is a walking advertisement for the business. For that advertisement to leave an impression on those who see it, you need a distinctive typeface for the store name, an eye-catching visual, or a combination of both for your logo. In time, the logo becomes a recognized symbol of that store. As soon as shoppers see it, it stirs their memories about the store and what it sells.

MAKE SURE YOUR STORE'S NAME SERVES A MARKETING PURPOSE

The best names define what the store sells, at least in the start-up phase. Manny's Toys can go by Manny's once the business is a local establishment. When establishing the store and creating an identity, that qualifier helps. Another thing to consider when coming up with a store name is where it falls in the alphabet. Believe it or not, this is an important determination to make, especially during the early stage of the business. A lot of people let their fingers do the walking and shop through the Yellow Pages. When they don't know the name of a store, they turn to the directory heading and work their way down the list of store names. Those listings appear in alphabetical order. The stores at the top of the list, in the front of the alphabet, get the calls first. If one has what the shopper wants and is conveniently located, there's no reason to shop further. If you can't define what you sell in your name, you may want to think in terms of the alphabetical listing. You're going to pay to have the name and logo turned into your symbol, so do all you can to get the most from that investment.

PUT YOUR NAME AND LOGO EVERYWHERE

Everything you do and everything that leaves the store should wave your store banner before the public. When you're giving away pens, pins, or any other premium, make sure whoever sees them knows who supplied them. When buying such premiums, selectively spend for those with the longest staying power. A pen or pencil promotes the store as long as it writes; the message adorning it can be easily missed. A desktop notepad stays around longer, and every time people use it, they meet your message. Refrigerator magnets with store name and number provide an in-home advertisement with years of service. A key chain may not last as long, but gets the store name before more people. Nicely done T-shirts with your name and number may cost more, but serve as walking billboards, carrying your message to places you could never reach with the marketing tools available to you.

MAKE SURE YOU MENTION ALL YOUR PRODUCTS AND SERVICES

Whatever you use, be it a giveaway or advertising paid for by you, mention what you sell and the services you provide. Someone who sees your message will need just what you're offering. In the newspaper and on the commercial airwaves, a share of those exposed to your ad may not need what you're promoting in that one ad, but they may need something else you do have. If they don't need it now, they may next week. While you're trying to harvest sales today, sow the seeds for tomorrow's business as well. You're paying for the ad space or airtime, so it's up to you to make the investment pay for itself.

DON'T FORGET THE SIDESHOWS

With in-store events, take your hint from the circus: There's the big tent and then there are all the sideshows. When you plan a big promotional event, make sure there are little events, little areas of activity, to spotlight what else goes on in the store. Your Grand Opening will generate a lot of hoopla merely because the doors are finally opening. It should be a celebration and sales event that spotlights everything you want shoppers to know, and tell their friends, about the store.

LOOK FOR, AND EXPLOIT, HIDDEN MARKETING OPPORTUNITIES

As the store owner, you decide how and where the money is to be spent for the good of your business. Always look for the hidden opportunity that will enable you to realize a promotional benefit from your spending. When paying to have your space renovated before you move in, make sure there's a sign outside telling people what's coming and when you expect to open. If you must buy a delivery truck, make it your mobile billboard. If you use your car for business, invest in a magnetic sign that tells the public about your store, its location, what it sells, and the services it provides.

CONDUCT AN AGGRESSIVE PUBLIC RELATIONS CAMPAIGN

An aggressive public relations program will benefit every type of business, even the retail store. It's the area where you shape perceptions about the store and your commitment to the local community. Public relations operates in two realms. There's the publicity angle, whereby you use every available resource to publicize your business. You can use these same tools and things you do, particularly community involvement, to create positive perceptions in the community about your business. Effective use of PR allows you to shape those perceptions to benefit your business.

The nice thing about public relations is that it costs relatively little to use, as long as you handle it in-house. You can handle most of this yourself, once you know whom to contact. But if you consider it worth the effort and expense, or you can't juggle your schedule to take on yet another responsibility, you may want to hire a PR consultant to help publicize what you're doing. Not many retailers use them, so your search will probably lead you back to the Yellow Pages. Use the same hiring criteria as with any other consultant. You want the person with retail experience first.

Then you want them to show you samples of work done for other clients, preferably retailers, and provide you with the names of business references.

PR agents work either by the project or on retainer. You may hire one only to help with your opening day event, or to handle all aspects of your marketing program through the first year. Rates vary, depending on where you live, the size of your market, and the project. The most important thing any PR agent brings to the task is a working knowledge of the local media. Good ones already have established contacts with media personnel. However, that won't necessarily make a difference in how much publicity they can generate for a client. If you're doing something newsworthy, reporters will be in touch as soon as they hear about it, whether they hear of it from you or a PR professional.

USE PRESS RELEASES AS YOUR MAIN PR TOOL

The basic tool for letting the media know is the press release. Here's where you must take a reckoning about your own skills. If you've never mastered the art of written communication, hire someone who has to write your press releases. The people who'll receive your releases are communicators, and will judge you and your business first on how it's presented in the press release. Poor grammar and misspellings raise doubts about professionalism more than they elicit a response.

The best press releases are short, preferably one page, and provide a concise summary of why what you're doing or what you have to say should be considered of interest to an audience. At the top of the page would be your store name and logo, address, telephone number, and the name of a person to contact for more information: you. A headline summarizing what the press release is about—"Grand Opening for Innovative Toy Store Set for Next Week"—should appear beneath the name and logo, followed by the body of the release: a few paragraphs explaining what's newsworthy. It's important the first paragraph contain as much information as the recipient needs in order to make a decision. Often what's said in those opening lines will determine what, if any, further attention your announcement receives. In a few sentences, the release must establish what is going on, where, when, and why it's important to the readers, viewers, or listeners of that news organization. In the paragraphs that follow, elaborate on each of the points contained in the opening, and then wrap up with an invitation to get in touch with the contact for more information.

Press releases should be sent out whenever something of significant interest occurs at the store. Believe it or not, completely filling the day's newspaper is often an arbitrary process. Sometimes things make it into the paper because there's a hole in the page to fill. The editor takes the first news item on hand—your release if it's available.

GET INVOLVED IN YOUR COMMUNITY

Community involvement should be regarded as the other side of your public relations strategy. Properly played, community involvement emphasizes the name of the store more than its business activities. The positive perceptions that result have beneficial impact on the business; people feel so good about what you're doing, they want to support your business for it. Community involvement is not a onetime deal; it requires an ongoing commitment that demonstrates you value your community and want to be a good neighbor to your customers. There are passive and active components of this program.

The passive activities ask minimal involvement on your part: You write a check once a year to sponsor a baseball team or you let a church group set up their cake sale on the sidewalk in front of your store. All these little activities contribute to a positive perception of your business and the person behind it.

Community involvement, to be effective, asks active participation as well. To be involved these days, you must demonstrate you're a good neighbor through action. When there's a clean-up of the local park, get your staff members to turn out, paying them for the time if you must. With protecting the environment such a concern for everyone in the community today, the store owner can set an example for all and profit from the endeavor. At the very least, set up a recycling bin for the packaging that comes with what you sell, and encourage shoppers to use it. Use recycled paper for receipts and bags. If it's appropriate in your specialty, stock a selection of the "green" products deemed environmentally friendly. Not everyone will want to pay the extra price these products usually command, but they'll feel better knowing that's an option available to them where they shop.

Community involvement also means being the spokesperson for what you sell. With all the debate over gun control in recent years, some gun retailers find themselves eagerly sought-out spokespersons of a particular point of view. Not everyone agrees with what they have to say. For those who do, their customers, the fact that these dealers are willing to represent their views strengthens the bond with the store. Of course, that's an extreme case, and community involvement on the political front poses as much risk as opportunity for the retailer. It can backfire. But when, by speaking out, you speak for your customers, you should consider it a duty and privilege to take the lead in espousing their views.

LOOK FOR WAYS TO GET FREE PUBLICITY

Publicity is a lot easier to come by than you think: It's just a matter of communicating with the right people at the right time, and then assisting them as best you can. When you read the day's newspaper or watch the local evening news, it's not always apparent how much work goes on behind the scenes to put that package together. The daily or weekly challenge for those who prepare those packages is filling them with meaningful and useful information. The news editors always need that fresh idea, that new angle on an old story that makes it relevant again. They look to people like you, or your PR agent, for useful leads. There's usually a little more involved than sending out a press release, but generating free publicity can prove as simple as that.

MAKE SURE YOUR NEWS ITEMS GET INTO THE RIGHT HANDS

Once you've got that release written, your next concern is getting it into the right hands. You can send it to the news department or to ''the editor,'' and you may get results. But putting a person's name on the envelope ensures someone will see it. And if it's not for her, she'll likely pass it along to the appropriate person. Before sending out a release, determine who should receive it. All media organizations employ people who specialize in particular aspects of the news. The bigger the organization, the more finely defined the categories. If you're in a small town, the editor, reporter, and salesman at your local weekly newspaper may be the same individual; at a nearby regional daily, there's probably an editor, managing editor, and specialists for sports, business, society, city hall, etc. A radio station may have one or two news staffers, while a TV station in the same market employs a producer, assignment editor, and the reporters you see on the screen each night. At a magazine you'll find an editor in chief, an executive and/or managing editor, and editors for each of the areas of news it covers.

Who should receive your press release depends on what you want to publicize. If it's a business concern—the fact that you're opening, a promotion on your staff, or sales trends—it should go to the business editor. If it's about what you sell, it should also go to the editor who covers that category: the sports editor if you've got big news about baseball mitts, for example. If you can't identify those people—all that's generally required is a telephone call to the news organization—then send your release to the name at the top of the staff listing. That's the editor or managing editor at a newspaper or magazine; the news editor for a radio station; and the assignment editor at the local TV station.

GO BEYOND THE NORM AND BECOME AN EXPERT SOURCE

If you want to make the most of your opportunities for free publicity, you'll need to be more involved in the process. Outside major metropolitan areas, the news personnel can be surprisingly accessible. Every reporter needs reliable, articulate sources for every story. Since you intend to be the expert in what you sell, make that expertise available to them.

Call the appropriate editor or reporter and introduce yourself. Always try and make a positive reference to past stories you've seen or read by the reporter in the course of the conversation. For all their hard work, the only time most media people hear from their audience is when there's a complaint. These people have egos like everyone else; your kind words will be remembered and serve as your best introduction.

After the formalities, explain a little about your store and your background and tell the reporter you'd be glad to talk whenever there's a need for someone in your field. Of course, it's to your benefit to approach the reporter with a specific story suggestion.

Watch and read the news, looking for ideas that might be expanded to include your store business. Human interest stories are always in demand, as are category-specific "how-to" pieces. These may demonstrate how to get more enjoyment from a hobby or interest, or simply show people what to look for when buying a particular item. Think creatively in terms of what people might want to know about what you sell. Not all your ideas will strike a chord with your media contacts, but when they do, it will help your business.

Talk shows on radio and local TV always need guests to fill their time slots. If you're a specialty dealer, there's probably a story to your business they'd love to feature. Even if you specialize in something that can be found in every town in America, you can add a local spin by showing listeners or viewers what's new or special about what's in your store.

Contact the show and try to wrangle an appearance. It won't hurt to try. If you're successful, and the appearance works for both you and the station, you could be asked on again, or given a monthly opportunity to share your expertise or field questions from consumers. You can't buy that kind of impact.

If there's enough of a local audience for what you sell, you may also be able to convince the area newspaper to accept a column written by you on the subject. The trick is to write in generalities even when being specific about your field. When you use your column to tout the benefits of particular products you're selling, it comes across as an ad, and your column's days will be numbered. The store will benefit enough just having the column written by you in print. It legitimizes your claims of being the local expert on what you sell.

Another way to generate free publicity is to create events, and not necessarily sales events. The appropriate activities depend on what you're selling but can range from previews and demonstrations of the new season's merchandise, to hosting some form of competition on-site. Also use your commitment to the community as a soapbox for garnering attention. Make a public event of your pledge or involvement, and challenge other retailers and businesses in the area to meet that commitment.

When working on any aspect of your marketing program, think

in terms of how you might strengthen its impact through freely generated publicity. Try to think like a reporter, always looking for a news angle behind what you're doing. Usually there's nothing there, but when there is, and you can convince the reporter of its interest, it will be the best marketing you never had to buy. Publicity is there for the asking, provided you learn how to ask. The people who can provide it for you want their next call to be from someone with a story worth telling. It can be you, if you step back from your business and reconsider it in terms of what's going on in the marketplace around you, and what your business has to do with it.

Persist, and know when to call. Timing can make all the difference. With any media, the half of the day leading up to deadline is a hectic time for staff members. For reporters on the morning paper, it's the hours after lunch and into evening; at the afternoon and evening paper, it's the morning hours until midafternoon. For the producer at your town's midday radio talk show, mornings are crunch time. Make your contacts during these hectic periods and your suggestions stand a good chance of being missed. Call in the slow periods, when the same people are unwinding from deadline pressure, and they'll have the time to talk and listen to what you have to say.

One final note. Free publicity should be exactly that. Free. You should never trade anything for coverage by a news organization. The majority of reporters have standards and wouldn't think of asking. If there's a request for a product to review, it should be filled by your supplier. Anything beyond that is wrong and will eventually catch up with that contact. Let that be someone else's problem. Any reputable news organization wants to cover a story worth telling, and nothing more. Your only obligation is recognition of the job well done.

USE PROMOTION TO GENERATE TRAFFIC

If public relations and advertising spread the word about you and your business, specific promotions provide those who hear that message with a reason to visit the store. Promotions work for the store in two arenas. In the retail marketplace at large, your promotions distinguish your store from all others by focusing on some aspect of what you're doing or how you're selling. Inside the store, promotion serves more to direct shoppers' attention to your merchandise and whatever you want to highlight.

The promotions that reach out encompass things you do to draw people into the store. You may use advertising and public relations to carry the message of your promotions, but the promotion stands alone. Promotional events, once conceived and created by you, generate excitement to focus attention on your business.

You begin with your Grand Opening and attendant festivities. Sure, you're celebrating that your store is finally open. The real purpose behind all the hoopla, however, is to get people into the store and let them see what your business offers them. Throughout the years ahead it will be up to you to come up with other special events that promote that kind of interest. Holidays, particularly long holiday weekends, lend themselves to promotions, as do seasonal activities like "back to school" shopping.

Other forms of promotion may not seem so obvious in intent, but help familiarize your target audience with your service and selection. Some retailers incorporate educational training and seminars into their promotional mix. A fabric store, for example, might sponsor sewing classes a couple of nights a week. It's no surprise the people who'll enroll bring with them a pressing need for the very products the store sells. Educational and training programs also help forge long-term interest in the category, ensuring the store a steady stream of customers for years ahead.

Promotions to the public need not be so subtle. People respond to any offer of free merchandise or significant savings. Either promotional approach serves as a subtle ploy for promoting the entire business. The gift or discount lures shoppers to the store. Once they're there, it's up to you to use your promotional skills to turn their curiosity into a sale.

That's what effective promotion does. It uses an activity or incentive to expose the customer to the store and what it offers in products and services. Participating in a local trade show promotes the business just as well as an annual inventory reduction sale does. You're using an aspect of your business to reach more consumers and expose them to everything else you do at the store.

A successful promotional strategy has two facets. The first part seeks to attract the shopper to your business; in the second part you try and direct their attention to a particular item or department. This works on the telephone as well as in person. When someone calls in an order and you mention the sale item of the day, you're promoting your business. In the store you can't just stand up and shout about what you want to move. Instead you'll rely on visual cues to direct the shoppers' attention to what you're trying to sell.

PROVIDE VISUAL CUES FOR YOUR CUSTOMERS

Everything about how you handle products on the showroom floor should figure in your promotional plans. Your suppliers can furnish you with counter cards, headers, point-of-purchase displays, and posters as part of their promotional support. Unless these sales aids are visible, and the products they promote easily accessible, they'll have minimal impact on sales.

One promotional tool that's often neglected is store design as it determines product placement. Your signage promotes in the sense that it directs shoppers to your departments. In the aisles, a product's position on the shelf or rack will directly influence sales. Those displayed at eye or ground level tend to get noticed more than everything in between. The same for products at the ends of the aisles.

You'll learn to use these to your advantage, as tools for creating visual cues to motivate the shopper. Use these spaces to highlight the products that need the promotion. Don't waste them on products that will sell consistently no matter where you place them. If you want to see this product-placement-based promotion carried to its most scientific, take a stroll around your nearest supermarket. If the store is part of a regional chain, you'll see promotional products at the ends of each aisle, the highest-profit items at eye level, and impulse items at the checkouts.

Place your biggest sellers, the high-demand products, at the rear of the store. On the way there, shoppers will have an opportunity to visually sample everything else you sell. You need to give accessories and impulse items as much visible exposure as possible. Use placement as a trigger to jog the memory and remind the shopper of things he may or may not need. With some products, allowing customers to handle as well as see them promotes the sale. When selling any type of equipment, it's better to have it out where shoppers can get hands-on experience. The same shopper who might hesitate to ask a clerk to unlock a case won't hesitate to pick it up and sample it unassisted. That may be all it takes to convince that shopper to buy.

Promotion is a process of developing awareness and interest in your merchandise, doing whatever it takes to encourage people to visit the store and buy. Effectively handled, it enhances the appeal of an item by giving the shopper incentive to buy now. Every form of a sales event is a promotion. Advertising carries the message, but the event is what draws the crowds. Everything you do to promote the store and individual products should have a beneficial impact on sales or strengthen perceptions of why consumers should shop your store.

Displays, on the showroom and in the shop windows, offer an ideal opportunity to promote your merchandise. A promotion, by intent, is a temporary activity. Promotion highlights a product by drawing the shopper's attention to it in some special way. If the spotlight always fell on the same product, it would be business as usual. By changing promotions—by highlighting this first, then that—you can create ongoing excitement. The shopper has a reason to visit the store, to see what's featured, what's new, and what's on sale. Every change in promotion gives cause for another visit.

Take advantage of the promotional opportunities available to you, free of charge, in your store windows. Set up displays that convey your enthusiasm about what you sell. Use seasonal themes to generate excitement. Keep the displays fresh, rotating them monthly at least to force people passing by to reconsider what the store has to offer. Your window may offer your best chance to communicate with them. It should be powerful and colorful enough to cause them to stop, and should invite them into the store for a better look.

So think of ways to use your display opportunities for maximum promotional benefit. By rotating the merchandise, changing the display to put the focus on a new item, you continually confront the shopper with new reasons to buy. Your create the motivation to look around and see what the store has now, to reconsider what it offers in terms of the shopper's own needs. The promotions that work inspire shoppers to continually rediscover what the store has to offer. It's still the same store, but effective promotion just gives the shopper a new way to look at it.

FORCE RESPONSES THROUGH ADVERTISING

No matter how effective your PR campaign, or how creative your promotions, the efforts will falter without a strong advertising program backing them up. This is the critical third element of your marketing program, the one that turns sales potential into retail power. With PR and promotions you put the word out; advertising carries that message directly to those you want to reach. The other two are more gradual processes; their impact is not always easy to assess. Advertising runs on a set schedule; you know when it hits, and when to expect results. With public relations and promotions, you can afford to learn as you go; with advertising, you pay as you learn. This is a necessary and basic expense of retailing. PR shapes perceptions, and promotion creates excitement. Advertising takes all that directly to the consumer in your attempt to force a response.

Mastering this crucial third of marketing is not as simple as buying some newspaper space or airtime, however. Unless the advertising vehicles you use convey the right message to the right audience, your efforts and investments will be wasted. Successfully advertising asks more than an occasional appearance. Think not in terms of specific ads, but of an advertising campaign. Although you may be promoting one product or one sale in any individual ad, you should consider every ad one component in an overall strategy to bring shoppers into your store.

IT'S ESSENTIAL TO GET THE MOST BANG FOR YOUR ADVERTISING BUCK

The real challenge to this process is to get the most effective use of each advertising dollar. Advertising poses an expensive undertaking in any market, any medium. As a start-up retailer, you'll need to spend more and get more from your ad budget. Sure, an established business needs to advertise, but not in the same way a newcomer does. Both want to attract shoppers into the store and broaden the customer base. The store that has been in business for a few years enjoys a reputation. People know where it's located. They've seen its ads before and have some preconceived notion of why they should shop there. You, as a start-up retailer, must use your early advertising to build that reputation, to grow from the unknown to a known and respected source. If you've got the only game in town, you approach the process as one of building awareness. When you're the latest entry in a developed market, you must build awareness and establish your store as a preferable alternative to the forces already at play.

When economic times are tight, when the economy slows, two theories of advertising prevail. One school holds that the retailer should reduce ad spending since there's nothing happening in the market anyway. The other school says the retailer should spend more, for an aggressive advertising program is all that will bring shoppers into the store. You'll have the opportunity to support either theory later when your business enters its first lull period. For the first year, though, every retail entrepreneur should consider him or herself a backer of the "spend all you can" approach. You're starting with zero sales. Much of your future depends on how fast and how far you can build on that in the short term. Public relations and promotion should make people aware of what you're trying to do with this venture and suggest why they should visit the store. Look to advertising to bring them there.

The challenge is to ensure you get the most result from what's available to you, in terms of media and money. You only have so much to spend, and you want to spend it wisely. You also want to spend it slowly. During certain periods of the year, during your peak sales season and in the months surrounding your grand opening, you'll increase ad spending significantly. But for a campaign to be effective, it must be an ongoing effort. Your advertised specials should change week by week, but you want to maintain a certain consistency in your advertising to make an impression. Present your store name or logo to people enough times and they'll know the store, whether or not they've reason to visit it. That recognition will help when you're promoting something that does interest them.

There's no exact science to advertising for the owner of the start-up store. Next year's effective campaign will be a response to this year's experiment in advertising. You can't escape your need to test the effectiveness of different media early in your game. It's a costly lesson but one of the growing pains of building your business. What you learn this first year will serve your business for years to come. The only way to gain that insight is by using a combination of media until you find the mix that works for your store. You can eliminate some of that risk by carefully comparing the options open to you against what you already know about your target customers. In the beginning, focus your efforts on the group you consider to be your core consumers. You need that core of supporters as a foundation before you can build the business.

TO BE EFFECTIVE, AN AD MUST DO THREE THINGS

Every advertisement should accomplish three things for the store: tell shoppers who you are, where you are, and why they should care. The last part is what gets them to the store. When you place an ad, it should motivate people to visit the shop. It may be for the weekend sale you're sponsoring or because you've got the best selection of whatever it is you sell. Your advertising communicates something about the store to potential shoppers. The goal, of course, is to communicate something so alluring that they rush out to respond with their wallets. The message should define a tangible benefit the consumer will enjoy only by shopping with your store. That could mean a low price, the first chance at new merchandise or the latest style, or an opportunity to consult with an expert to find the right solution for a special need. An effective ad has an impact, even if it only makes shoppers aware of the new store in town.

The quality and appearance of your advertising contribute to consumers' perceptions of the store. Anything that comes across as cheap, cluttered, or pushy works against what you're trying to achieve. Spend what it takes to do it right.

There are many places to take your spending discussed below. Before deciding on any, consider the merits of each in terms of a total campaign, comprised of different elements, each reinforcing the messages carried in the others, and all working together for the good of your store.

SIGNS ARE THE MOST EFFICIENT FORMS OF ADVERTISING

The cheapest and most necessary form of advertising is the sign that hangs outside your storefront. It should be neat, easy to read, and well lit. If the store name doesn't readily define the nature of your business, list what you sell on the sign. When your business sits on a street, always give the store phone number prominent display on the sign. Some retailers treat their windows as a second sign, identifying the store with name and logo or highlighting what the store sells. Every sign should be neat and easy to read from a reasonable distance; across the street or across the mall corridor. If you're not an artist yourself, hire a professional sign painter to do the job. Unless you're selling vegetables from a roadside stand, your homey touch won't help your endeavor. The sign comes to be considered as much a symbol of the business as what you stock and sell. You'll probably be living with it for a long time. Make sure it says all you need to say in the best way.

A sign works for the store every day. People walk or stroll by, and there it is announcing your name and what you sell to all who pass that way. After a while, though, people get used to it and that sign becomes part of the landscape. The only ones who notice are those new to the area. The sign should be distinctive enough to serve as an enduring symbol of your business, reminding people that you're there and what you sell.

BILLBOARDS REACH VERY BROAD AUDIENCES

When you're starting the business or when you want to reach the broadest possible market, you may want to consider the merits of billboard advertising. Billboards communicate something to everyone who passes that way. They can be expensive to use, however. Cost is a matter of the size of the sign, the production costs involved, and the visibility of the location. Most billboards constitute roadside attractions along highways and byways. In recent decades the billboard concept has evolved into more of an ever-present advertising medium. Walk the streets of any large city and you'll face paid advertising: on the sides and insides of buses, taxis, and trains; lining the platform at commuter rail stations; and gracing sidewalks, bus stops and buildings. Even indoors, billboards have found a place for themselves in poster-sized advertisements to be found wherever people might see them, including rest rooms.

You might think with so much signage vying for the consumer's attention, the message of a billboard would be lost in the clutter. The human eye, though, constantly seeks out new stimulation in the environment. A billboard provides that stimulation. When it's new, just about everyone who passes that way will notice the message. Since these signs usually end up in places where crowds pass and linger, a good share of those exposed to the sign will investigate what it has to say. Unlike your store sign, which must stand and identify your store for years, the same billboard advertisement in the same location will lose its impact over a much shorter period of time. People will soon fail to notice it. If you plan to use these signs as a means of advertising, change your message regularly, or rotate the same message through different locations periodically.

The message you carry on any outdoor advertising medium must be one that can stand the test of time. Remember these paid-for signs will remain in the same place for weeks or months. Therefore, billboards, indoors and out, are not a good forum for promoting a product at a price. Better to tell shoppers about what you have in general. Use them as a tool for building awareness more than cultivating interest in any single product. Consider them more a forum for generic advertising that directs the shopper's attention back to the main business. That's why a billboard warrants serious attention when you're opening the business. You'll miss a share of your audience with your advertising in newspapers or on the airwaves, but a billboard at a busy intersection lets everyone who passes that way know your store has arrived.

Your first thoughts may be to display that message where it will be seen by the widest possible audience. Before you do, take a look at the demographic profile of where your audience lives and works. The billboard at the town's busiest intersection may put the store name before more people, but one closer to their neighborhood speaks directly to the people you want to reach.

Your decisions on whether to use a billboard, how many to use, and where to place them will be a product of the local cost for use of that space, the production fee for your ad, and the amount of your advertising budget. Larger signs can prove an extremely costly form of advertising, especially when your budget is limited. A pair of billboards in two busy intersections will get your name before many more people. The venture could also consume a disproportionate share of your media budget in the process. Better to go to smaller signs and back them up with a campaign in other media.

Consistency and frequency are what make any advertising campaign effective. If you shoot your budget blanketing the area with billboards that are here one month and gone the next, you may push your store toward a similar fate.

Billboard advertising makes sense for you, provided it represents only one aspect of a cohesive advertising campaign. To find out what's available in your area, check in your Yellow Pages under the listing "Advertising—Outdoor." Better yet, next time you see a sign or billboard where you'd like to have your message displayed, step up to it and read the fine print. You'll usually find the name of the company leasing that space and a telephone number. Most of these companies handle everything from the rental to the production of your ad. If not, they can refer you to someone who will provide whatever services they don't.

SELECT THE MOST EFFECTIVE FORMS OF PRINT ADVERTISING FOR YOUR STORE

Mention advertisement and most people immediately think of something that runs in the local newspaper. For retailers, newspaper advertising is, and will likely remain, one of the preferred means of reaching customers. The major problem with newspaper advertising, however, is one shared by all conventional media: It carries your message to a broad spectrum of the local populace, only a few of whom may be the people you need to reach. This tends to dilute the effectiveness of your advertising spending. Newspaper advertisements in the largest markets, served by the large-circulation newspapers, may seem excessive by your budget standards.

In recent years, some of these same newspapers launched what are called *zone publications,* special sections of the paper included in editions destined only for households in certain zip code areas. If you have demographic data that indicate the people you want to reach live only in certain parts of town, these sections can prove a cost-effective way to get your message across. Another viable alternative worth investigating is the weekly newspaper. Any community, even a good-sized neighborhood within a city, has its own weekly newspaper. Again, if it's distributed where those you want to reach live, it will provide a way to stretch your advertising dollar and reach only those you need to reach.

When investigating your print options, don't think only in terms of area newspapers. Many other publications provide an inexpensive alternative to spending with your major daily. Freely distributed shoppers, Penny Savers, and local entertainment guides all accept retail advertisements that will be seen by a large number of people. If your store targets a particular age group, you can save money and strengthen your message by talking directly to them in publications only they read. College newspapers provide an ideal and relatively cheap forum for reaching young consumers.

Some communities have their own papers for mature readers, or specific ethnic groups.

Magazine advertising, particularly in slick regional or city publications, represents an entirely different tool from newspaper advertising. For one thing, space in these publications carries a higher price, and they don't lend themselves to the same types of ads. A newspaper ad, like the newspaper, carries a sense of immediacy. Reading a magazine is a more relaxing undertaking. The newspaper will be read in a day; the magazine may be around the house for a month, or at least until the next issue appears. Therefore, it's not the place for the price-based ads you'd use in the newspaper. The magazine, like the billboard, works better as a forum for generic advertising, for perception building. With a magazine you'll also be reaching a more exclusive audience. If you want to reach affluence, you can do it on those glossy pages. If your business is geared more toward Everyman, stick with the newspaper.

IT'S CONSISTENCY THAT COUNTS MOST WITH PRINT ADVERTISING

Whatever print media you settle on, consistency is what counts in your advertising. Even where everyone reads the newspaper, not everyone reads the paper every day. The occasional ad is often missed. If you advertise consistently, sooner or later your ad will be seen by all. With a monthly or weekly publication, the decision on when to advertise is already made: Put an ad in every issue. With a daily newspaper, though, you must be more selective. Your ad should appear at least once a week. Which is the golden day? Most papers have a higher circulation on Sunday, so that may make it the day of choice. But that's also the day the newspaper has the most ads vying for the shoppers' attention. If yours is small, it could be missed. The papers toward midweek grow fatter as grocery stores place their ads. That helps increase readership, but again there are lots of ads in competition.

There's something good and bad to be said about advertising any day of the week. What you, as your store's advertising agent, need to do is decide what day of the week you'll advertise, then stick with it. Don't leave the ad placement up to the newspaper. Request that your ad run in the section of the paper you expect your customers will read most closely: for example, the business section if you're selling office equipment, or the society pages if you specialize in fine china. Run the ad in the same place on the same day every week. After a while, the people you want to reach will turn there automatically to see what you're offering this week.

Print advertising should always present shoppers with a compelling reason to visit the store. The message may be a new product, a sale price, or a three-day event, but the ad should convey a sense of urgency that will motivate the shopper. In competitive industries retailers often use "laundry lists" of product names, key features, and prices in their print ads. The message is simple and direct: Here's what we're selling and here's what it will cost you. Other retailers highlight a particular product at an attractive price as a means of attracting as many customers as possible to the store. Some larger retailers feature "loss leaders": products they're selling at or below cost to attract shoppers into the store. Once there, they hope to step shoppers up to a higher-priced product, or get them to buy something that's not on sale. Whatever strategy you use, your print ads should always promote a particular item and event, and the store in general.

If mail-order sales figure prominently in your business plan, you'll probably be placing your ads in a variety of specialty publications, "buff books" that cater to the interests of a highly specialized audience. In many retail specialties, mail order is the most competitive part of the marketplace. Unless yours is a one-of-a-kind store catering to a select customer base, you can lose your hide going head to head with national mail-order retailers. Price is their only game; if your price isn't the lowest among the ads, you won't get the sale. If you must rely on mail order, you'll be advertising in specialty publications. Use the ads there as a forum for promoting the unique selection at your store and the specialty aspect of the business. If your category is restricted, enough people will respond just because they know your store is a source for the special products they need.

ADVERTISING ON THE AIRWAVES IS DIFFICULT TO MASTER

Advertising on commercial airwaves, be it radio or TV, can prove a more difficult process for the retailer. For one thing, commercial advertising on television in general, and radio in the major markets, is even more expensive than putting your message in print, and the need for advertising frequency is greater. Once it appears, the print ad remains accessible to your audience as long as the paper or magazine remains around the house. With broadcast media, however, the inattentive consumer may miss your full message the first time he or she is exposed to your ad. And there's no guarantee everyone you want to reach is listening or watching any single time the ad airs. In order to reach them all, it must run several times throughout the day, or the week. The expense quickly adds up. Add to that the high cost of production. A poorly produced ad on television reflects back on the retailer in a negative way. Even if you could afford to have your commercial professionally produced, you probably can't afford to run it often during those prime viewing hours when your customers sit before the tube.

Some retailers use cable television advertising as a more cost-effective way of reaching their audience, running a series of ads on the channel or during the program that has a direct connection with their core business. It makes sense for the crafts store to advertise during the "How to Paint" half hour, and for the hardware store to state its case during the home improvement show.

But even these targeted efforts can prove costly for the retailer on a limited budget. And the impact of the advertising may not be measurable for some time. You're better served by trying to wrangle a guest appearance on the local talk show to discuss basic techniques. Or to spend your time and money putting together your own instructional program to air on the local cable-access channel. Later on, when your business is well established, you can afford to spend for TV advertising. In the beginning, your money may be better spent with radio.

One of the nice things about radio is that it's easy to segment the market. There are as many station formats as there are customer types: jazz, rock, adult contemporary, easy listening, gospel, all news, all talk, all sports, country, etc. Your target customers probably listen to only a combination of a few.

But even if you can make an educated guess as to what stations your shoppers listen to, guessing when they listen poses a bit more of a challenge. If they're morning listeners, when in the morning? Some people drive to work, others commute by train. Are they listening between 6:00 A.M. and 7:00 A.M., or between 7:00 A.M. and 8:00 A.M.? Any doubts means your commercial should air both hours, and every day during the week. Radio gets results, as long as your message is consistent and airs on a regular basis. But be careful, you can expend your whole budget working toward that.

When an ad appears in print, people must refer back to it. Similarly, the first time someone hears or sees an ad over the airwaves, they probably miss part of the message, or aren't completely sure of what it said. They need to be exposed to it more than once for it to have an impact. Even then, unless you're shouting about some sale of a limited duration, it may be a while before they respond. And that response is difficult to measure. When you're operating on a tight budget, and trying to stretch the impact of your ad dollars, the commercial airwaves can quickly use up what you've got to spend. Unless your store is situated in a very small market, the cost of airtime is expensive. And that expense is compounded by your need to get that message on the airwaves as often as possible.

TV and radio commercials work when you want to make that big initial splash or your store's success allows the budget to fund an ongoing broadcast advertising campaign. These expenditures should figure into your total marketing campaign, but not as its major components. There's just too much at stake and too little to spend for you to take the chance.

DETERMINING HOW MUCH YOUR ADVERTISING WILL COST

Before you select your media mix, you need to determine what it will cost you to advertise. Contact the advertising department of the print and broadcast media that interest you and request their media kit. Those that don't have a media kit should be able to supply you with a rate card. As the name implies, it details the rates charged for ads of different sizes in print, or lengths, with broadcast media. Advertising, like everything else, is cheaper when you buy in bulk. When you commit to a schedule of several ads, the total package will be higher, but the cost per ad will be significantly lower.

The rate card tells only half the story, though, about what you're getting for your money. Every media representative should be able to furnish you with a market profile: a demographic description of the audience you'll be reaching by advertising through that vehicle. Never agree to any ad schedule until you've had a chance to compare that profile with what you've already determined about your target customers. The closer the match, the better the choice. When none exists, or there are so few people you'll be reaching, you may want to consider alternative approaches to advertising.

DIRECT MARKETING

Many retailers, through a costly process of trial and error, now consider direct mail advertising to be their most efficient tool for communicating with their target audience. The wisdom of this approach should be immediate and obvious to the retailer opening a specialty store.

Other forms of advertising take their message to a wide audience, in hope of reaching the few who might buy from the store. Direct or target marketing focuses the effort only on those you know to be your best sales prospects. You may also use this to target a special promotion at a specific demographic group. This is one of the ways building a database of customer names can help your promotional efforts. When you have something special to promote, you need only spend to reach those people who already demonstrated an interest in what you sell by buying from you. There are two ways to do this.

REACHING INTERESTED PARTIES THROUGH DIRECT MAIL

When you've something to promote, and you know who you need to reach and where they live, the easiest way to make sure your message gets through is by sending it directly to them. A simple postcard, containing the same information you'd include in an ad, may be all it takes. In many cities and suburbs, marketing companies put together promotional packages containing coupons from a variety of businesses, sent to all the households in the area. Whether you buy into one of these packages or conduct your own direct mail campaign, it's always good to include a coupon as it allows you to measure the effectiveness of the effort.

Direct mail can prove even more effective when you combine your advertising with information that will be of interest to the recipient. Since you know the people on your mailing list are interested in what you sell, you should present yourself as the expert in that category. An informative newsletter describing trends in the category, highlighting new merchandise, and demonstrating how the recipient may get more from that interest will strengthen perceptions of the store and keep the channels of communication open between you and your customer.

REACHING INTERESTED PARTIES THROUGH TELEMARKETING

People who enjoy hearing from the store in the mail probably won't appreciate hearing from you over the telephone. Most people resent a telephone call from a stranger as an unwelcome invasion of privacy. Telephone sales, as a means of attracting new customers or strengthening ties with the old, are a risky venture. Unless you're sponsoring a special event for special customers—by invitation only—consider the telephone dial off limits for promoting the start-up. It's one thing to take orders by phone, and another to try and get them.

There has been so much backlash against telemarketing in recent years, with all the talk of telephone scams, that a telemarketing program can do little, if anything, to enhance the stature of the new retail business. When an advertising venture draws negative responses, it's hurting the very business it was meant to help.

BE AWARE OF THE EMERGING MEDIA CHOICE

As new information technologies present themselves and become the norm in American households, they'll present you with many more ways to take your message directly to shoppers. Some will offer you the ability to target your message to a particular group with even greater precision than direct mail does today. Others will provide innovative ways to reach the broadest possible audience in hopes of attracting the few who will buy from you. Already the stage for the promotional future is being set with tests of new marketing tools.

The growing popularity of home shopping ushers in the potential for shopping any store from anywhere by telephone, fax, or computer. Many on-line services now carry scrolling electronic billboards that tout products and stores. Activate another screen and users can learn more from the store, and place an order.

The paper catalog, cherished by generations of shoppers, is already yielding to its electronic replacement, distributed on CD-ROM. People are learning to get product information by computer connection or on the home screen, via dedicated retail shows and networks or a video "infomercial." Readers of tomorrow's electronic morning newspaper will predetermine content, and the paper they view will carry advertising specific to their income, interests, and household demographics.

As an advertiser, you may one day be able to specify who gets your message in print or over the airwaves, using your customer profile as a guide. Your bill will tell you how many consumers received your message, and who they are.

Marketing professionals also continue to devise new ways to package advertising messages for the general public. Some stores and businesses take the moment a telephone caller is on hold as an opportunity to talk about their business or services. Expect to be able to buy "hold time" over the telephone lines as you would buy commercial time on the radio today. Supermarkets and grocery stores already experiment with electronically activated video screens that promote products as the shopper walks past them in the store. That same screen could carry sales prompts for other products and businesses as well.

There's already talk of celestial billboards, drawn by satellites, that could illuminate the heavens with nightly sales pitches within a few years! Let's hope it doesn't happen.

As you explore the new marketing tools of the information age, be sensitive to the fine line between service and nuisance. Promotion serves when it provides information the consumer wants. There's much talk now about relationship marketing in the future, and of targeting the consumer with marketing messages for particular products and services based on that consumer's or household's purchase profile. While there's truth in trends, the retailer must also keep in mind that shopping is one of the principal ways we exercise our individuality in our society. Assume too much about the consumer, to the point that you begin to dictate what he or she should be buying, and you're courting a backlash.

The promotional push that has worked and will continue to work is telling shoppers everything they need to know about the store and its products, without dictating they buy there. People want to make that decision themselves. Your promotional push should *convince* people they're making the right choice when they shop with you.

PUTTING IT ALL TOGETHER

Equipped with a working knowledge of the basic promotional tools available to you, you can start devising a marketing program to tell the world about your store. The best strategy operates as a coordinated effort in the three spheres of promotion. You want to generate as much free publicity as possible through public relations, come up with the creative ideas that lend themselves to effective promotions, and use the appropriate advertising media mix to get your message to the right people.

During your first year of operations, approach your marketing strategy as a two-phase program. First, you pull out all the marketing stops to create as much attendant excitement you can around the store's Grand Opening. Make it an event. Mail out a release announcing your store, what it sells, and when it will open. Run special ads announcing the celebration, and invite local dignitaries for the ribbon cutting. Then build on that with an ongoing promotional push to nurture a strong base of customer support as you address the unique marketing challenges of the start-up store.

IT'S VITAL TO MEASURE YOUR MARKETING SUCCESS

In all you do to promote business during your first year, it's especially important you track and record the effectiveness of each component of your marketing effort. You must experiment before you can identify the promotional mix that best serves your store, so you want to test the effectiveness of each marketing option as you use it. What you learn now will guide your future campaigns.

With PR, keeping track is relatively simple. Send out your releases, and wait and watch for results. Track all the news organizations receiving your release to see if it's been picked up. If you have any doubts, call the station or paper and ask the news or business editor if the information was used, and if so, when and where. Keep a scrapbook of clippings and notes of appearances and inquiries. Promotions prove more difficult to gauge, much of it a matter of monitoring store traffic and measuring how individual promotions, in media and at the point of sale, affect sales of the featured items. With advertising in any form, one of the best ways to measure effectiveness of individual ads is to build in an enticement that encourages feedback. The easiest way is to include a coupon in the print ad or newsletter, or offer some incentive—say, 5 percent off if the ad is mentioned—with your broadcast commercials. Featuring coupons in your advertising will help you track the impact of your message and media, and boost sales. An attractive coupon offer gets people shopping. You'll see how well it's working by counting the number of coupons redeemed.

You can make this job easier if you have a computer system and customer database in place the day you open the doors. Ask each customer what brings her to the store, and enter a previously determined code for the response. Tally the responses for an exact indication of what you're getting for every promotional dollar spent. Of course, you can ignore the need to track your advertising, but then you'll always be guessing at your strategy and never really know what's working.

That's why it's important to write up an advertising strategy and budget for the first year, and keep detailed records of what you spend, where, and when. Then compare each investment with the shopper responses it generates. What you'll learn from your customers should guide you on spending and where to put your promotional dollars. If a third of customers tell you they learned of the store from a billboard, and it only represents 10 percent of your spending, you'll know it's an especially effective medium. It's also one in which a substantial increase in spending might be justified. Sometimes the results of your advertising may be immediately apparent: Your commercials start airing on radio, and the next day there's a line outside your door. That would mean it's time to shift more of your budget to radio.

By the end of the first year, the records you keep, detailing the direct impact of advertising on store activity, combined with monthly breakdown of sales, will enable you to devise a promotional strategy based on realistic expectations and need, by the month or even week. The promotional budget and what it allows will differ for every retailer in every market. Planning ahead, budgeting your promotional spending, and setting up a system that allows you to measure its impact will enable you to take much of the guesswork out of the promotional process.

SETTING UP YOUR OPENING DAY MARKETING PROGRAM

Determining your marketing needs begins with an assessment of your budget. You can only afford what your resources allow. Return to your business plan and consider the numbers factored in for your annual marketing budget and the Grand Opening. Remember: Opening day should make a big splash, and the marketing wheels should be turning at least two weeks before the event to guarantee a crowd.

Work up a press release about the store opening and send it to area media. Use this to explain what the store will sell, its hours of operation, and when the store officially opens. Describe anything special you're doing for the Grand Opening, like free balloons for the kids, giveaways, contests, and the like. Advise recipients of the release when the ribbon-cutting ceremonies will take place and what local dignitaries will be on hand for the festivities. If it's a slow news day, the papers will send a photographer out. Make sure you hire your own photographer for the occasion just in case they don't. If you can submit a quality photo of the ribbon cutting to the paper, with everyone in the picture identified, odds are in your favor it will be used. Of course, the better known the dignitaries in attendance, the better your chances of getting the picture into the newspaper. Send invitations at least two weeks before the event, and follow up with a phone call to their offices.

A Grand Opening tends to promote itself and always attracts a share of the curious, to see the new store and what's being given away free. Order your premiums well in advance, looking for those with staying power. Your immediate promotional challenge is to get the store name out there in front of as many people as possible. Make sure you have bags with the store name and logo printed in time for the occasion. Consider what you can do to make the event a sure draw. A contest with hourly prizes always encourages good turnout and can help get your database started. Have store visitors fill out a form and drop it in a bowl. Offer top prizes of merchandise and gift certificates, and secondary prizes of walking advertisements, such as shirts, hats, or canvas bags with the store name.

It helps to make your grand opening a sales event, with sales keyed around a featured product. Storewide sales for the start-up can work against you at this point as they establish shopper expectations for discounts. Better for prices to start high and come down than to start low and climb. Feature a few key items at opening day sale prices to kick off what should be the store's cyclical sales program.

When planning your opening day promotions, remember who your store aims to serve. If your specialty appeals to a more afflu-ent, sophisticated audience, consider the merits of a more subdued grand opening celebration. Host a tea or a wine and cheese party that's more a showcase of what you sell than a daylong selling circus.

Advertising is the toughest part of the kickoff and the element that will cost you the most. The advertising attending your Grand Opening must promote the event and let the world know you're finally open for business. Get your signs around the store in place as soon as possible, and make sure there's a big one in the store window announcing the Grand Opening and the date. It will probably work to your benefit now to invest in a high-visibility billboard for at least four weeks preceding and following your big event. It should feature a generic message about the store, its location, and your specialty. Include a teaser in one corner stating "Coming soon," with the date of the Grand Opening. On that date the teaser should change to "Now Open."

Two weeks before the store opens, spend for another teaser in your paper or papers of choice. Again announce "Coming Soon" with a description of the store and what you'll sell. Raise the readers' expectations; don't be afraid to brag. Give the when and where, with your phone number. Repeat the ad the following week, and launch a heavy print campaign, at least every other day, for the week leading up to the event. These ads should promote the Grand Opening and special sales, and invite the curious to come in, see the store, and participate in the festivities. Continue your Grand Opening advertising for at least a week after the event, then start rolling back your schedule, first to three, then two days a week, keeping your ad in the Sunday paper and your weekday of choice. Eventually you may want to roll back to either one of these days as your weekly newspaper ad. When you want to increase advertising for special events or your peak selling season, advertise on both days.

If there's an identifiable core group of shoppers you're targeting with the store, contact them through the mail. Design the card so it looks like an invitation, and encourage them to bring it in for a special contest. Collect the cards and you've got a list of people who responded to your first direct mail effort.

If your budget allows, sample the effectiveness of broadcast media with commercials announcing the store opening. Use the station's or stations' market breakdown to decide which to use, and pay for the heaviest campaign you can afford for at least a week, commencing at least one day before the opening.

If the broadcast campaign is to have any impact, your commercials must air for at least a week or there's no guarantee your ads will have any impact. Remember, the broadcast media represent the most expensive advertising vehicle in most market areas. Make sure you've thoroughly investigated less expensive but reliable alternatives like print or billboards before committing to a commercial campaign. If you decide to use TV or radio, use this as an opportunity to test the impact of the media and stations in your area. Track the results.

That's as far as you want to go experimenting with advertising media for your Grand Opening. Spend on the medium that's already proven first. Opening day is not a time to play. You want to use those tools you have a reasonable assurance will deliver shoppers when you open the store.

Once you've got the business up and running, you can afford to play with some of your alternative, or more expensive, advertising options. Early on, you want guaranteed impact for every ad dollar you spend.

DON'T FORGET TO ASK YOUR SUPPLIERS FOR HELP

You can alleviate the cost of some of your marketing spending and increase its effectiveness by checking in with your suppliers first. It's their job to help the retail network spread the word about their products. You may find them ready and eager to help you in your promotional effort now (and throughout your career in retail). How much they're willing to assist depends on the size of the company. The largest suppliers offer a marketing arsenal of in-store sales aids to promote their products on the showroom floor. These include counter cards, floor displays, posters, and a variety of premiums.

Ask about any premiums before your Grand Opening. You may be able to save yourself the cost of the giveaways by getting them from your supplier and having your store name imprinted. These freebies are a chance to advertise your business. You want to be sure and use that first to your benefit, and then to your supplier's. While you're talking about premiums, hit up your suppliers for a prize to be given away during your Grand Opening festivities.

It's your responsibility to stay informed about what your suppliers are doing on the promotional and advertising fronts. Large suppliers create contests around products during the year as a means of building awareness. When you know what they're doing, you can revise your plans as needed to make that promotion work for you. The same is true with advertising. Make sure your sales rep keeps you up-to-date on his promotional plans. You want to be able to localize the national campaigns so they'll benefit the store. You need to know what's being promoted, when, and how, and when the company will feature its products in special packages like the freestanding inserts that regularly appear in Sunday papers.

One area where your suppliers can really help you is with advertising. When major manufacturers have a product they want to push, they can be very accommodating in terms of advertising support. Some localize their national campaigns on TV, radio, and in print with dealer tags. The ad promotes the product and tells the public where to find it, listing local retailers stocking the product by name and telephone number. Many suppliers also have pools of co-op funds available to dealers. These funds can be used to help defray the cost of advertising that features the manufacturer's products. Sometimes the co-op funds may be used only for ads highlighting a specified product, sometimes for ads featuring the product among many others. You may even be able to pool the co-op funds from several suppliers to pay for a store ad featuring all their products. Some restrictions usually apply on the use of co-op money. The amount of money available to the retailer depends on how much business the store does with the company. Be sure to follow the manufacturer's guidelines or you could lose the support. The same is true with other promotional materials and in-store sales aids.

Whether or not you're using co-op funding in your advertising program, look to your suppliers to supply you with ad slicks and camera-ready art to use in your own campaigns. Ad slicks are fully prepared print ads, in a variety of sizes. The only thing you need to drop in is your store name, logo, and address. Camera-ready art includes photographs and line drawings of a product for use in your print ads. Even suppliers who can't provide these materials should be able to provide you with a copy of their logos for use in your advertising and promotions. Make sure you're aware of any restrictions regarding the use of a logo. Most major manufacturers will also provide you with promotional literature for their products. Some will imprint the material with the store name for free; with others, you'll need to cover that cost yourself. It's a necessary and worthwhile expense.

If you solicit marketing support from suppliers, you may be surprised to learn how much is available. The money and materials are there for those who learn to use them. You should, from opening day on.

BUILDING ON YOUR OPENING STRATEGY

Carefully planned and effectively promoted, your store's grand opening should kick your business into gear. You want to do all you can to maintain and build on that momentum with your marketing program. Right now, think in terms of a one-year plan, with quarterly and midyear assessments of what's working best for the store. During the first year you'll become aware of sales and traffic trends you may not now anticipate. At the end of that year, you'll be able to look at your sales records and know, statistically, how much business you realized in each month. With those figures as a guide, you can then adjust your ad spending in response to anticipated sales activity.

As you approach your first year in business, you don't enjoy that insight. For now, assume your store will experience a peak sales season, with a couple of major sales weekends, and several lull periods. That peak sales period, the fourth-quarter holiday season for most retailers, will require more ad spending than any other period of the year. You want to make sure your message is heard when customers' minds are on buying. If you don't know what to expect from that period, in terms of a percentage of your total sales volume, start with a figure of 20 percent. That means you should commit at least 20 percent of your ad budget to your key month of the year. Again, for most, that's either November or December. Then take what's left and divide it by eleven to give you a monthly marketing budget for the rest of the year. Look at that amount as your base allowance. Remember, you want to sweeten that fund as much as possible by taking full advantage of every available form of marketing support from your suppliers.

Next, think in terms of what you want to accomplish with that monthly allotment. Your need to advertise consistently is only compounded by the need to experiment during this first year. How you go about that is a function of your budget and the advertising expenses in your area. At the very least, you want to keep the store name in print every week of the year. One month you may want to accomplish that with an ad in a newspaper, another month with a series of billboards. Of course, it's even better if your budget allows for both. At any rate, you want to use a mix of media until you start seeing measurable impact on sales from what you're doing.

Experiment by the week and month, and by location and advertising vehicle. When testing different print media, use the same ad, otherwise you won't know if your customers are responding to the ad or what it's promoting. And try different approaches to print. For the cost of your newspaper ads one week, you may want to invest in a direct mail piece.

Experimenting with broadcast media poses much more of a challenge because of the expense involved. If your ad budget allows this luxury, use your commercials to advertise something not carried in your print campaign. It will give you a clearer idea of how television or radio is helping business. Remember, to use radio or television effectively, you need to run a schedule of ads over a period of a few days or weeks.

An effective advertising program in any medium requires consistency. Until your store develops a local reputation, you must consistently spend to keep its name before the public.

As you spend, you must do everything else within your power to give shoppers a reason to visit the store. Selling gift certificates is a simple way to accomplish this and an easy program to administer. Offer them to customers from day one. Many store owners learn to use cross promotions with other noncompeting retailers as a way to increase store traffic. Usually the promotion involves two businesses indirectly related: the clothing store and an area dry cleaner, for instance. By mutual agreement, each participating store owner refers customers to the other's business. That referral usually includes some form of additional incentive such as a discount or special offer.

In all you do to promote the business, think creatively: The future of your retail business and your retail career depends on how well you succeed in attracting as many people as possible to the store.

REMEMBER THAT IT'S WORD OF MOUTH THAT MATTERS MOST

Ultimately, however, it's what happens after the consumer steps into the store that will have the greatest impact on your business. The promotional push is all about motivating shoppers to visit your store. There, you directly determine the results of your marketing effort. Your best publicity, your best promotion, and your best advertising is a satisfied customer. Getting people to the store is the marketing challenge; getting them to come back is yours. Nothing works for or against a retail business as much as word of mouth. As you attend to the varied promotional chores, don't lose sight of why you're in business, and how you can succeed. Keep your customers satisfied. Provide them the selection, service, and assistance that make shopping your store a pleasure, and they'll spread the word.

⋙ 14 ⋘
OPENING DAY AND BEYOND

Even if you do everything within your power to guarantee your store its best start, the night before opening day will still be one of the most gut-wrenching, nerve-racking evenings of your life. When opening day dawns, your efforts and intentions are on the line; you've gone too far with the venture to turn back. You're in business for yourself, with your own store, responsible for your future. Whether the future brings success or failure, it will be to your credit or blame, entirely.

As much as opening day symbolizes, it is the weeks and months following this milestone that should be of real concern to you now. Opening day provides the retailer with a definite, definable target to work toward. You set the date and throw yourself into making it a resounding success. By the time you close the doors that first night, you'll know how well you succeeded. But that's only the starting point.

Win or lose on opening day, the real anxieties of running your own business begin the following morning. From there forward, the tangible goal is surviving long enough to realize the potential you planned and built into this retail venture. Your business opens with potential; each day beyond measures how well you're doing to turn that promise into retail power. The faster that pace, the stronger the foundation that will allow you to realize your vision of a career in retailing.

Retailing, by its nature, is a competitive venture. Even the store owner who opens a one-of-a-kind shop should expect competition. The challenges confronting the retailer this first year of business should equip you for that future. Some aspects of your retail business will run smoother than you can now imagine; others will throw that proverbial spoke in the wheels that promises to overturn the operation. As personal as this entire project is, the retail entrepreneur must work not to get personally involved. This is your business, your dream and your future, but is a separate entity from yourself.

When you get too caught up in the effort, and personalize the problems of the business, you lose the ability to judge clearly and to make the right decisions. Expect a tough first year, and you'll be prepared to handle whatever providence throws your way. That attitude will always serve your plans and aspirations. When you're prepared to deal with challenge, you're mentally equipped to make the right decisions.

EVOLVING WITH YOUR BUSINESS

After opening day, you'll quickly learn that even the best, most accurate business plan only hints at the realities of the retail marketplace. Your store may meet expectations from day one, but retailing in theory and retailing in practice offer entirely different perspectives to the store owner/operator. Numbers and projections on paper describe a finite world of measuring cause and effect; your market will reveal itself to you as a dynamic interplay of people and products, response and action. The best map can't begin to describe the journey. With your eyes on the map only, you'd miss the scenery. That's what makes the road worth traveling, where you learn and grow. Think for the moment of your retail venture as a trip. Everything you do leading up to the store opening amounts to packing your bags and loading up the car. Opening day you cleared the city limits. The retail journey begins there with you, the retail entrepreneur, in the driver's seat.

Where are you heading? You've already indicated where you want to end up in your plans and goals. But your business plan, your goals, only begin to describe what awaits you in the retail marketplace, and it's a best-case scenario at that. The experience getting there will teach you to be a better retailer. Your plans and priorities may change as you gain a better understanding of your market. Allow yourself the freedom to learn, to sharpen your retail skills from what the market teaches you. But maintain enough distance from your business so you can make the right decisions and recognize opportunity where it presents itself.

Track your progress in a journal or notebook through the year. Write down your insights and what you learn and observe as your business builds. Compare these notes on actual experience with your written expectations. How are they similar, and how do they differ? The answers should serve as a resource for adjusting your business plan and strategy to the realities of your market.

The retail entrepreneur keeps with his plans but evolves with the business. Survival is a hard-won result of timing and action. You can't get that from a plan on paper. Success reflects your ability to interpret and respond to the reality of running your own business.

THE SIGNS OF SUCCESS

Success can prove easy to describe but hard to hold. Your business plan outlines tangible goals for your business, long- and short-term. Along the way you want to look for additional assurances, the ongoing endorsements your business is on the right track. The easiest measure of success reveals itself at the cash register. When sales receipts match expectations, you're reaching the parameters you've set for your own success. Cherish the moment.

The other side of retail success is a story told by your customers. There are two things you want to see in your store: an ongoing increase in the number of shoppers, and some of the same faces returning to buy again and again. The new face in the store is always welcome, but continued prosperity depends on a loyal following. When people return to the store, it says you're hitting the right chord, giving them what they want. You'll also know you're on the right track when you can see the immediate impact of your advertising; when, through your customer polling and their comments, you know your message is reaching its targets.

Of course, the bottom line to your business is money. In your financial records, and your profit-and-loss column, you'll really be able to measure the breadth and extent of your success. Return to your business plan by the week and month, and compare how well your store is faring against projections for sales and profits. Obviously, the faster you accrue profits, the quicker you can relieve yourself of debt, and the better equipped you are to build on the core your store represents.

Look also for signs of your success in how your competitors, direct and indirect, respond to your presence. If they're suddenly running scared or increasing their advertising effort, you know you're hitting the mark with your strategy. Don't make the mistake of surrendering your advantage by rolling back your own effort.

Regard the success that greets your business as a starting point, the appropriate beginning of a retail story you will write through your continued dedication to the retail vision behind your store.

SIGNS OF TROUBLE

Your first year as a retailer will likely include some setbacks. As store owner/operator, it's up to you to continually monitor your business so none of those challenges develops to the point where it threatens your livelihood. Any indication of trouble in any aspect of your business demands an immediate response. Trouble, like success, will reveal itself at the cash register and in your showroom.

The surest sign of trouble for a retailer is an empty store or an idle phone. Without floor traffic, without consumer inquiries, there won't be any sales. If the crowds are thin from the start, reconsider your marketing strategy. Misdirected promotions mean either you're not reaching the right people or there aren't enough of them receiving your message to support your business. Your best response: Step up your ad spending. You know what isn't working; pull out all the stops and blanket the area with your message in other media. Either crowds will follow and you'll know what media to use or you'll know it's time to reconsider your business and its location.

Slow traffic could also signal that, despite your careful research, you've ended up with a good store concept in the wrong location. The location simply might not be the draw it seemed when you selected it. Check with nearby retailers and compare notes. Closely monitor area traffic of shoppers on foot and in cars. If you're one of the first tenants in a new shopping mall or strip, with construction going on around you, people may not yet realize you've opened your doors. Get the message out and watch for a turn in the tides. If nothing happens and you've done all you can to attract shoppers, recognize your obligation to yourself to reconsider the location. Give yourself at least six months before giving up, though. It may take longer than you envisioned to establish your store. Once you're convinced the place will not live up to its promise, start planning a move—the sooner the better. Throughout your retail career, you must be honest with yourself and learn to accept the lessons of the marketplace.

If there are crowds in your store but no one seems to be buying, take the hint from your customers. Either your prices are too high or your selection too limited. Step back and consider how competitors handle similar merchandise in terms of pricing and selection. Look first at pricing. Check theirs against yours. If theirs are lower, make sure the goods they're carrying are of comparable quality. If so, you may have no choice but to respond by lowering your prices. Try a moderate price reduction first, without any acclaim. No more than 10 percent. If that doesn't help increase sales, lower them again. When forced to lower prices, do it gradually until you reach a level at which consumers respond. You're not in business to beat any price around. Just track shopper response to see where your prices need to be.

When it seems your limited selection may be dampening sales, try expanding it in every direction. Add variety to your good-better-best selection, with more merchandise at each pricing tier. At this point, go for breadth, not depth, until you identify the merchandise mix shoppers in your area seem to prefer.

Until sales activity picks up, play with your product display, rearranging inventory and placement until customers seem to respond. During the first few months your store is up and running, do everything you can, spend whatever it takes, to get your revenues up and running as well. If consumer response is not immediate, it's your job to force it. The process may take longer than you expect, but you can't wait too long. Look for the signs of success or trouble from day one, and act as needed. To sit back and wait for something to happen is to neglect your responsibility as owner/operator. Your future is at stake here, and yours alone.

For this reason, regard all your plans as outlines of preferred activity, easily revised as needed. It's important to build some flexibility into your plans, and leave yourself an easy way out when market reality doesn't match your expectations. Running your store should provide a learning experience from day one. Adapt your plans to what that experience teaches you. Your store requires a certain level of sales activity to realize its potential. The sooner that foundation is in place, the better. It's up to the owner alone to move it along, to do whatever it takes to give the store a proper start.

As you work toward that goal, remember the successful entrepreneur is one who recognizes her limitations. If the initial challenges to your store seem insurmountable, turn outside for help. Signs of trouble in your business do not signal failure. They are indicators that require your immediate attention. Not to respond is failure. If you do all you can, but cannot seem to get the business running, seek the advice of the experts who helped you into business. Ask your attorney, accountant, and any other consultants for insight and suggestions on what you're doing wrong.

Talk to your customers and hear what they say about your business. They've got no financial stake in its future and may be able to point you to the problem immediately.

Success will present itself to you in full bloom. The roots of trouble in your retail operation will prove more difficult to identify. You must scratch around and shed light on any problem before it develops into a threat to your future. You've planned too much and worked too hard bringing this business to life to let it slip away through neglect. It's your duty to contain the problems, and turn the challenges of your business into new opportunities.

RESPONDING TO THE COMPETITION

Whether you stand alone or are the latest among many retailers of the same products in the area, you will face competition. Recognize it for what it is. Competition is a form of flattery, a sign you're doing things well enough that others feel threatened by your presence. That compliment carries thorns, of course. Competition is all about getting to the top at another person's expense. How you address the efforts of your adversaries early on will set the tone for the retailing future that awaits you.

The biggest mistake any retailer can make is to get caught up in the cycle of competition based solely on price. If your entry compels other retailers to start slashing prices, let them. There are no victors in that retail arena, only survivors. Your retail store should mean something entirely different to shoppers. The successful specialty retailer, the small store owner with a future, is the one who offers customers much more than the lowest price in town. The consumers who will support your future value the service and convenience that can only be found with a specialist like yourself. Price is important, but the lowest price will not support your business.

Your best response to competition: Emphasize the strengths you bring to the market. Anyone can cut prices. What is it about your business that customers can't find anywhere else? Be it service or selection, that's what you want to tell your customers about in advertising. Play the pricing game and you'll find yourself sucked into a downward spiral of diminishing returns. First your profits get squeezed, then the entire business. Before long your dream is just another casualty of the retail price wars. Return frequently to your outline of why you are in business and who you want to serve. In what you've written you should find all the reason you need to forge ahead in the face of competition.

As a retailer you must respond to what your competitors do and say about you. Your best response is a reaffirmation of your business strategy, and what you want to do for the shopper that your competitors can't. Use sales and promotions to give shoppers extra incentive to visit your store. But stick with the philosophy and strategy that convinced you that you could offer consumers something they need in a retail store.

MANAGING STOCK AND INVENTORY

During the early days of your business, closely monitor what happens with your inventory. Sales, by product and category, should provide an indicator of where to broaden your retail horizons. One of the secrets to retail success is having what the customers want, when they want it. This is another of your responsibilities as store owner/operator, one that helps set the pace of your success. You have one chance to win the customer: whenever he is in your store. If you don't have what he wants when he wants it—epecially an item at the core of your selection—he'll go elsewhere. If he gets what he needs there, you can only hope he'll find a reason to visit your store again.

For opening day you ordered merchandise based on your best expectations. From opening day on, your orders must be based on what has already happened in the store. After the first month you should know what most interests your shoppers and what you should have in stock for the next quarter. Over time, your experience will teach you what to order, when, and what you need in terms of quantities. That skill will help you cut your operational costs as you learn to run a tighter, more efficient operation. During these first few months you develop this skill through a process of carefully observing your sales transactions. Over time you'll gain an instinctive sense of when to start price reductions on certain merchandise to move it out of the store in the beginning of the product cycle rather than at the end. There will always be the surprise winners and losers on the sales floor. Managing inventory effectively means you eliminate the amount of surprise by knowing instinctively, from experience, what your customers want, and when.

BROADENING YOUR HORIZONS WITH PRODUCTS AND SERVICES

The retailer who closely tracks sales performance learns to recognize opportunities for expanding the business. Regard your store on opening day as the core of your future, and always look for ways to build on that. Respond immediately but proceed cautiously. Once your store is established, you have the ideal forum for field-testing new products and services before making a commitment to any expansion. When adding inventory, look first for those products that promise the greatest profit potential. Accessories and impulse items serve as logical extensions of your main product categories and the best direction to move when first broadening your sales offerings. As high-profit items, they also strengthen the store's total profit picture to provide enough economic base to allow business expansion on a much broader basis. When you add any product, use display and placement to highlight it for your customers. Put it where they can't miss it. Talk it up. Make sure everyone who enters the store knows what else is now available from you.

A strong customer service program will prove among your best tools for establishing a loyal customer base. New services, like new products, require that you proceed with caution. Start with the familiar, the necessary enhancements of what you're already doing; the things that will broaden the store's appeal and strengthen your relationship with customers. Begin with those services that represent a logical extension of your core business.

When looking for new sales and service opportunities, listen closely to what your customers say. If you find yourself frequently explaining you don't stock a particular item, maybe it's time you did. When your customers turn to you for help locating parts or service for their products, maybe you are missing opportunities when you refer them to someone else. Your commitment to your customers should lead you to the services that will serve your own goals for building a business with staying power.

As you investigate ways to expand your business, remember your best resource is your customers. Speak honestly to the people you serve, and solicit their opinions. You'll get plenty of suggestions on how you could and should expand the business. After all, they're the people who know best what your store could do for them. What they have to say in a few moments could save you hours of agonizing over how to make yours a better business, the store that stands apart on the retail landscape, the store with the satisfied customers.

RETAINING EMPLOYEES

Every business requires a strong support structure before it can prosper. For the retailer, that structure is provided by staff.

Whether your store is a one-man shop or employs scores of people, its future growth and development depend on how well the owner equips the business organization with qualified personnel. An expanding business is one with an ongoing need for skilled personnel. Every time you lose an employee, you must go through the hiring and training process again. It's a drain on your time and resources. You'll escape some of that process by doing all you can to keep staff turnover to a minimum. While you won't be able to hold on to everyone, there are a few people you'll want to keep, people who can grow with the business into positions of greater authority.

There are no secrets to retaining staff. All that's required are the same management skills and sensitivity that go into effective team management and leadership. Recognize those you hire for their contributions to the business with words and dollars, and they'll know they are appreciated. Some will demonstrate interest in the business as soon as they join your team. Look for enthusiasm and the willingness to give that extra effort, to stay with every job until it's completed. Those who demonstrate it are people you want to work to keep. Involve them in the decision-making process, soliciting their advice and opinions. Unless yours is the one-man or one-woman shop, you can't be in touch with every customer. But you want to know what every customer has to say. Listen to what your staffers tell you, and their opinions about the business. You'll learn who has the insight, the business sense that makes for a stronger team. Realize, even in the earliest days, that you'll need the help of others.

Over time, as soon as the business starts to take off, recognize their contributions with cash rewards. Give people some form of incentive for staying with the business. Let them share in profits, or provide a bonus or pension program, and they'll think twice before leaving. That kind of involvement also encourages people to work harder for the good of all.

SHARING YOUR RESPONSIBILITY

As an entrepreneur, it isn't easy for you to share responsibility. That runs against your grain. You entered into business to be the boss, and once you're there, it's tough to trust others with the authority to make decisions regarding the business. You must, though, if you want your dreams of retail success to realize the potential you've built into them. You can't guide an ocean cruiser with a rowboat mentality. At the start, your retail business is like that humble little craft on this wide ocean of business opportunity. You may have a staff, but you're the one pulling the oars. Everything about moving the craft through the water is your responsibility. Step into a larger boat, and it takes more than your effort alone to navigate the waters. You alone still set the course and direction, but you cannot get there entirely of your own efforts. The bigger the ship, the larger the crew; but there's never any doubt there's a captain in charge.

This retail venture is your ship to prosperity. But you can't get where it can take you entirely on your own effort. Plan from the very beginning to share your responsibilities. That doesn't mean you'll be giving up any final authority. Rather, you'll be making your own job easier and putting yourself in a better position to build your future. As your store grows and you look to expand it, you'll be faced with new responsibilities. Cultivate and train a staff who can help you manage your business. Enter business knowing you will share your responsibility. Your effort alone can bring you success, but with the help of others, you'll find it much easier to broaden the horizons of the business. Giving up some of your responsibility may be one of the toughest things for you to do as the owner and founder of the business. It's also one of the most necessary.

BUILDING ON YOUR SUCCESS

For those who possess the entrepreneur's drive and spirit, a retail career will always promise the opportunity to make your own way through the world. As much as the retail business of the 21st Century may differ from the retail store of the past, retail businesses will always be, in essence, businesses whose existence is based on serving the needs of a buying public. You will face new channels of competition and will need to learn to adapt new technologies to address that challenge. You'll need to explore every avenue of distribution and marketing in the search for those tools that will allow you to better serve an audience that is at once more demanding and less forgiving. The tools of technology may change the trade, but the basic business will not.

Success for the retail entrepreneur is not an end, but a process. Those building a future for their stores will learn to adapt their skills to the times, taking full advantage of the new tools of distribution and communication to seize new opportunities from the marketplace. Your store should mark only the beginning, the foundation for success that will follow your best efforts. Whether yours is a dream for a store that will support your present lifestyle, or an international retailing empire, what you bring to the endeavor, in terms of personal determination, perseverance, and vision, will set the horizons on your accomplishment.

No matter how far this venture carries you, no matter what your retail future holds, you will not face another day as filled with promise and challenge, nor as rewarding, as when you finally hang that sign that says "Open for Business."

❖ Appendix A ❖
BIBLIOGRAPHY

Here's a listing of other books you may find helpful in starting your own specialty store.

- *Business Plans That Win Venture Capital,* by Terrence B. McGarty (Wiley, 1989)
- *Buying & Selling a Small Business,* by Michael M. Coltman (International Self Counsel Press, 1989)
- *Buying & Selling a Small Business,* by Verne A. Bunn (Ayer, 1979)
- *Buying or Selling a Business,* by Dana Herbison (Success, 1990)
- *Buying Your Own Small Business,* by Brian R. Smith and Thomas L. West (Viking Penguin, 1985)
- *Crafting the Successful Business Plan,* by Erik Hyypia (Prentice-Hall, 1992)
- *Fifty-Nine Response-Profit Tips, Tricks & Techniques to Help You Achieve Mail Order Success,* by Galen Stilson (Premier, 1984)
- *Finding Money for Your Small Business,* by Max Fallek (Dearborn, 1994)
- *Free Money: For Small Businesses & Entrepreneurs,* by Laurie Blum (Wiley, 1988)
- *From Dogs To Riches: A Step-by-Step Guide to Start & Operate Your Own Mobile Cart Vending Business,* by Vera D. Clark-Rugley (MCC, 1993)
- *Getting into the Mail-Order Business,* by Julian L. Simon (McGraw, 1984)
- *Getting Money: A Getting-into-Business Guide* (International Self Counsel Press, 1991)

- *How I Grossed More Than One Million Dollars in Direct Mail & Mail Order Starting with Little Cash & Less Know-how,* by Tyler G. Hicks (International Wealth, 1993)
- *How to Control & Reduce Inventory,* by Burton E. Lipman (Bell, 1988)
- *How to Finance a Growing Business,* by Royce Diener (Fell, 1974)
- *How to Start & Run a Successful Mail Order Business,* by Sean Martyn (McKay, 1980)
- *Inc. Yourself: How to Profit by Setting Up Your Own Corporation,* by Judith H. McQuown (Macmillan, 1988)
- *Jumpstart Marketing for the New Business Owner,* by Peter Evans (Colonial, 1993)
- *Mail Order Legal Guide,* by Edwin J. Keup (Oasis, 1993)
- *Mail Order Moonlighting,* by Cecil C. Hoge, Sr. (Ten Speed, 1978)
- *Mail Order Riches Success Kit,* by Tyler G. Hicks (International Wealth, 1993)
- *Mail Order Selling: How to Market Almost Anything by Mail,* by Irving Burstiner (Prentice-Hall, 1989)
- *Money in Your Mailbox: How to Start & Operate a Successful Mail-Order Business,* by Perry L. Wilbur (Wiley, 1992)
- *Procurement & Inventory Ordering Tables,* by Jerry Banks and Hohenstein, Jr. (Franklin, 1977)
- *Raising Start-up Capital for Your Firm,* by Gustav Berle (Wiley, 1990)
- *Recent Developments in Inventory Theory,* by Moshe F. Friedman (Pergamon, 1981)
- *Security for Small Businesses,* by David Berger (Butterworth-Heinemann, 1981)
- *Small Business Management Fundamentals,* by Dan Steinhoff and John F. Burgess (McGraw, 1993)
- *Small Time Operator: How to Start Your Own Small Business, Keep Your Books, Pay Your Taxes & Stay Out of Trouble,* by Bernard Kamoroff (Bell Springs, 1988)
- *Start-up Money: How to Finance Your New Small Business,* by Michael McKeever (Nolo, 1986)

- *Starting on a Shoestring: Building a Business Without a Bankroll,* by Arnold S. Goldstein (Wiley, 1991)
- *Successful Mail Order Marketing,* by Linda Hebert (Gibraltor, 1988)
- *The Bootstrap Entrepreneur,* by Steven C. Bursten (Nelson, 1993)
- *The Entrepreneurial PC,* by Bernard J. David (TAB, 1991)
- *The Essentials of Small Business Management,* by Thomas W. Zimmerer and Norman M. Scarborough (Macmillan, 1993)
- *The Radical New Road To Wealth: How to Raise Venture Capital for a New Business,* by A. David Silver (International Wealth, 1990)
- *The Small Business Security Handbook,* by James E. Keogh (Prentice-Hall, 1980)
- *The Start-up Business Plan,* by William M. Luther (Prentice-Hall, 1991)

⋖⋗ Appendix B ⋖⋗
ASSOCIATIONS

Here's a list of small business associations that might be helpful both before and after you've launched your own specialty store:

- American Association for Consumer Benefits: Promotes the availability of medical and other benefits to small business owners, their families, and employees. Plans to conduct charitable programs. Phone, (800)872-8896.
- American Small Businesses Association: Supports legislation favorable to the small business enterprise; organizes members to collectively oppose unfavorable legislation. Informs members of proposed legislation affecting small businesses; conducts business education programs. Operates scholarship program. Phone, (800)235-3298.
- American Woman's Economic Development Corporation: Sponsors eighteen-month training and technical assistance program. Provides management training, on-site analysis of businesses, volunteer advisers who work in specific problem areas, assistance in preparing a business plan, and continued support after the program is completed. Nine-week miniprograms are also available. Provides seminars. Staff is composed of experienced businesspeople and specialists from university business schools and major corporations. Phone, (800)222-AWED.
- BEST Employers Association: Provides small independent businesses with managerial, economic, financial, and sales information helpful for business improvement. Maintains a Washington, D.C., office to assist small businesses working with federal agencies. Conducts research on pending tax

and government regulations affecting small businesses. Fax, (714)553–0883.

- Business Coalition for Fair Competition: Seeks to eliminate unfair advantages of tax-exempt organizations that sell and lease products and services in the commercial marketplace. Works to change regulations and legislation through Congress and regulatory agencies, primarily in the IRS and social services. Fax, (202)887-0021.
- Coalition of America to Save the Economy: Works to protect the rights of small businesses by opposing the practice of national discount store chains demanding that suppliers discontinue the use of independent manufacturers' representatives. Promotes fair and open competition. Works for favorable legislation, regulatory policies, and legal decisions. Phone, (800)752–4111.
- Independent Small Business Employers of America: Works to assist members in keeping their businesses profitable and maintaining good employee relations. Phone, (800)728-3187.
- International Association of Business: Seeks to secure for members benefits that are usually reserved for larger companies and corporations. Conducts seminars. Fax, (817)467-0807.
- International Council for Small Business: Fosters discussion of topics pertaining to the development and improvement of small business management. Holds regional seminars. Fax, (314)658-3897.
- National Association of Private Enterprise: Seeks to ensure the continued growth of private enterprise through education, benefits programs, and legislation. Promotes the common interest of members. Bestows scholarships. Phone, (800)223-6273.
- National Association for the Self-Employed: Acts as a forum for the exchange of ideas. Promotes political awareness; conducts educational programs. Endorses group insurance programs. Sponsors charitable and self-help projects through the NASE Foundation. Fax, (800)366-8329.
- National Business Association: Promotes and assists the

growth and development of small businesses. Aids members in obtaining government small business and education loans; makes available insurance policies and software in conjunction with the U.S. Small Business Administration. Maintains career, educational institution, and scholarship information program for members and their dependents. Makes available printing grants for government agencies involved in small business assistance. Sponsors seminars and trade shows. Phone, (800)456-0440.

- National Business Owners Association: Promotes the interests of small business. Provides government relations services and member benefit programs. Disseminates information. Fax, (301)913-0001.
- National Small Business Benefits Association: Offers discounts on group dental and life insurance, nationwide paging and travel programs, car rental, fax equipment, office supplies, and cellular phone services. Provides specialized services including business overhead analysis, management consulting, accounting services, marketing, public relations, and owner-to-owner networking. Bestows awards; maintains speakers' bureau and library; conducts seminars and research program. Fax, (217)544-5816.
- National Small Business United: Purposes are to promote a sound national economy, and to foster the birth and vigorous development of independent small business. Serves as administrative and legislative coordinator of Small Business Legislative Council. Phone, (800)345-6728.
- Network of Small Businesses: Aims to obtain expansion funding, new sources of supply, and low-cost cooperative advertising for members. Stresses support of inventors, innovators, scientists, and engineers. Offers health insurance programs, liability insurance funding, and loan assistance; provides legal advice and employee benefit counseling. Conducts forums to discuss experiences, common problems, successes, and setbacks. Serves as a unified voice on political issues relevant to small businesses. Maintains speakers' bureau; compiles statistics; bestows awards. Fax, (216)449-3227.

- Small Business Foundation of America: Conducts education programs. Fax, (202)872-8543.
- Small Business Service Bureau: Provides national assistance concerning small business group insurance, cash flow, taxes, and management problems. Offers legislative advocacy, group benefit services, group insurance, and group health plans. Fax, (508)791–4709.
- Support Services Alliance: Provides services and programs such as group purchasing discounts, legislative advocacy, and business and financial support services. Phone, (800)322-3920.

❧ INDEX ❧

BUILD YOUR OWN BUSINESS LIBRARY

with the

21ST CENTURY ENTREPRENEUR SERIES!

HOW TO OPEN A FRANCHISE BUSINESS
Mike Powers   77912-9/$12.50 US/$16.00 Can

HOW TO OPEN YOUR OWN STORE
Michael Antoniak   77076-8/$12.50 US/$18.50 Can

HOW TO START A HOME BUSINESS
Michael Antoniak   77911-0/$12.50 US/$16.00 Can

HOW TO START A SERVICE BUSINESS
Ben Chant and Melissa Morgan
                                 77077-6/$12.50 US/$15.00 Can

HOW TO START A MAIL ORDER BUSINESS
Mike Powers   78446-7/$12.50 US/$16.50 Can

HOW TO START A RETIREMENT BUSINESS
Jacqueline K. Powers   78447-5/$12.50 US/$16.50 Can